MW00795580

The Cultural Dynamics of

Democratization in Spain

The Cultural Dynamics of Democratization in

SPAIN

Peter McDonough

Samuel H. Barnes

Antonio López Pina

with

Doh C. Shin

José Álvaro Moisés

CORNELL UNIVERSITY PRESS

Ithaca and London

This book is published with the aid of a grant from the Program for Cultural Cooperation between Spain's Ministry of Culture and Education and United States Universities.

First published 1998 by Cornell University Press.

Printed in the United States of America.

LIBRARY OF CONGRESS CATALOGING-IN-PUBLICATION DATA
McDonough, Peter.
    The cultural dynamics of democratization in Spain / Peter McDonough, Samuel H. Barnes, Antonio López Pina, with Doh C. Shin, José Alvaro Moisés.
        p.   cm.
    Includes bibliographical references and index.
    ISBN 0-8014-3516-1 (hardcover) : alk. paper)
    1. Spain—Politics and government—1975-   —Public opinion.
    2. Democracy—Spain—Public opinion.   3. Political participation—
Spain.   4. Public opinion—Spain.   I. Barnes, Samuel H. (Samuel
Henry).   II. López Pina, Antonio.
JN8210.M39   1998
306.2'0946'09048—dc21   98–15273

Cornell University Press strives to use environmentally responsible suppliers and materials to the fullest extent possible in the publishing of its books. Such materials include vegetable-based, low-VOC inks and acid-free papers that are recycled, totally chlorine-free, or partly composed of nonwood fibers.

Cloth printing   10 9 8 7 6 5 4 3 2 1

In memory of Kenneth Organski

Contents

Preface

This book is about Spanish citizens during their voyage from the era of Franco to political democracy, economic prosperity, and membership in the mainstream institutions of Europe. Our focus is not on the epic journey itself but on how the public reacted to it, on what people have thought about their changing political world, what they have done about it, and—this is always the enigmatic dimension—why they have thought and acted as they did. Our basic data come from four national surveys taken in 1978, 1980, 1984, and 1990, a period that extends over the critical years of the transition to and consolidation of democracy in Spain.

At the core of the book are three questions: What are the foundations of the new regime's political legitimacy, compared to the economic pragmatism of the preceding authoritarian order? How did Spanish democracy manage the change from the conservative center-right coalition that engineered the transition to the socialist government that consolidated it? And finally, what accounts for the striking deficit in political participation and civic engagement across the Spanish public?

Political legitimacy, we argue, deepened as the new regime took on a life of its own, surpassing that of the early days of the transition, when it benefited from the vivid contrast between dictatorship and democracy. As for the shift from the center-right government to the tenure of the socialists, that change represented a transition within the transition, from an agenda centered on the resolution of foundational issues to one that privileged economic and social concerns. Instead of splitting between outright reaction and radical fervor, Spaniards opted for social democracy.

In order to pinpoint the causes of Spain's participatory shortfall, we compare the country with Korea and Brazil, two post-authoritarian settings where political involvement is higher. Part of the answer to the puzzle can be found in a pair of structural conditions. Spain's chronically high unemployment rate, together with an extraordinarily low rate of labor market participation among women, dampens participation. Added to this factor is the historical decision taken by the Catholic church, in contrast to its strategy in other recent episodes of democratization, to remain largely neutral during the transition. The result was to withdraw a vital stimulus from mass mobilization.

The project of which this book is the culmination goes back a long way. The existential sources were the efforts of universities, governments, foundations, and individuals to expand the invisible colleges, the international consortia of scholars with similar interests and shared assumptions about theory and method in lines of inquiry that have developed since World War II. Those efforts took Antonio López Pina from Spain to Germany and then to France and finally to Ann Arbor on a Ford Foundation grant for the 1964–66 period. The same spirit took Peter McDonough to the Peace Corps in what is now Bangladesh, then to Michigan, and then to several years of fieldwork in Brazil. For Sam Barnes it involved research in Canada, a post-doctoral Fulbright in France, research in Germany, Italy, and Britain, and a cross-national research project involving several European countries.

These diverse careers came together in the Institute for Social Research and the Department of Political Science at the University of Michigan. This experience gave us a common exposure to the importance of surveys as research instruments and an acquaintance with some of their limits, and it alerted us to the substantive role of the public's attitudes and behavior. Events in Spain in the mid-1970s intrigued us as an opportunity to examine the cultural dynamics of democratization, to apply to the Spanish experiment theories and methods that had been developed in the study of advanced democracies.

In democratic theory citizens' attitudes and behavior are crucial. But in the literature on democratization, the importance of the public is, to put it charitably, a matter to be investigated, not a factor to be assumed. Interpretations of the Spanish transition commonly emphasize the importance of elites and play down the role of the public. This diagnostic turnaround is perhaps the most important revision that research about democratization has made to naive understandings of mass politics, and it is generally consistent with earlier work by the Michigan school that gave cause for skepticism about the depth and constancy of belief systems in mass publics. All evaluations, however, see Spanish leaders as consciously striving to direct events so as to minimize the potential for conflict, to craft a transition that would not stir up the demons in historical memory. Their consensual strategy required careful regard for the views of ordinary Spaniards, their reactions to events, and their aspirations and fears. No other transition has been conducted with so much attention to public opinion and polls as the Spanish.

Still, why bother to study public opinion during the course of democratization? Partly because it is there. The views of Spanish citizens were monitored with astonishing frequency and on a massive scale throughout the course of democratization. Public opinion became a presence, one that was taken into account, even if participation was poor to middling. Spaniards were entered into the data base of democracy. The citizenry may have been relatively passive. But it was not inert or powerless.

Another reason for taking the mass politics of the transition seriously is that it includes behavior as well as beliefs. Sometimes it is hard to see what was behavioral about the behavioral revolution in political science; so much of it looked rather like a psychometric diversion, correlating attitudes with attitudes, with hardly a glance at behavior. In our view, the cultural dynamics of democratization in Spain have involved not only changes in symbolic capital and cognitive style—in the icons of nationhood and in habitual ways of framing lines of conflict. The transformation has also encompassed changes in what used to be called mores or customs of association, now known as social capital, and in various forms of collective action and expression.

A third reason for viewing the transition from the bottom up concerns the complex relationship between institutions, both cultural and political, and mass behavior. Does the fact that participation has faltered in Spain signify that the public matters little more in democracy than it did under dictatorship? Whatever the answer, the fact of low political engagement itself cries out for explanation. We try to pinpoint the organizational as well as the structural determinants of the deficit in social and political involvement in Spain. We stress the paradoxical role of a cultural institution, the Catholic church, in reinforcing the peaceful nature of the transition while it exerted, by the same strategy of refraining from the mobilization of old antagonisms, downward pressure on participation.

Fourth, imagine what our picture of the Spanish transition would look like if we omitted public opinion. An occasional corollary of the assumption that political culture doesn't count for much is disbelief in one or another of the extravagant claims associated with the construct—for example, that democratic values must be firmly in place before democracy gets consolidated. Assertions in this mold have their counterpart in attempts to reduce the new institutionalism in political science to the idea that democratic regimes can be installed pretty much regardless of structural conditions. Once such mantras and obiter dicta are set aside, we can get on with exploring some genuine mysteries—for example, the curious mix of political moderation and low participation.

Finally, aside from these more or less sensible rationales for the study of democratization from ground level, a dose of contrariness serves to challenge scholastic orthodoxies. Hermann Goering may or may not have said that when he heard the word *culture*, he reached for his gun. No political scientist has gone on record in support of statements in this vein, though a few have come close. Some favor the notion—to paraphrase a view attributed to an American commander in Vietnam—that when you have them by the institutions, their hearts and their minds will follow. Our investigation of the cultural dynamics of democratization, we trust, involves more than making strong statements about vague things.

One mild eccentricity of the book may be worth explaining. We often use author-date citations to refer to collateral literature rather than factual sources. Most of the time, our purpose is to alert readers to comparable theories about or findings in countries besides Spain. Those not interested in this sort of cross-national allusion may accept or dismiss the device as the equivalent of popcorn at the picture show.

In a project carried out over a long period of time we have accumulated a large number of debts to individuals and organizations. First we thank Doh Chul Shin and José Álvaro Moisés for enabling us to include data from their studies in South Korea and Brazil that paralleled our indicators on several important dimensions. These scholars collaborated with Peter McDonough on their study designs, providing similar formats for critical questions on several aspects of participation in politics. We also owe a special debt to Roger Haydon of Cornell University Press for his encouragement and unfailing good humor during the course of writing and rewriting. We are also indebted to Barbara Salazar and Joel Ray for putting a technically baroque, table- and figure-laden manuscript in shape.

Data collection and analysis were made possible by grants from the Spain–United States Bi-National Commission, the Tinker Foundation, the National Science Foundation, the Instituto de Estudios Fiscales of the Spanish Ministerio de Economía y Hacienda, and the Banco Hipotecario de España. We thank those organizations for their support. We also thank individuals who encouraged and supported us, in particular Pablo Barrios, Ramón Bela Armadio, José Borrell, Guillermo De la Dehesa, Julio Feo, Julio Rodríguez, Francis Coughlin, Edward Elly, John Geer, Christopher Lundry, Kenneth Maxwell, Thomas Middleton, and Martha Muse.

We also appreciate assistance received from the Institute for Social Research at the University of Michigan, Arizona State University, the Center for German and European Studies at Georgetown University, and the Autónoma and Complutense universities in Madrid.

We dedicate this volume to our wives—Josefina Figueira-McDonough, Anne Barnes, and Annegret Piesch—for their patience with our travels and tribulations in this project over two decades.

P. McD.

Tempe, Arizona

S. H. B.

Washington, D.C.

A. L. P.

Madrid

The Cultural Dynamics of
Democratization in Spain

Introduction: From Maximalism to Moderation

Spain shows signs of Democracy Lite. Democratic procedures are solidly in place, but participation seems to have stagnated. On the one hand, a culture of compromise has replaced a tradition of lethal antagonisms. The maximalist fantasy of strangling the last capitalist with the guts of the last priest has evaporated. On the other hand, only about one-third of Spanish adults belong to any voluntary association, and more than two decades after the passing of Franco the fraction of the public identifying with a political party of any stripe stands at about the same low level as in Eastern Europe after the fall of communism. Civic anemia appears to be endemic in Spain.

Why? A partial answer comes in the form of a paradox. The participatory deficit in Spain is a by-product of the ethos of tolerance and bargaining that pervaded the transition from Francoism. The viability of Spanish democracy has been achieved at some cost to its quality. The good news—the efflorescence of tolerance—is partly responsible for the bad news, "the extraordinarily low levels of mass-level involvement with politics" (Gunther, Puhle, and Diamandouros 1995: 22).

This is not the whole story. We need to know what exactly it is about comity that might depress participation. And it is quite unlikely that a single factor, moderation or anything else, accounts for all or even most of the shortfall of participation in Spain. Consider two other, more mundane causes.

One obvious culprit is unemployment. The economic restructuring that accompanied democratization in Spain produced a jobless rate that has stayed in the high teens and low twenties since the late 1970s. Such displacement was unheard of under the Franco regime, and the level of unemployment in Spain remained at about twice that in most other parts of Europe through the eighties and much of the nineties. Joblessness during this period tracked the stagnation in political participation closely.

1

The other structural condition that has contributed to low political involvement is the lag in labor market participation by Spanish women. Technically the problem is not unemployment but entrance into the labor force in the first place. Despite increases, female labor force participation in Spain continues to be the lowest in Europe (*Situación de la mujer* ... 1994; Méndez 1994).

These conditions have exerted powerful downward pressure on political participation in Spain. Early in the transition, unemployment shot up, and it has stayed at very high levels. The labor force participation of Spanish women, though it has improved since the days of Franco, still ranks at the bottom of the European community. On both counts, Spain is a deviant case, and the political participation of its citizens appears to be extraordinarily low.

The trouble with this argument-by-correlation is not that it is wrong but that it omits something important. One other factor makes Spain stand out from countries that have democratized since the mid-1970s. In contrast to what transpired in the Philippines, Poland, South Africa, Brazil, and numerous other new democracies, organized religion in Spain stood aside from the transition. The Catholic church in Spain did not oppose democratization, and it did facilitate some of the contacts that developed between the old regime and the opposition (Linz 1991).[1] But it stopped short of spurring the faithful to mobilization against the authoritarian system and it declined to back efforts to organize a confessional party. "Like the House of Lords during World War II," one participant observed, "the Spanish bishops did nothing, and they did it very well."[2] The result was to leave the link between popular devotion and political abstention intact. This strategy was the reverse of the activism espoused by churches during the seventies and eighties in Latin America, Eastern Europe, and parts of Asia (Smith 1996).

Moderation in general was a hallmark of the Spanish transition, and forbearance around a specific flash point—church-state relations—almost certainly dampened participation. In transitions where the church set out to mobilize the faithful—in Poland, for example, or the Philippines— participation was higher. Each of these conditions taken separately—high unemployment, low female labor force participation, and the relative neutrality of the church—is distinctive though not unique to Spain. Taken together, they form a singular nexus of forces that subdued mass participation.

What motivated such restraint? For many Spaniards, democratization meant awakening from a nightmare of overwrought worldviews and dogmatic enthusiasms, and the collective memory of this debacle made the country receptive to a political strategy that, while not hostile to civic engagement, was often indifferent to it.[3]

The emphatic moderation that characterized the Spanish transition has another implication, one that concerns the nature of democratic legitimacy rather than political participation. A leitmotif of the regime change that got under way with the death of Franco in 1975 has been depolarization—essentially, the fading not only of religion as a cleavage but of other lines of conflict such as class and, to a degree, region. The process of reform rather than *ruptura* raises questions about the normative content of Spanish democracy. What does the new regime signify for ordinary citizens, aside from a delegitimation of extremism, expressed through apparently mediocre political participation? Does democratic legitimacy amount to more than a side-effect of depolarization?

The style of democracy that took hold in Spain constitutes not only a refutation of authoritarianism. It also stands as a rejection of "maximalism," and with it of attempts to impose a substantive, programmatic democracy that goes beyond the formal, procedural variety. After all, it was, many felt, the menace of the radicalism propounded by the Second Republic that brought on Francoism. This time around, all parties to the transition wanted to avoid the mistakes of the past, the chief of which was thought to be an insistence on foisting quixotic ideals on a befuddled, reluctant citizenry. But how was this cool incrementalism to be distinguished from the limited pluralism of the Franco years (Linz 1964)? Along with political participation, democratic legitimacy is a primary theme of our book.

Our third theme is the evolution of political support for and opposition to successive governments in the post-authoritarian period. We are concerned not just with the legitimation of the transfer of power from Francoism to the democratic regime in the late seventies but also with what, at the time, seemed to be the equally momentous collapse of the center-right coalition, whose leadership orchestrated the transition, and the rise to power of the socialists in 1982.

This triad of questions—the ambiguities of democratic legitimacy, the shifting grounds of political support, and the puzzle of low participation—arose sequentially as we followed democratization in Spain from its inception. At the outset our energies were focused on thinking through ideas about political legitimacy. By the mid-eighties, as this problem seemed to be in hand, we became interested in the implications of the shift in the political agenda from crisis resolution to economic management, in how this shift affected the mass base of the made-over socialists, who were beginning their long tenure as incumbents. Meanwhile, we had been expecting political participation to pick up. When it became clear that this wasn't happening, we prepared to examine participation more attentively.

Each cluster of questions can be addressed on its own, and though democratization may throw one or another of them into relief—for example, clarifying the realism of an otherwise abstract concept such as political legitimacy by pitting democracy against a still vivid authoritarianism—each has been studied in ongoing democracies, without special reference to master constructs such as regime transformation. Instead of a single *explicandum*, we have three dependent variables: political legitimacy, political support, and political participation.[4]

At the same time, it should be clear that what we call "depolarization" or its near equivalent, "moderation," is a thread common to these major themes. The phenomenon is associated with, though not identical to, political legitimacy. It conditions the bases of support for specific governments. And it modulates political participation. Depolarization is a core ingredient, along with "legitimacy," "support," and "participation," of our treatment of mass politics in Spain. Except for political support, a fairly transparent construct that boils down to satisfaction with or the intention to vote for a particular government, these are splendid polysyllables in need of concrete referents. We consider each in turn.

FUNDAMENTAL CONCEPTS

"By the mid-seventies," observed Pérez Díaz (1996:27),

the intense ideological conflicts of contemporary Spanish history had been notably reduced; a good part of the right as well as the left tended to accept political compromise with their adversaries and to adopt an attitude of moderation; and, even more important, the majority of Spaniards at the time, better educated and less habituated to the ideological debates of the past, had gone through the experience of living, up to a point, with socioeconomic, sociocultural, and educational institutions typical of civil society, which provided incentives for negotiation and compromise, and which allowed them to participate in innumerable accommodating rites [*ritos pacificadores*], dialogue, and conversation. . . . These Spaniards, who had daily experience of conciliation, were in search of a language of public discourse consistent with this experience. They found the normative language of a modern and European Spain, which left behind, once and for all, the drama of the civil war and which, logically, had to be post-Franquist and democratic.

Depolarization refers to what has come to be called the end, or close to the end, of ideology. A classic manifestation of this involves a progressive disengagement of once overlapping lines of conflict. In much of Mediterranean Europe and particularly in Spain, a symptom of this delinking is the gradual separation of left-vs.-right attachments from secular-vs.-religious orientations. The tie between political conservatism and religious devotion and, conversely, between political liberalism and secularism, unravels. The matrix of cleavages is transformed and so, too, is the political culture.

Figure I.1 illustrates the general point. It depicts the dynamics of the correlations between the popularity of King Juan Carlos I and the location

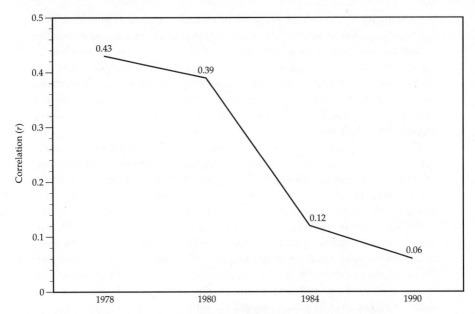

Figure I.1 Correlations between left-right placement and popularity of the king, 1978–1990

of Spaniards on the left-right continuum. Strong positive correlations indicate that the popularity of the king goes with right-wing inclinations and, conversely, that the left is inclined to hold the monarch in disfavor. As the correlations tumble, so does the connection of the king with either ideological camp.[5]

The circumstances behind the growing separation of the figure of the king from any ideological *tendance* are well known. During the attempted coup of February 1981, when elements of the military occupied the Cortes (the building in Madrid that houses the representative assembly), Juan Carlos came down on the side of democracy. His popularity, already high, soared. His decisiveness severed the traditional connection between the monarchy and political reaction. Democratic imagery did not become associated, as it had been in the thirties, with radicalization and the exclusion of the right. The steadfastness of the king endowed the moderation of the new system with respectability (Podolny 1993).

The episode throws light on two related changes. First, depolarization in this instance was identified with the emergence of judicious pragmatism, of moderation over intransigence. Though they may not have signified a transcendent political legitimacy, pragmatism and tolerance were touched with an assertive, even heroic air. Depolarization in the early days of the transition was not reducible to a drab expediency.

Second, depolarization didn't just happen in Spain as the result of "modernization." The hegemony of moderation issued from calculated, courageous political action. The consolidation of democracy was not the inexorable outcome of long-term structural transformation, although such change, together with widespread recognition of the futility of fratricidal conflict, helped (Rustow 1970). Far from being a predetermined scenario, the commitment of the king to democracy reflected deliberate choice at a tipping-point—one that helped turn the political culture of the country around (Di Palma 1990).

Our use of "depolarization" understood as the attenuation of once-overlapping lines of conflict, follows an approach embodied in the historical analysis of cleavage structures by Lipset and Rokkan (1967) and Moore (1966), and it has the advantage of concentrating on relations among variables, which are probably less subject to adventitious fluctuations than the variables—that is, opinions on issues—taken one by one. Another approach to polarization, pioneered by Dahl (1971), contrasts "conflictful," distributions of opinion on single issues with "less conflictful" unimodal distributions of other issues. Polarization is depicted as the clustering of opinions toward the poles of a continuum, giving the distribution a U shape, with the middle ground emptying out.

We employ versions of both approaches. In addition to documenting the delinking of various cleavages—between the popularity of the monarch and left-right leanings, for example, and between left-right placement and religiosity—we posit three classes of issues marked by differing degrees of volatility: "identity," "ideological," and "interest" conflicts (McDonough 1995). Our point of departure is a distinction between extremely touchy foundational issues on the one hand and relatively manageable conflicts on the other. Typical of the conflicts falling in the first category are those bristling with religious, regional, linguistic, racial, or ethnic allegiances (Jalali and Lipset 1992–93; Linz and Stepan 1992; Marty and Appleby 1997). The second category is made up of mostly economic controversies. Some of them may be severe but many of them, given a minimum of resources, can be dealt with through tangible payoffs. The first type of conflict involves *identities*, and often pits rival ways of life against one another. The latter variety involves relatively fluid *interests*. These interest-based conflicts raise "functional" questions characterized by more-or-less gradations rather than all-or-nothing splits (Hirschman 1977; Holmes 1993: 40). Honor, self-hood, survival are not involved (Gilmore 1987; Nisbett 1993).

It is also instructive to imagine an intermediate type of conflict that engages *ideologies*: belief systems that incorporate overarching principles about property, developmental strategy, or institutional design. The divide between command and free-market visions of the economy serves as the classic ideological conflict (Comisso 1991; Randolph 1996; Sachs 1992, 1993). Battles involved in the shift from single-party monopoly to multiparty competition represent corollary conflicts in the more strictly political realm.

On the eve of democratization in Spain and through its early years, some loosening of seemingly intractable conflicts—mainly, those associated with regionalism and "micronationalism"—took place. Geographic mobility and, later, the astuteness of the institutional design negotiated by the protagonists of the transition helped avert the dismemberment of the country. The categorical coordinates of identity conflicts didn't crumble but they became less rigid. And ideological disputes over grand economic principles incited even less *odium theologicum*. These changes facilitated a procedural consensus on the rules of the political game. There would still be plenty of reason for dissension on substantive matters, which more often than not turned out to be interest conflicts involving questions of incremental change rather than root-and-branch transformation.

An important hypothesis can be coaxed from our classification of types of conflict. Positions on relatively nonthreatening interest conflicts, more than anything else, have determined the popularity of post-authoritarian governments in Spain. By the onset of the eighties, Spaniards approved of the central government for political reasons and voiced criticism of it on economic and social grounds. This assessment was roughly the reverse of the public's views toward the end of the Franco years, when Spaniards enjoyed an economic boom but were put off and embarrassed by authoritarian politics.[6] During that period, the lines of authority were also, in effect, the main lines of conflict. The architecture of power was itself a matter of confrontation. With the onset of democracy Spaniards learned to live with identity conflicts and had become bored with ideological tensions, and their concerns focused on economic performance. The political culture itself had been transformed.

Changes in the hierarchy of conflict implicit in identity, ideological, and interest issues give concrete expression to "depolarization" and "moderation," conditions which in turn set the stage for the legitimation of regimes and the viability of governments. The classification has a further advantage. There is a theoretical payoff to imagining the mix of more or less conflictual, more or less manageable issues in cross-national contexts. Some fledgling democracies happen to inherit less daunting configurations of cleavages than others. The desperate cases, concentrated in though scarcely confined to post-communist countries, are those with longstanding identity and ideological conflicts and few material resources to finesse interest conflicts (Bratton and Van De Walle 1994; Jowitt 1992; Petro 1995).[7] By the middle of the 1970s, Spain was a promising mixed case. Its economic progress had put it near the outskirts of the top ten industrial powers. Still, depolarization was not a sure thing. Much of the drama beneath the pragmatic actions of the players in the Spanish transition, and much of the suspense that was never far offstage, derives from the uncertainty built into the mix of identity, ideological, and interests conflicts.[8]

Whether we understand depolarization as the dissociation of traditionally intertwined axes of conflict or as the ascendancy of interest over ideological and identity conflicts, the process approximates a slackening of passions: movement toward a negotiation of conflicts whose stakes have been altered (Mitchell 1990). But depolarization, it should be remembered, is the harbinger of political legitimacy, not the thing itself.

Legitimacy, as an academic construct, shows astonishing resilience in the face of two difficulties that would spell the death of most ideas in political science. One of its key premises—that government popularity is separable from regime support—has never been firmly established. And what practical difference legitimacy might make to the survival of political systems, democratic or otherwise, remains unclear (Useem and Useem 1979).

Democratization puts within reach a solution to the first of these problems. For about a decade or so after the death of Franco, before memories of the old regime began to fade, most Spaniards could compare authoritarianism and democracy from firsthand experience. And once the socialists had taken over from the conservative democrats, ordinary citizens could make distinctions between different democratic governments as well as between democracy and what had gone before. One sign of the meaningfulness of political legitimacy would be a perception on the part of the public that inter-regime contrasts were of a different order than contrasts between successive democratic governments. During this period, then, Spain met all the conditions for a test of political legitimacy that was more realistic than the speculative exercises conducted among citizens lacking a grasp of nondemocratic alternatives within living memory.

The temporal proximity of the Franco and the democratic systems facilitates the test of legitimacy but does not guarantee its outcome. Democratization in Spain was characterized by ambiguous moderation. The exit from authoritarianism involved a movement toward the neutralization of flammable passions. In avoiding a wholesale rejection of the old regime, Spanish democracy drew on the "backward legitimacy"—a kind of legitimacy by association—that came with a degree of continuity, particularly with regard to material growth (Di Palma 1980). The economic accomplishments of Francoism were not repudiated. Such respect for the old regime raises the question of what might be democratic about whatever legitimacy the new regime enjoys.

This question is complicated by two other developments. Ironically, by the time Spain was beginning its transition, in the aftermath of the sixties, the institutions that were identified with earlier waves of democracy, such as political parties, were showing signs of fatigue (Pizzorno 1981; von Beyme 1996). And the third wave of democratization, rising in the wake of the oil crisis, was getting started under less auspicious economic circumstances than had prevailed during the boom that followed World War II. The institutional maps inherited from the heyday of European social democracy, and the expectations associated with the good times of the postwar period, furnished uncertain guidelines for the experiment in redemocratization (Berger 1981; Berger and Dore 1996). For all the seeming desirability of democracy, some confusion existed about what it meant and what it could deliver (Schmitter and Karl 1991).

The serious question is not whether Spaniards managed to distinguish democracy from authoritarianism but how they did so. It was easier for Spaniards to agree on what they disliked than to come to a consensus on a positive model of democracy. Two options were off the table: a continuation of fascism and a return to maximalism. Beyond this, it is difficult to make out the popular bases of democratic legitimacy in Spain, especially if one is looking for fully articulated principles.

It is possible, however, to discern three rules of thumb. Perhaps foremost is the veneration for moderation itself—simply put, centrism. Depolarization in this sense nurtures a respect for procedural democracy. The economic pragmatism of the last decades of the Franco regime and the limited pluralism it nourished were steps away from the old absolutism, as was the abandonment of frantic egalitarianism on the part of the left. The coming of procedural democracy was a step beyond functional pragmatism, which Francoism had begun to cultivate, toward impartiality as the rule of law, which was absent from the old regime (López Pina 1994). Because both authoritarian and post-authoritarian regimes have been associated with a commitment to economic development, the democratic system cannot lay claim to that as a distinctive prop of its legitimacy. But it can expect to be evaluated for protecting the rights of citizens and for its adherence to the rule of law (Foweraker and Landman 1997).

Two other tenets are part of the vernacular of political legitimacy in Spain in the sense that governments can violate them only at the risk of popular rejection of their democratic credentials. One is a sense of what can be called "social fairness." In the main, this consists of a widespread expectation of equitable treatment in the material as well as judicial realms. A livelier component of democratic legitimacy in continental Europe than in the Anglo-American tradition, social fairness traces its lineage beyond Francoism to the class hierarchy of early industrial Spain (Baldwin 1992; Lipset 1983; Huber, Rueschemeyer, and Stephens 1997).

The third ingredient is "trust." The challenge confronting governments in Spain during the transition was not only to restore a sense of social fairness, without reviving the specter of maximalism, but also to hold the country together. On the one hand, respect for procedure, impartiality—that is, for the rule of law—distinguished democracy from Francoism in public opinion more than did a subfusc pragmatism, which may be as much a property of developmental authoritarianism as of neocorporatist democracies. On the other hand, many aspects of procedural democracy are remote and abstract, too rarefied or constitutionally complicated for the public to grasp (compare Beetham 1991, 1992; Beiner 1992; Jones 1996). Trust is a conviction that leaders, working through institutions, are striving to do the right thing, even if the workings of these institutions are sometimes incomprehensible and frequently inefficient (Hart 1978).

Trust in institutions, we will see, is often mediated through perceptions of the character and actions of individual leaders. It is the lesson drawn from emblematic narratives, of which the story of the king's behavior during the 1981 coup is a prime example. The evocation of feelings about such acts is an important characteristic of mass opinion not only in cases where identity conflicts, such as those prompted by region, aggravate centrifugal tendencies, but also in cases of corruption, which elicit cynicism about "the political class."[9]

Of the three ingredients—moderation, social fairness, and institutional trust—two things can be said for now. Trust and, to a lesser degree, moderation fit pretty well in mainstream treatments of political legitimacy. But the sense of social fairness may smack more of substantive than procedural democracy, tying an immaculate legitimacy to performance and outcomes. Such is not necessarily the case, however. What is at stake is the perception that the regime is trying to be equitable; whether it actually succeeds in being so is another matter. However this may be, there are clearly cultural differences, slow to change though not immutable, in the theories about democracy entertained by ordinary citizens (Feldman and Zaller 1992). In rejecting maximalism, Spaniards left room for a type of democracy that was more than minimalist. One of the forms this takes in practice is an elevated set of expectations about the role of government in social problem-solving.[10]

Second, all three ingredients are probably not invariant components of democratic legitimacy. Again, it is the sense of social fairness that seems most susceptible to vacillation. What counted as equitable in the late seventies and through the eighties may have begun to undergo redefinition as the political limits of distributive policies approached in the nineties in Spain.

Participation is the ultimate puzzle of our study. Our contention is that the depolarization of Spanish politics, particularly as expressed in the reluctance of the Catholic church to promote mass mobilization, did little, in conjunction with high unemployment and low rates of female labor force participation, to foster civic engagement.

Explanation of the participatory deficit in Spain can be aided enormously by a comparative approach. Except at the extremes there are no set criteria of what constitutes high or low participation. Cross-national evidence at least provides an empirical range for what cannot be assessed as "high" or "low" beforehand. But in order to calculate variability in the *amount* of participation, we need to spell out guidelines that are sensitive to similarities and differences between *types* of participation. Not unexpectedly, because of differences in how it is conceptualized and measured, there is some controversy about whether political participation is really as low as it seems in Spain. And, apart from the obstacles to estimation, internally as well as cross-nationally, not much is known about the causal side of the equation, about what raises and lowers participation in Spain.[11]

A sensible initial strategy would seem to be to compare Spain with other European countries that have Latin, Catholic backgrounds—Italy, for example, or France. But neither of these countries has gone through extended authoritarian episodes in the recent past. By this standard, within the Western European orbit we are left with Greece and Portugal. But both these countries must be eliminated for lack of comparable data.[12] A little thought about the diversity of participation quickly reveals that the logistics of measurement and the spotty availability of comparable indicators for the varieties of participation and their determinants place constraints on estimation and explanation.[13]

We proceed by considering first the selection of countries for comparison and indicating how they help us sort through the possible causes of variation in participation. Then we take a closer look at the varieties of participation itself. Judgments about the amount of participation presuppose clarity about the forms that participation, a notoriously multidimensional phenomenon, takes (Verba, Nie, and Kim 1978).

Our analysis of low-to-middling levels of participation is fleshed out by bringing Spain into comparison with two other new democracies, Brazil and Korea. The triad is not as exotic as it may seem. All three democracies represent recent post-authoritarian settlements. The Spanish transition got going in the mid-1970s, Brazil started a decade later, and Korea in 1988. The crucial similarity is not just one of timing, though the countries are close enough in this respect, but of political antecedents. The totalitarian repression associated with communist regimes is usually judged to have had a more toxic effect on civil society, poisoning the wellsprings of participation, than its authoritarian counterparts (Zang 1994). However else they differ, the recent authoritarian ancestry shared by Spain, Brazil, and Korea eliminates the totalitarian-vs.-authoritarian divide as an explanation for the participation gap.[14]

What's more, the countries are disparate in systematic ways, and these differences enable us to discard other initially plausible factors as causal agents behind the participation shortfall in Spain. For example, the fact that Brazil lags in economic development but is relatively high on mobilization belies any linear consonance between material progress and political participation (Del Campo 1994; Dos Santos 1990; Helliwell 1994). Nor are there institutional arrangements or legal prescriptions that might condition mass political involvement from one country to another (Casado et al. 1992).[15]

One factor which we have suggested does directly affect rates of civic engagement involves differences in women's participation in the labor force. The rate at which Spanish women compete in the job market rose sharply in the sixties and seventies, beginning from a very low level, then tapered off in the eighties (Garrido 1993). The involvement of women in the Spanish work force still trails comparable rates in peer countries. The percentage of Spanish women defined as economically active (22) is not only the lowest in Europe; it also ranks significantly behind female work-force participation in Brazil (30) and South Korea (40). As it happens, the deficit in female employment is in line with the low level of political participation and social voluntarism when Spain is compared with Brazil and Korea (Lesthaeghe 1995; Nelson and Chowdhury 1994; Roh and Mun 1994; Roh, Kim, and Mun 1994; United Nations 1995: 104ff.; compare Anderson 1975; Anderson and Cook 1985; MacDonagh 1982).

It is when we consider the religious factor that even more intriguing similarities and differences emerge across Spain, Brazil, and Korea. There is, first of all, an underpublicized similarity between Latin-Catholic Spain and Brazil and Confucian-Buddhist Korea. About 30 to 40 percent of the Korean population is estimated to be Christian—a proportion far higher, and much faster-growing, than that in any other East Asian nation (Johnstone 1993; Kang 1997). At the elite level, the primary opposition figures during the waning years of military rule, Kim Dae Jung (elected president in 1997) and Kim Young Sam (the president elected in 1993), are respectively a devout Catholic and Protestant (Jung 1987). Church leadership has been in position to catalyze participation at multiple rungs of Korean society (Cheng and Kim 1994; Han 1990; Wells 1995).

Recognition of the size of the Christian constituency in Korea may qualify cultural stereotypes, but this quantitative presence is not at the heart of the puzzle of participation. Rather, the mystery arises from the different ways in which religious practice is connected to political involvement in Spain, Korea, and Brazil. What was once thought to be the typical—in effect, the continental Western European—pattern corresponds to the tendency for the impact of religiosity on participation to be powerful, and usually negative, in industrial societies: the more religious, the less political (De Vaus and McAllister 1989).[16] This is the opiate-of-the-masses hypothesis. But the impress of religious devotion is more circumstantial. Its effect on participation goes one way (negative) in Spain and the other (positive) in Brazil and Korea.

Figure I.3 conveys the gist of the participatory puzzle. In Korea political participation increases, mildly but significantly, with religiosity. The same goes for Brazil, after one takes into account the moderately high level of participation among the irreligious—a twist likely to be found in all soci-

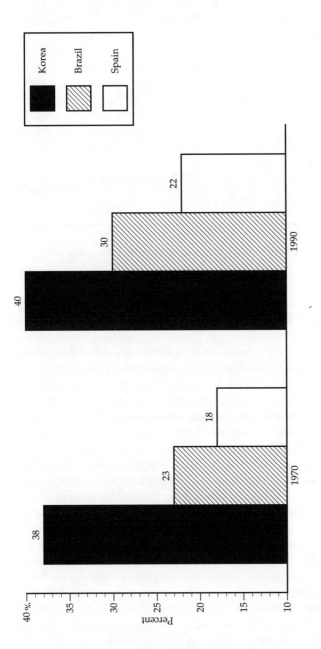

Figure I.2 Economic activity rates for women: Korea, Brazil, and Spain, 1970 and 1990

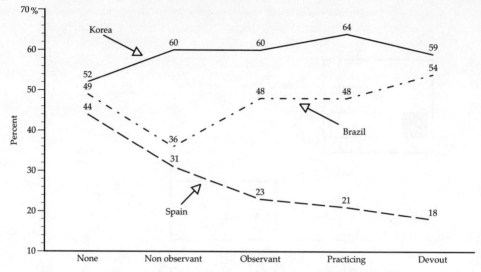

Figure I.3 Percent reporting high political participation, by religiosity: Spain, 1990; Korea, 1991; Brazil, 1993

eties with histories of anticlericalism. Spain, where political participation falls off regularly as religious devotion increases, follows the classic route.[17]

The Spanish pattern is not unlike that found in other, mostly Catholic countries of continental Europe, where the expectation is that with modernization the connection will slacken and the role of religion as a determinant of political attitudes and action will continue to decline (Whyte 1981; Dobbelaere and Jagodzinski 1995; Jagodzinski and Dobbelaere 1995). Religion's impact on participation is supposed to move from the negative to the neutral (Davis 1987). But Spain is in the minority not only in our sample of three countries but among other recent instances of democratization, such as Nicaragua, Poland, and the Philippines, where religious attachment has galvanized political participation (Youngblood 1991).[18]

The explanatory clue, we propose, lies in the specific histories of church-state relations, particularly the strategies of mobilization sponsored by churches during the course of democratization. In the wake of a legacy of catastrophic violence, proponents of the Spanish transition refrained from fanning religious passions and anticlerical enmities. In Brazil and Korea, on the other hand, the churches chose to mobilize their constituents against authoritarianism. In these countries, as in several others undergoing third-wave democratization (Arjomand 1993), church-affiliated movements and church-activated interest groups fostered participation (Cavendish 1994; Della Cava 1993; Ensor 1986; Kim 1989; Lee 1992; Mainwaring 1986).

The cross-national differences call attention to the discretionary political elements embedded in the religious factor, as contrasted with the more heavily sociological, structural inertia behind the operations of employment and gender. The reversal in the association between religiosity and political behavior in Brazil and Korea, by comparison with Spain, alerts us to the contingent, organizationally shaped nature of mobilization, over and above the longer-term forces, such as involvement in the labor market, that also drive participation (Edwards 1994; Laitin 1986).

Having spelled out what might be responsible for cross-national variations in participation, we must turn to a logically anterior question, one that we have finessed so far: how we define and operationalize participation. This is not a lexical exercise but a live issue with interpretive consequences. As interest in social capital, civic engagement, and allied manifestations of participation has risen, and as alarm has spread over supposed declines in associational life, debate over the definition and measurement of participation has heated up (Edwards and Foley 1997; Foley and Edwards 1996, 1997).

We concentrate on three kinds of public activities, with a fourth important variant. One of three major types is explicitly political. The other two encompass forms of social capital. The fourth variety, as we'll see, is not so well mapped empirically, but it merits careful attention because for some it represents the future of political participation.

We treat mass *political behavior* as a set of activities that are for the most part designed to influence public policy—contacting politicians, attending town meetings, and so forth (compare Knoke 1990a, 1990b). By this standard, Spain comes up short again. Our indicators can be summed to form an index of "conventional" political participation and, taking Spain as the norm, divided into quartiles. Thus, 27 percent of the Spanish respondents report high political participation. Using the same cutting points yields estimates of 49 percent claiming high participation in Brazil and 58 percent in Korea.[19]

Another kind of participatory contact—the local relations of everyday life expressed in interaction with neighbors—may seem so removed from political activity that they hardly qualify as civic engagement of any sort.[20] Yet *neighborliness* can function as a mobilizational resource. In the least it serves as a baseline against which to gauge the extent of more plainly political and social *civisme* (Logan and Spitze 1994).

In sharp contrast to the cross-national differences in political participation, the level of neighborliness varies hardly at all between countries. The percentage of Spaniards reporting close relations with their neighbors (21) is about the same as in Brazil (25) and Korea (24), so there is no intercountry variation to explain. But neighborliness is not static. It declines steadily *within* each country among younger cohorts. Not only is the level of neighborhood ties remarkably similar across countries; so is their rate of decline.

These prepolitical ties are conditioned by macrostructural dynamics—for example, urbanization, social mobility, education—that operate in a nearly uniform manner across countries.

In between overtly political behavior and the closeness of backyard and street-corner ties come indicators of *civil society*: membership in voluntary associations, in groups that extend beyond the purely local and informal but that do not typically carry as much political content as activities guided toward policy (Curtis, Grabb, and Baer 1992). Table I.1 summarizes the evidence for cross-national variation in what has come to be termed social capital, understood as membership in voluntary associations and movements. It suggests not only that about a third of the Spanish public claims to belong to such groups, and that the figure in Spain is significantly below the involvement reported in Korea and Brazil, but also that such civic engagement held steady, at a low level, from the onset through the consolidation of democracy in Spain. If anything, membership in voluntary associations has fallen off a bit from the first to the fourth survey.[21]

These three types of involvement—closeness to neighbors, membership in voluntary associations, and conventional political participation—cover a reasonably broad spectrum of civic and not-so-civic engagement. How are they connected? To what extent do political activities build on membership in voluntary associations or on neighborhood ties? Membership in voluntary associations is convertible, after some slippage, into political participation. But the two are sufficiently distinct to warrant separate analysis. And neighborhood bonds tend to be independent from, though not in opposition to, both voluntary association membership and political participation.[22] So, rather than treat them as a bloc, we deal with neighborhood ties, membership in voluntary associations, and political activity as tiers along a gradient of civic engagement, running from parochial to civil to political society, with each requiring explanation in its own right. These constitute our dependent variables in the study of participation.

One other question remains. Ample as our coverage may be, it conceiv-

TABLE I.1. Membership in voluntary associations: Spain, 1978–1990; Korea, 1991; Brazil, 1993 (percent)

	Spain				Korea	Brazil
Number of associations	1978	1980	1984	1990	1991	1993
None	64%	65%	60%	69%	13%	34%
One	23	20	25	22	31	28
Two or more	13	15	15	8	56	38

Note: In this and subsequent tables, column or, when applicable, row totals may not sum exactly to 100 percent because of rounding error.

ably overlooks certain informal vehicles of political behavior—for example, protest activity—that gained prominence in the sixties and that, some would argue, have continued to play an important role in grass-roots politics since then. Besides, the anarchist current and its variants represent a long tradition in Spain (Esenwein 1989; Kaplan 1977). While involvement in protest activities is difficult to monitor, failure to do so might contribute to a significant underestimation of informal, intermittent expressions of participation.

We gathered information on protest activity in the most recent Spanish survey, so that the amount of this activity and its determinants can be estimated.[23] We also obtained usable though not exactly equivalent information from Brazil.[24] Though we have no such information from Korea, estimates of the incidence of protest behavior in some Western European countries are available, and some idea can be obtained of where Spain stands cross-nationally in this regard (Gundelach 1995; Topf 1995).

Examination of this fourth variety of political behavior yields ambiguous results. This is not just because the evidence is scattered. It is unclear, on theoretical grounds, what the empirical clues we do have tell us about the types of collective action that can be expected to develop in Spain in the wake of democratic consolidation.

On the one hand, whatever the actual incidence of "unorthodox" political activity, approval of such behavior runs high in Spain. In this sense the political culture harbors a potential for protest, and the syndrome probably does reflect traces of the anarchist legacy. Moreover, even though the number of formal strikes has declined markedly since the very early days of the transition, just after the death of Franco, Spain still ranks high—second only to Greece in Europe—in the time lost to "work stoppages." And when protest behavior in Spain is set alongside such indicators as we have for Brazil, the country turns out not to look so politically lethargic as it does in terms of associational membership and conventional participation. On the other hand, the only data on protest behavior reasonably comparable to ours, drawn from the World Values Study (1994), indicate that activity of this sort may have receded in Spain from 1980 to 1990.

So one challenge is simply to put together credible figures on the level of direct political action from country to country. Then, if such estimates can be worked up, we need to gauge the forces that shape involvement in protest behavior. Ideally, we would like to be able to separate the causal elements that drive such participation everywhere from those that are country-specific. Increasingly, scholars have noted, protest behavior that was deviant in the break from the fifties to the sixties may have entered the repertoire of normal political action (Dalton and Kuechler 1990). Once an expressive style for the few, certain types of protest may have become fashionable, and instrumental, for many. The diffusionist argument has merit, but it runs into trouble with cross-national variations. New forms of political behavior may have spread, in general, as an inheritance of the sixties, but this overall tendency, such as it is, doesn't account for differences in participation between countries. The concluding analytical chapter takes up these factual and conceptual countercurrents, with the focus on Spain in comparative context.

THE EMPIRICAL BACKGROUND

Most of the data come from four national surveys we conducted in Spain in 1978, 1980, 1984, and 1990. This series is unique for its scope (3,000 personal interviews at each time) and temporal extension (taking us from the days of the conservative-led transition through the glory days and incipient decline of the socialists). Fifty percent of the people interviewed in 1978 were interviewed again in 1980; this continuity enables us to trace the dynamics of mass politics during the inchoate days of the transition.[25]

Another body of data is composed of national surveys, modeled after the Spanish design, carried out in Korea (1991) and Brazil (1993).[26] The Korean and Brazilian data are deployed almost exclusively for the cross-national analysis of participation. These materials help us gauge in what sense and to what degree participation in Spain is actually low or below average. Then, having established the magnitude of the gap, we marshal evidence from all three countries to test a causal model of cross-national disparities in participation.

One other type of data, contextual information on the Spanish transition and its aftermath, is crucial to interpretation. A capsule history is in order, to give an idea of the political events and cultural developments that molded public opinion over time.[27]

Francisco Franco died in his bed on November 20, 1975, but the transition can be said to have begun in earnest, and ominously, nearly two years earlier, when Prime Minister Luis Carrero Blanco was blown up in a car-bomb assassination in the center of Madrid five days before Christmas, 1973. The military rebellion across the border in Portugal, dating from April 1974, that overthrew the regime Marcello Caetano had inherited from Antonio de Oliveira Salazar, was another sign that the old order might be crumbling. In October 1974, at a party congress held in exile in France, the socialists elected a labor lawyer in his early thirties, Felipe González, as their first secretary.

On November 22, 1975, two days after Franco's death, the Cortes proclaimed Juan Carlos de Borbón king of Spain and, as head of state, successor to Franco. In May 1976 the first issue of El País, the newspaper of record for the oncoming transition, appeared in the streets of major cities. On July 3, 1976, the king appointed a former civil governor and functionary of the Falange, Adolfo Suárez, as prime minister. A few days later,

Suárez announced a program of reforms, including elections scheduled for mid-1977. Suárez would stay on as prime minister until his resignation in January 1981, overseeing the most delicate years of the democratization process (Simons 1995).

In November 1976, less than one year after Franco had died, the Cortes passed the Law of Political Reform, which promulgated the dismantling of the old corporatist structure of governance. The law was approved in a national referendum held the next month; turnout was just over 80 percent, and 94 percent of ballots cast were for approval. In February 1977 all political parties except the communists were legalized. And in April, on Easter Sunday, 1977, the Communist party itself was legalized.[28] On the same day, Luis Buñuel's film *Viridiana*, made in 1961, was shown for the first time in Spain. One month before, unions had been given the right to organize and to strike.

In June 1977 national elections—the first democratic elections since 1936—were held as scheduled, returning Suárez's Unión de Centro Democrático (UCD) to power.[29] These elections also chose, in effect, the delegates who drafted the constitution that would be approved by referendum a year and a half later, in December 1978 (Gunther, Sani, and Shabad 1985). In July 1977 Spain submitted its formal application for membership in the European Community. In October 1977 the Moncloa Pacts (named after the prime minister's residence in Madrid) were signed by politicians and by labor and business leaders. These were the first in a series of accords designed to curb wage demands and stem inflation.

A month earlier, in September 1977, the king issued a "preautonomy" decree to Catalonia; in December a similar pact was negotiated with the Basque provinces; so, in March 1978, was a pact with Galicia. By the end of 1978 Spain had been divided into seventeen *autonomías*.[30]

In March 1979, three months after the Spanish people had voted to approve the new constitution, the UCD was again successful at the polls. Soon after, however, *desencanto* (disenchantment) set in because of deteriorating economic conditions—inflation was running at 25 percent—and tensions surrounding what some in the military called "the dismemberment of Spain." On February 23, 1981, less than a month after Suárez had resigned and before his replacement could be elected, a faction of the military seized the Cortes. The uprising failed once the king broadcast his defense of democracy through television facilities that troops loyal to him had regained from the insurgents.

In July 1981 divorce was legalized. Just over four years later, in August 1985, the abortion laws were liberalized as well.

By 1982 the UCD was in a state of collapse. The Partido Socialista Obrero Español (PSOE) won a parliamentary majority in elections held in October of that year, with Felipe González as head of the party.[31] The socialists would remain in power until 1996.

Toward the end of 1983 fragmentary newspaper reports began to appear about the government's antiterrorist operation, directed mainly at Basque separatists. It was not until the early nineties that these activities erupted into a full-fledged scandal.

At the beginning of 1986 Spain was admitted to full membership in the European Community, and the economy began a run of prosperity, lasting through 1990, that matched the spurt of the 1960s. The socialists won another parliamentary majority in the 1986 elections. However, relations between the PSOE and the major (communist and socialist) labor unions grew testy because of the government's moves to implement economic restructuring policies as well as because of persistent high unemployment. In December 1988 the unions called a nationwide general strike, forcing the government to reconsider the pace of its reforms.[32]

Another watershed was reached in the referendum about membership in the North Atlantic Treaty Organization, approved by a narrow margin on March 12, 1986, just a few months after Spain had entered the EC. The government's advocacy of membership in NATO represented yet another reversal of socialist orthodoxy; González had opposed the initiative when it was launched by the UCD government in 1981.[33]

In October 1987 two top leaders of the Union General de Trabajadores (UGT), the socialist labor organization, quit their positions as deputies in the Cortes, protesting the economic policies of the González government.

In 1989 the conservative Alianza Popular coalition changed its name to the Partido Popular (PP). The Communist party of Spain had already, starting in 1986, tried to broaden its base as the Izquierda Unida (United Left). In April 1990 José María Aznar was elected president of the PP; he would become prime minister, defeating the socialists, in 1996.

Also in 1989 the PSOE lost its parliamentary majority, winning exactly half of the seats in the Cortes. With this decline, the regional parties, primarily the Catalans, became pivotal alliance partners in sustaining national governments.

Nineteen eighty-nine was also the year of Pedro Almodóvar's *Women on the Verge of a Nervous Breakdown*, which opened in March, capturing the spirit of the hip, hyperkinetic *movida madrileña*—roughly, the night-life scene of Madrid.

In June 1989 the Spanish peseta was keyed to the European Monetary System. With the signing of the Maastricht Treaty in December 1991, Spain underscored its commitment to the "rationalization" of its economic system.

The World's Fair was inaugurated in Seville in April 1992. In July of that year the Olympic Games opened in Barcelona. The PSOE managed to form a minority government, again with the support of Catalan nationalists, after the 1993 elections. But the hold of the socialists continued to weaken, from its peak of 202 seats in the 1982 landslide to 159 seats after the 1993 elections. By March 1996 the socialists were out of office. In June 1997, at the 34th party congress, Felipe González chose not to run again for the position of secretary general of the PSOE.

1

Rethinking Democratic Legitimacy

... on a road in the mountains somewhere in southern Spain [a] small car traveling just ahead of me suddenly crashed into the large nose of an incoming lorry. The car contained three members of the *guardia civil* police force and the leader of the three men, a general distinguished by the ribbons and medals that decorated his dark uniform, was sitting in the front passenger seat, so that when the collision took place he was thrown forward, his head hit the windshield and he suffered a mild concussion. The other two men were unharmed and I watched as they hurriedly clambered out of the car and began to heave the passive body of their superior onto the road. His face was deathly pale, but although it was without expression it still looked rather dangerous, as if the owner might at any moment open his jaws and bite.
— Julia Blackburn, *The Emperor's Last Island*

The 1970s were promising years for democracy. The oil crisis of 1973 shook dictatorships in Argentina and Brazil that had taken credit for stimulating economic growth. In 1974, for reasons having more to do with the impasse of a colonial war than with economic stagnation, the authoritarian regime that had held power in Portugal for nearly half a century collapsed (Baklanoff 1992). A great wave of democratization was starting to build. It would course through Latin Europe and much of Latin America, over many of the newly industrialized countries of East Asia, and culminate in the disintegration of communism in Russia and Central and Eastern Europe (Huntington 1991, 1997).

At the start, however, what was to became a trend seemed more like a trickle than a tidal wave. Events during the first half of the seventies called into question the link between political repression and economic progress without sending an unequivocal message about democratic governance as an alternative to despotism and economic backwardness. The boom experienced under dictatorships in East Asia argued against outright rejection of rule from the top (Scalapino 1989), and turmoil in Portugal in the wake of the revolution of the carnations (as the transition there was called because of the peace-and-love tenor of its earliest phase) gave observers in Spain pause about the wisdom of "premature" democratization (Graham and Makler 1979).

Graffiti and posters covered the walls of Lisbon. Citizens once noted for long-suffering parked their cars and motorbikes where they pleased in defiance of a police force too cowed to issue tickets or solicit bribes. The tessellated sidewalks of the city fell into disrepair. A constitution mandating the nationalization of numerous industries and extensive redistribution of resources was being drafted by deputies in need of sleep. Impromptu people's courts and assemblies cropped up and vanished and reappeared. The only consensus that emerged from the roundtable talk shows that filled the evening hours of Portuguese television was that the wearing of neckties was dangerously out of fashion. Estates belonging to the landlords of the south were threatened with confiscation. Drugs and miniskirts flourished in once-decorous urban quarters. Marriages collapsed, especially, it seemed, among the better families. Spaniards who signed up for tours to the Lisbon production of *Hair* were of two minds about importing such material back home. Happenings across the border had an unseemly third-world flavor (Maxwell 1995).

It was not just that Spaniards feared a return to the bloodbath of the 1930s—the executions, the reprisals, the terror. Reactionaries drew dour lessons from the cultural radicalism of the sixties which they saw working its way into Spain through tourism, consumerism, the media, and the assorted effronteries of mass society. Among the old guard—some older, rural, religious Spaniards in addition to the scandalized "bunker" itself—democracy was seen as a carnival of impudence, immorality, and bad taste, and some conservatives had doubts about the approach of a free-wheeling capitalism that smacked of something beyond an avocational going-into-trade under protected conditions. Permissiveness threatened the strictures of an entire way of life.

From another, more common perspective, however, the problem was material and political rather than one of cultural apocalypse. A burgeoning middle class had done well during the last years of the Franco regime. Prosperity deepened their skepticism about visionary democracy, and in particular about socialism as an ideology identified with bureaucratic centralism and confiscatory taxation. Their quarrel was not with modernization in general but with the restoration of ways of thinking about the economy that were identified with the old left.

Many Spaniards acknowledged the desirability of balancing political reform with measures designed to foster not only economic liberalization but a measure of social fairness. Substantive as well as procedural democracy was at issue. Alarm about the coming of democracy involved more than equivocation about permissiveness and challenges to authority. It included fears about the implications of the political transition for the arrangement of economic power and expectations of social distribution. Modest as the ambitions of youthful reformers may seem in retrospect, social democracy at the time appeared to be, as it did among postwar French intellectuals addicted to prophetic purities, "the politics that dared not speak its name" (Judt 1998: 30).

The crux of the problem was a profound self-doubt on the part of Spaniards about their capacity to pull off a reformist program, moderate though it might be. The historical rarity of moderation in public life made political actors nervous about the chances of implementing democracy as a venture in pragmatism (Cebrián 1985). Reform had too often gotten out of hand, spiraling into the terrible simplifications and irreconcilable antipathies of class warfare. With the prospect of democracy imminent, anxieties about the maintenance of authority and continuity could not be dismissed as rightist hysteria or antiquarian melancholy. Uncertainty and ambivalence were not simply a consequence of the dialectical nature of economic growth that undermined the political controls and social hierarchies through which development had been channeled for decades. They reflected reservations about how the coming of democracy was to be handled without jeopardizing the achievements and some of the privileges of the past. Spain had yet to undergo a political transition in the twentieth century without pitting implacable radicalisms against one another; the record of dashed aspirations bordered on the perverse. "Spain's only previous experience with democracy," Richard Gunther notes (1998: 268), "lasted just five years (1931–1935) and ended in civil war."

> Indeed, this episode was only one (albeit by far the most violent) manifestation of political instability that dated back to the end of the Napoleonic era: in little over a century, Spain experienced seven pronunciamientos (military uprisings), four monarchical abdications, two changes of monarchical dynasty, two dictatorships (one lasting nearly four decades), two republics, and four civil wars (1833–1840, 1846–1848, 1872–1875 and 1936–1939).

By the 1970s, then, outside of a few corners in the military and the church, the defense of hierarchy as an absolute tenet seemed less pressing in Spain than the need to preserve a modicum of continuity and a minimum of control over the unfolding of the new era. For most Spaniards democracy was no longer a profane, impious conceit (Lilla 1993: 152). It might even be desirable. But was it feasible?

Democracy in principle, as some sort of loosening of outmoded restraints, was less threatening than democratization from below. Scripted in social movements and mass resentment, this latter scenario threatened to let the bats out of the attic of Spanish maximalism. Moderate democracy meant a managed transition. In enlightened quarters, democratization was seen not only as a good in itself but as a strategic imperative to preempt the radical antics and raucous mobilization that myopic elites, like the Portuguese and others of the bunker, might bring on themselves, letting government fall in the streets.

Lessons about the futility of confrontation, drawn from the explosiveness of Spanish politics of previous generations, did not cause old antagonisms to vanish overnight; statesmanship and self-confidence did not automatically overcome the fratricidal rivalries of the past. Structural fault lines and historical grudges continued to jeopardize the reformist scenario. Divisions between regional, ideological, and economic groupings predated the Civil War, and these cleavages had formed venerable scars (Barnstone 1995). The fear was that confrontational democratization—*ruptura* was the buzz word—would rip open scabs that had covered but not healed these wounds. Though the modernization experienced by the country since the early sixties had taken some of the edge off these conflicts, memories died hard. At the time of the transition, after more than a generation during which the organized expression of antagonisms had been repressed, the political momentum of such memories might be difficult to control. The old demons might be resurrected, leading to polarization (López Pina and Aranguren 1976; López Pintor 1982).

THE EVOLUTION OF DEPOLARIZATION

The conceit that the fading of ancient cleavages diminishes the propensity to extremism and encourages bargaining and compromise is axiomatic in political sociology. The possibility that countries might make a go of democratization anyway, in the face of terrible antagonisms, should not obscure the likelihood that the reduction of such tensions eases the process. Depolarization approximates a necessary condition for the consolidation of democracies that do not rely on formal consociational settlements—that do not, in other words, make special provisions for minorities defined as ethnic, linguistic, or religious identities or in terms of ideological labels (Sartori 1994). Depolarization operates in the cultural sphere as the socioeconomic prerequisites of democracy—growth in the GNP, urbanization, literacy, and so on—function in the structural realm (Diamond 1992). It establishes the groundwork for the institutionalization of competition in place of conflict *à l'outrance*.

Yet the softening of ancient cleavages may not in fact precede the onset of democratization. What appears to have taken place in Spain was an erosion of the structural bases of the earlier political combat that left recollections of these conflicts vivid but disembodied. The smoke of battle hung in the air even as the demographics had altered. Almost all political players recognized that the remnants of old cleavages still smoldered. This awareness, together with memories of the terrible consequences of fanning the embers, placed a premium on restraint as a preventive to conflagration, even if it didn't guarantee that such learning would actually be converted into sensible action (Aguilar 1995). The cooling of political passions did not simply happen or exactly precede the consolidation of democracy in Spain, even if it was foreshadowed by favorable economic and social transformations—none of which guaranteed that the Spanish temper would overcome its grudges or that leaders would strategize astutely. But the disjuncture between structural modernization and cultural obsession cut elites some slack and, eventually, encouraged the renunciation of mortal combat.

The menacing feature of political culture in Spain was not only the abundance of antagonisms or memories of them but the fact that they overlapped. Polarization in its exacerbated form stems from the intertwining of conflicts; one division reinforces another. A classic instance of this in Spain has been the meshing of ideological, left-vs.-right leanings and secular-vs.-religious dispositions. In this case the overcoming of cultural rigidities involves an exercise in pulling apart knots that have grown hard with age. It entails not just a change in this or that attitude but a rearrangement in cultural proclivities—in the ways of relating political signals to one another. A sea change in political habits occurs.

A disentangling of such ties would signify depolarization, which would in turn foster political tractability. If a primary characteristic of polarization involves the interlocking of lines of conflict, then one sign of depolarization is the attenuation of this linkage. The correlation between religious and ideological sentiment, for example, should drop over time.

Examination of the rudimentary evidence doesn't yield many clues about the polarization of public opinion. No significant change is detectable in either religious attachment or left-right placement from our first through our fourth surveys.[1] In 1990 about eight out of ten Spaniards claimed to be "believers," a percentage that if anything had edged up a bit from the benchmark year.[2] Ideologically, Spaniards continued to tilt to the center-left, at least until the end of the eighties.

Two other indicators, however, display impressive change. Figure. 1.1 graphs measures assessing satisfaction with "the way democracy is working," with the present government and with the Franco regime.[3] Satisfaction with the government went up from the time of the UCD (center-right) governments of the early days of redemocratization to the ascent of the center-left PSOE in the early eighties and into the high tide of prosperity toward the end of the decade. Satisfaction with democracy parallels good times.

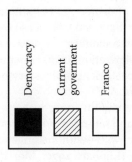

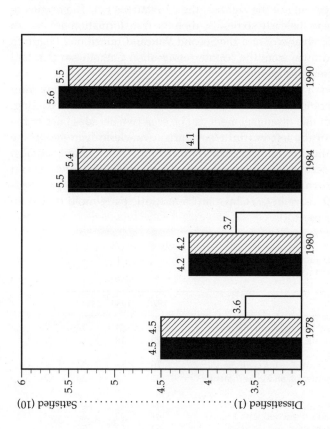

Figure 1.1. Mean satisfaction with "the way democracy is working," with current government, and with "last ten years of Franco regime," 1978–1990

Note: Franco item was not asked in 1990.

Such trends are not wholly self-explanatory. One would like to know more about what Spaniards mean by "left," "center," and "right" (Díez Medrano, García-Mon, and Díez Nicolás 1989; compare Miller, Hesli, and Reisinger 1997). In addition, what exactly economic growth contributed to support for the government and to the binding-in of democracy has still to be determined. Nevertheless, it is reasonably clear that trends like these reflect a boost in government popularity and in regime stability.

Table 1.1 gets directly at the question of depolarization; it documents the correlations between cultural indicators. The coefficients tell a story of a gradual though not quite steady drop in antagonisms.

The top-row correlations for 1978 and 1980 are about the same as the associations regularly reported between religiosity and left-right orientation in other Latin countries—Italy and France, for example—with histories of ecclesiastical triumphalism and anticlericalism (Lijphart 1979; Martin 1979). With the passing of the eighties, the correlations fall. The origins of this delinking lie in the early sixties. By then the transformation of Spanish society was well advanced, and the Second Vatican Council had begun to promote a withdrawal from the counterreformation Catholicism that had buttressed the Francoist regime.

To the chagrin of hard-liners, the church had started to back away from its embrace of Francoism about a decade prior to the dictator's passing, and the results of this disengagement can be seen two decades later in the decomposition of the left-vs.-right/secularism-vs.-clericalism syndrome (Linz 1991). By the time democratization was in full bloom and a socialist government undertook the reformulation of laws governing divorce and abortion, the church in Spain had neither the will nor the capacity to organize a counteroffensive in the Christian Democratic party mold (Callahan 1992; Pérez Díaz 1991a).

TABLE 1.1. Correlations between religiosity, left–right orientation, government support, and satisfaction with democracy, 1978–1990

	1978	1980	1984	1990
Religiosity and left–right orientation	.45	.51	.42	.29
Left–right orientation and satisfaction with democracy	.20	.10	-.13	-.13
Religiosity and satisfaction with democracy	.20	.11	.00	.01
Left–right orientation and government support	.30	.24	-.29	-.24
Religiosity and government support	.30	.20	-.03	.03
Religiosity and satisfaction with Franco	.41	.43	.40	*
Left–right orientation and satisfaction with Franco	.62	.62	.56	*

* "Satisfaction with Franco" not asked in 1990.

The shrinkage of the association between religiosity and both support for the government and satisfaction with democracy gives further evidence of a thaw in cultural hostilities.[4] By 1984 there is simply no relation between religious devotion and either of these political learnings. Nowadays religious attachment seems to have little to do one way or the other with popular attitudes toward democracy or toward the government in Spain. This dissociation does not exclude the possibility of indirect connections between religion and politics generally or even of some impact of positions regarding religion-related issues, such as abortion, on evaluations of the government. But the days of mobilization against the political system, on the basis of religion as an institutional counterculture, are over.[5]

A subtle but significant pattern also emerges in the differential connection of left-right placement with support for a specific government and support for the regime. On the one hand, the link between left-right leanings and satisfaction with the government is obvious. Those toward the right are somewhat happier with conservative governments and those toward the left are a bit more content with socialist rule. The corresponding link between left-right placement and satisfaction with democracy turns out to be weaker. This distancing hints of a partial distinction between support for the government and support for the broader system. In Spain democracy is much less inflammatory, less a matter of partisanship than it used to be. Not only has depolarization set in but government and regime are not so fused as in the days of revolution and counterrevolution.[6]

The mildness of perceptions regarding the center-right and center-left governments and the democratic settlement under which they have operated contrasts with the intensity of popular attitudes toward Franco. The correlations between religiosity and satisfaction with "the last ten years of the Franco government" are higher than the equivalent coefficients for the democratic governments and the democratic regime, and the associations between left-right placement and feelings toward Francoism are stronger still. The diminishing numbers of Spaniards with memories of the Franco years tend to feel passionately, both pro and con, about these decades. The authoritarian past is more polarizing in memory than the democratic regime is in the present. Whatever the shallowness or depth of popular commitment to democracy, the old regime evokes harsher feelings, with connotations of atavism and ferocity, than does the new dispensation (compare Gibson 1996).[7]

All told, these instances of attenuation between the indicators of religiosity, left-right placement, political satisfaction, and the like form a remarkable pattern. Francoism was as much a cultural talisman of devotion to and sins against hierarchy, of garish monumentality and repressed sensuality, as it was a system of economic and political control (Higginbotham 1988; compare Brownlee and Gumbrecht 1995). If democratization is understood in part as a process of differentiation between political, economic, and cultural domains that once were intertwined, the hold of the symbolic tentacles of the old regime was clearly weakening by the time the political and economic transitions got underway. This shift represented a cultural transformation in itself, clearing the air and encouraging a pragmatic style that would shove aside an expiring way of life.

Almost all countries that have democratized since the 1970s have gone through or attempted to pull off dual transitions. The twofold nature of these changes is clearest in transitions from communism, where democratization has involved not just political liberalization but a shift from command to market economies. A less dramatic transformation is evident in transitions from authoritarianism such as those experienced by Spain and Brazil, where privatization and other variations on industrial restructuring are leitmotifs of the political economy of democratization (Bermeo 1994; Geddes 1995; Haggard and Kaufman 1995; Hojman 1994).

What happened in Spain was a *triple* transition—cultural, economic, and political (compare Edles 1995). The thick tangle of religious conviction set against a rigid secularism came undone, and geographic mobility took some of the edge off regional enmities. Cleavages that once overlapped became differentiated. Depolarization gained momentum. By the onset of democratization in the 1970s a fresh generation of leaders, many of whom were indistinguishable from their predecessors except by reason of their youth, saw fit to gamble on moderation.

Here again, some important ramifications of depolarization and possible countercurrents remain to be explored. Nothing has been said about regional antagonisms, and class hostility has been touched on only glancingly through reference to the left-right split. Our evidence serves merely to introduce the point that a calming of political passions occurred during the course of democratization. The task now is to specify the implications of this development for the legitimation of Spanish democracy.

CONCEPTUALIZING LEGITIMACY

"Depending upon one's views," the historian Paul Kristeller remarked, "the Renaissance would seem to have lasted as much as four hundred years, or only 27 years, not counting the view of those scholars who think that the Renaissance did not exist at all" (1990: 2). A similar elusiveness afflicts the idea of political legitimacy.

Consider two opposing approaches. The strong view treats political legitimacy as the product of a civil religion, that is, of a consensus on an ideal of the good polity. The model may or may not, as in theocracies, be democratic, and it is questionable how extensively and deeply consensus runs across the citizenry. In the democratic case this civil creed is supposed to constitute a characteristic set of norms—the dignity of the individual, social equity, and so on—that make up the standards by which the legitimacy of governments is assessed (Bellah and Hammond 1980). The essential distinction is between concrete governments and the prescriptive abstractions that compose a higher regime, set of rules, or meta-institutions. This distinction introduces political accounting by dual criteria. Governments are judged by their performance, on the grounds of efficiency. They may also be judged normatively, according to the appropriateness of their policies and actions—by how well they live up to a common understanding of justice. The implication is that governments may perform poorly for some time without jeopardizing the legitimacy of the regime which they incarnate. Conversely, sound performance alone—getting the trains to run on time, and so on—doesn't guarantee the legitimacy of the political system.

In contrast to full-blown legitimacy, the stripped-down view focuses on political support or popularity, based mainly on instrumental payoffs and assessments of material performance. Even if, like faintly alarming ghosts or occasionally comforting spirits, norms have a cultural existence apart from the political realm and exercise certain boundary-marking functions (in defining criminal behavior and deviance, for example), political legitimacy is seen as a side issue among the host of more tangible factors that determine the viability of governments. Norms and the like may exist, but they don't count for much politically (Jackman and Miller 1996). Governments and regimes weather prolonged slumps in performance not because they draw on a mythical reservoir of legitimacy but because of skilled gamesmanship on the part of political and economic interests (Rogowski 1974; compare Remmer 1995). Political culture is fluff.

The contrast between these approaches to political legitimacy, one tied to a full-service version of the construct and the other deeply skeptical of the conversion of psychocultural forces into politically consequential behavior, points up the dichotomous nature of theorizing on the subject. Just this dualism happens to be pertinent to the Spanish case. The Don Quixote-Sancho Panza interplay captures a historical division between the supposition, shared until recently by many protagonists in Spain, that political differences could best be understood as rivalries between world views and ways of life, and on the other hand a no-nonsense realism according to which it is the payoff and not the principle that's at stake. The first persuasion evokes a cosmology of the wicked and the redeemed, not just of winners and losers. In the second, intractable identities and salvific ideologies give way to negotiable interests.

The contrast makes for a fundamental division in political culture (Gracián 1647/1953). The tradition of harsh polarization and intolerance has not enjoyed a monopoly in Spanish political life (Kamen 1988). It can be argued that the political culture of Spain is dualistic not in the customary sense of being polarized between left and right but by reason of being divided between one culture that takes ideological discourse with deadly seriousness and another that persists in a bemused matter-of-factness.

The story behind the waning of the political animosities we traced at the beginning of this chapter is one of the passage from panoptic ideologies to pragmatic mentalities. Only a few decades ago, moderation went against the folkloric grain. When the transition was getting started in the 1970s, after the stirrings of cultural liberation in the sixties, to embrace bargaining and compromise meant rejecting the pathological specters of the past. The change was aided by generational replacement among the elites, and even some of the old guard underwent historical detoxification (Morán 1996). The de-dramatization of Spanish politics has been real enough. But it has not been without perils of its own.

Rejection of the posturing, grandiloquence, operatics and gratuitous cruelty of *espagnolisme* has run the risk of replacing a sense of honor and public service with narrow self-seeking and of reducing not just the survival of governments but the quality of democracy to market transactions. For some the democratic ethos is indistinguishable from a business ethic. Overcoming the heroic, tragic manias of *la España atormentada* might entail acceptance of a treadmill expedience that admits no public space or collective purpose.

If the history of Spanish politics has been one of extremes, one of the ironies of the democratization of the post-Franco era has been a nearly obsessive avoidance of extremism that may have drained incentives to political mobilization. Though political quiescence doesn't undermine the stability of democracy, its effect on the quality of democracy—on the extent of civic engagement, in particular—may be damaging. The depolarization of mass politics in Spain raises an important question about the nature and the consequences of democratic legitimacy. It is doubtful whether the disappearance of the once lethal clarity of Spanish political culture has produced a new civic vision; depolarization might just as well generate indifference or apathy as stimulate the adoption of democratic ideals.

But this is to get ahead of our story. We need to come up with a working definition of political legitimacy, one that permits us to verify its existence in the minds of ordinary citizens, before making claims about its impact on political behavior. Three elements will occupy us here: legitimacy by multiple criteria, legitimacy based on the retrospective comparison of regimes, and legitimacy as a function of trust.

Dimensions of Legitimacy

The theoretical convention, we've noted, has been to split the objects of political support and legitimacy into lower and higher levels: concrete governments whose popularity hinges on effectiveness and broader regimes based on diffuse commitment (Beetham 1993). Without abandoning this split completely, suppose we shift the spotlight from the objects to the criteria of support. Instead of forcing an a priori partition between supposedly higher and lower conceptions of the state, we attend to the values by which governments are judged.

Imagine that political systems—whether governments or regimes, or both—are evaluated by standards that emphasize *political, economic,* and *social* functions. The democratic regime (if such an entity exists in the eyes of the Spanish public, apart from the various governments that have made it up) might find approval on social grounds for reducing, or trying to reduce, disparities between rich and poor. In this case the standard would be one of equity or fairness (Tyler 1984).Yet it might be regarded as wanting by political standards—for failing to maintain law and order, for example. Similarly, it might be viewed positively along economic lines, for promoting growth, while falling short on one or both of the other criteria. Several permutations are imaginable. The new regime might be judged as adequate on both social and economic grounds while it is seen as no more or perhaps even less satisfactory politically than the Francoist system.

Legitimacy, then, may be understood according to its range or scope as well as by its depth or levels (Walzer 1983). The political component of the "system" may be legitimate, while the economic and/or social components are not, or are only partially so, and vice versa (Dahl 1985; Vidal-Beneyto 1984). The differentiation of evaluative dimensions is an empirical as well as a theoretical question, as is the supposed separation of a specific government from a broad regime.

We are accustomed to thinking of political legitimacy holistically, as a package, or as some qualitative, categorical entity, an ideal type or marmoreal absolute. But the theoretically stylized can be the enemy of the politically real. Breaking legitimacy down into functional components is no more farfetched, and may be more comprehensible to ordinary Spaniards, than expecting them to distinguish between governments of the here-and-now and abstract political systems or regimes. It is reasonable to expect some citizens to evaluate governments, and perhaps regimes, on a selective basis, emphasizing certain criteria more than others. In the Spanish context this possibility has the ring of reality. The authoritarian system and the democratic regime that followed it are not mirror images. Democratization was gradual rather than abrupt. The nonrevolutionary nature of democratization leaves open the possibility of a selective, less-than-total separation between the two. The question becomes: after breaking them down into specific domains, do citizens put the regimes back together again as contrasting systems?

Why these particular dimensions? Economic, social, and political criteria clarify the complex differences between and convergences of authoritarian and democratic capitalism—the two systems that constitute the poles of the Spanish transition. If the differences were blatantly harsh—as stark, say, as that between Stalinism and market democracy—then going to the trouble of sorting out the component elements, on the hunch that there would be significant overlap between them, would be a waste of time. But because of the gray areas between authoritarian and democratic capitalism, analysis of this sort makes sense in the Spanish case, as it does in other instances of incremental democratization such as Korea and Brazil.

In the simplest post-authoritarian scenario, most people give priority to political freedom over order or control and favor social distribution over economic development (though post-communist scenarios differ a bit in the latter respect). However, to the extent that democratization proceeds by reform, these priorities do not take the shape of zero-sum tradeoffs (Munck and Leff 1997). If they do, polarization is likely to be perpetuated. But if, on the other hand, the sense of tradeoffs is minimal, depolarization may be so pervasive that regimes can hardly be distinguished.

In the end, Spaniards either recognize the democratic regime as a political system, separate from the authoritarianism that preceded it, or they do not. This judgment must outweigh perceptions of similarity between the regimes with regard to one or another of their operations. It is when Spaniards give priority to the division between authoritarian and democratic systems, over and above the putative differences between separate governments and beyond possible discriminations between either governments or regimes on the basis of one or another functional standard, that we can begin to speak of a legitimacy that resonates in popular consciousness.[8]

If on the other hand practical functions or policy domains are perceived as more salient, we would probably be faced with considerable indifference to political form in both the short (government) and longer (regime) term. Outputs of the governments, whether similar or different, would be viewed as the main thing, to which constructs like "regime" would be incidental. There would be a real question about popular understanding of the supposed differences between democratic and antidemocratic institutions.

Again, this is not a mere fancy. The Franco regime wasn't all bad, the democratic system has not been uniformly benign, and the transition from one to the other showed important continuities, for example, in economic strategy ("Veinte años después" 1995). This being the case, perceptions of resemblance along this or perhaps another dimension might conceivably overcome a judgment of difference between the regimes by other criteria.[9]

The postulate that political legitimacy is neither monochromatic nor categorical but multidimensional and a matter of degree has two tangible implications for understanding the mass dynamics of the Spanish transition. One is that while we should be able to pick up some overlap in perceptions of the regimes—for example, with regard to economic performance—they are almost certainly going to be set apart on criteria related to political freedom and social fairness. The former quality amounts to a commonsensical distinction whose failure to register would indicate political cynicism at a level astounding even by Mediterranean standards.

The latter, dividing the regimes by expectations regarding social fairness, is a bit more subtle. A few authoritarian regimes—in East Asia, for example—have done well enough by their citizens socially that they constitute a tough act for democracies to follow in this sphere (Jones 1990). In the Spanish case the contrast between authoritarianism and democracy is not so problematic, for "democracy" evokes antihierarchical sentiments that trump the antiegalitarian paternalism of Franco.

The second implication of our treatment of political legitimacy concerns depolarization. The dilemma raised by depolarization and by attendant phenomena such as retrospective legitimation is that they may come close to rendering the authoritarian and post-authoritarian regimes indistinguishable. As a result, moderation might swamp any uniquely democratic legitimacy, just as moderation may dampen participation.

A simple test is available to check this eventuality. Francoism and post-Francoism tended to be seen as remarkably continuous in the early days of the transition. But as the years went by, even with continued depolarization, we would expect perceptions of past authoritarianism and present democracy gradually to grow apart. In this scenario, democracy would attain cultural autonomy and, hence, political legitimacy in its own right. This is precisely the dynamic that repeated surveys permit us to monitor.

Evaluating the distinction between depolarization and political legitimacy in this way presupposes real-time comparison between alternative regimes. This is the approach to legitimacy we consider now.

Legitimacy and Retrospective Comparison

Attempts to pin down legitimacy have been severely ahistorical. In long-established democracies where most studies of regime support have been conducted, few citizens have direct experience of alternative regimes. Answering questions about hypothetical political systems in the absence of familiarity with all but one of them requires an exceptional act of imagination and presupposes extraordinary interest in the matter besides. The lack of palpable options or of an existential sense of difference regarding political systems makes the exercise all but meaningless. Most studies of political legitimacy are experiments without control groups.[10]

Spain presents a different picture. Francoism is a living memory for a significant though shrinking portion of the population. Comparisons between authoritarianism and democracy are more than speculative exercises. And because there have been different governments since the transition, with the conservative UCD yielding power to the socialists in 1982, it is possible to verify whether Spaniards distinguish between regimes as a whole as well as between particular governments. In this sense Spain is a natural laboratory for the study of political legitimacy.[11]

How might legitimation by retrospective comparison work? From the time of the transition onward, there is probably a period of around a decade before questions about predemocratic politics begin to sound arcane. Within this period, our investigative tack resembles the multiple-criteria strategy outlined above, except that the before-after comparison becomes explicit. The approach involves a two-step sequence in which Spaniards are asked, first, how they feel about the current government and then how they feel about the same government "*in comparison with* the last ten years of the Franco regime." The first query concentrates on the here-and-now, on stand-alone popularity. The second sets the present in the context of what's gone before. The difference between the two approximates an indicator of legitimacy. It represents the bonus which a democratic government may receive—or the deficit it may be burdened with—when citizens take the longer view, considering its antecedents.

Legitimacy and Trust

There are two potential flaws in the approach to legitimacy by way of retrospection. Both concern the fact that it may not travel well. First, however suited it might be to *democratization* in which over-the-shoulder comparisons come as a matter of course, the method of contrast makes little sense in *democracies*, and in nondemocracies for that matter, that have been around for a long time.

Second, just as our approach is context-dependent, there is some ambiguity about the content of democratic legitimacy. The temporal proximity of authoritarianism and post-authoritarianism privileges common sense over speculative imagination as a demarcator of regime differences. It is relatively easy for Spaniards to separate the systems because the contrast between them is experientially intelligible. At the same time, although Spaniards rejected maximalism, we have indicated that a sense of social fairness may be as much a constitutive element of democratic legitimacy in Spain as a sense of procedural impartiality. Whether this condition applies with equal weight in other democratic cultures is debatable.

At any rate, something more "universal" may be missing from our construction of legitimacy. This something has to do with affective, precognitive attachment to governments.

So far we have had little to say about one of the standbys of the literature on political legitimacy: the notion of "trust in government." Measures of political fairness, honesty, trust and the like have yielded mixed results. They appear to separate governments within the democratic system at least as sharply as they distinguish between authoritarian and democratic systems; they look more like indicators of support for and dissatisfaction with particular governments than assessments of the legitimacy of regimes.

But trust construed in down-to-earth terms, with an eye to its variations in a Latin setting, may be a meaningful component of legitimacy. The stereotype of the French, the Spanish, the Italian, the Argentine citizen—of the generic Latin *Homo politicus*—is of a supreme individualist who trusts only a few familial intimates, and he rarely turns his back even on them. "If there's a government," the saying goes, "I'm against it" (compare Wilson and Banfield 1971). The trouble with this caricature is that it obscures real-life departures from the ideal of hermetic privatism. It leaves no room for a middle ground or for more or less graduated constructions of political allegiance or of its converse, privatism: citizens are either fully committed or completely alienated (Dealy 1977, 1992). Our point of departure is the simple contention that *confianza*, with its connotations of "faith," "dependability," and "loyalty," varies across public and private spheres, along a continuum.

The logic of this perspective resembles that used to revise categorically dualistic treatments of legitimacy. The notions of continua and multidimensionality are essential. Keeping open the possibility of variation around central tendencies and "modal personalities" not only restores realism and nuance to the distinction between the private and the public, but will also enable us to search out connections between these orientations and political legitimacy.

We do not depend solely on questions about "confidence in government." Our analysis starts by asking Spaniards how much or little they trust a whole series of things, from the government and politicians to their colleagues at work, their family, themselves, and God. The initial task is to calculate the highs and lows across this range. Then we estimate how specific objects of *confianza* might be arrayed along a private-public continuum and what this continuum might have to do with legitimacy.

Our interest lies less in the absolute levels of trust assigned to particular referents than in determining how Spaniards might express zones of trust along the political and social sectors that form clusters on a public-private continuum. Viewing the continuum as indicative of kinds as well as degrees of "public-regardingness" (Wilson and Banfield 1964) gives us a fresh perspective not only on legitimacy and the autonomy of the state from immediate pressures but, conversely, on the ways in which citizens insulate themselves from politics. That some spheres—for example, family life, kin relations, and the like—tend to be reserved for "private trust" and the intimacies of the personal does not mean that the public sphere tends to be associated uniformly with distrust. That would be simplistic. The outward linkages of trust—the connections of this sentiment with public institutions and political leaders—are questions of degree.

The argument for legitimacy as trust hinges on the possibility that some form of emotive and largely inarticulate identification or commitment, usually thought to be confined to kin, small communities, or ethnic groups, extends outward and binds large numbers of citizens to democracy. It is at this point that trust-based treatments of political legitimacy usually get bogged down in attempts to link benevolent sentiments with abstractions such as "the political system." In Spain this connection is supplied by the figure of the monarch.

Ever since King Juan Carlos's speedy intervention on the side of democratic forces during the aborted coup of 1981, his popularity has been enormous, and his dual role as both psychological anchor and symbol of democratic ideals has been widely recognized (Allman 1992). Royal popularity is easy to document. What merits a closer look is the *association* between feelings toward the monarch and democratic norms within social strata—for example, older, comparatively religious Spaniards—whose allegiance to democracy might be shaky were it not for their liking of the king.

The search is not for strictly causal linkages. Instead we are looking for associations that stand out as propitious for legitimacy, amid a field of neutral or potentially hostile cultural syndromes. It is the perceived nonpartisan connection of the king with sentiments about legal procedures, above the triumphs and defeats of particular governments, that we seek to isolate. Like a president in a predominantly parliamentary system (Portugal, say, or Ireland), the Spanish monarch stands for principles and continuities, for institutionalized rules, in a way that the rules themselves sometimes cannot do (Braga da Cruz 1994).

It is not attachment to the monarch or to the monarchy that matters but the relationship between such sentiments and attitudes toward the forms and procedures of democracy. Connections of this sort are similar in form, though different in content, to the analogical thinking, common in authoritarian settings, that sees correspondences between family structures and "the larger family" of the state (Nuccio 1979). Rather like one of the Founding Fathers of the American experiment, the king is looked upon as a figure to be trusted, a protector of democratic principles, even when these principles are feebly grasped and the institutions of state seem remote (Fliegelman 1982).

Democratization puts political theory in reach of ordinary citizens. Distinctions between systems of government that might remain at the level of abstraction become part of lived experience during political transitions. Yet it is not certain that—more accurately, how—a clear-cut demarcation will take hold in the public mind between soft authoritarianism and a democracy born of moderation and bent on pragmatic accomplishment. Pacted, arranged transitions admit a certain equivocation into political legitimacy. Incrementalism is rarely a galvanizing vision. How do new democracies, crafted through reform, distance themselves from their authoritarian predecessors in the eyes of the public? Where is the tipping point?

One way to approach this set of questions is to acknowledge that transitions by reform are not clean breaks. The opportunity to compare authoritarianism and democracy in real time doesn't mean that the contrast will be black and white. Some continuity is bound to prevail between judgments of the past and present. The result is a motley legitimacy, one with significant if understated traces of appreciation for the accomplishments of authoritarianism, and these ambivalent memories may be compounded by the fact that the process of consolidation may itself be less than fully democratic, giving only a modest role to bottom-up mobilization. Nonetheless, as the new regime attains institutionalization and time passes, ties with the authoritarian past are likely to get weaker and weaker.

Second, moderation and pragmatism—the benefits of depolarization—are probably not enough for legitimacy, even when "pragmatism" is understood to be more than mere opportunism but rather a culture or value-style itself (Dirks, Eley, and Ortner 1993; Merelman 1992; Schneider 1993). "The life of even the most democratic polity," notes Peter Dews (1995:11), "will degenerate into oppressive and purposeless routine unless the transcendent sources of ethical energy and moral inspiration are periodically renewed." Though they fail to get the measurement straight, and though they show a weakness for categorical, usually dichotomous thinking, traditional theories are correct, we believe, in their claim that democratic legitimacy propagates distinctive norms. The trouble is that these principles are hard to articulate. Our contention is that such values become embodied through their connection with trust in the visible institutions of democracy—a trust that may be more sentimental than cognitive—and through identification with heroic figures who incarnate democratic ideals. The myth of democracy is transmitted by its icons, including the icon of "the people" (compare Morgan 1988).

Third, just as there are different types of democratic regimes, it may be that there are different brands of democratic legitimacy. Around a core of respect for democratic procedures, we can imagine another standard, of social egalitarianism, whose ranking on the agenda of values varies from democracy to democracy or indeed from one period to another in the same democracy. In other political cultures, such as those in parts of East Asia, the accent may be on communitarian understandings of legitimacy (Fukuyama 1995). At any rate, it is hard to escape the impression that during the seventies, the eighties, and the beginning of the nineties in Spain social equity was not just a question of delivering the goods by which individual governments might rise or fall but a criterion by which the legitimacy of the new regime was sealed, along with its procedural impartiality. This elasticity challenges the old notion that democratic legitimacy is everywhere all of a piece and unchanging; it may expand and contract.

2

Gauging Political Legitimacy

Now the two officers obviously had to try to behave correctly in the presence, albeit the unconscious presence, of such an important person, and so instead of leaving him lying there helpless and unattended, they heaved him up from the hot naked road and, with one of them holding him by the feet while the other grasped him under the arms, they went to discuss the accident with the lorry driver. There they stood for what seemed like an interminable length of time, in the heat of the day, with that heavy body hanging between them, the medals glinting lopsidedly in the sun, the socks exposed and a military hat balanced on a gently heaving chest. At last they had worked out who was to be blamed for what and with tottering steps they returned to their car, pulled and pushed the general along the length of the back seat, climbed in themselves and continued on their interrupted journey. It was tempting to think that for a brief moment I had seen the unconscious man open his eyes and stare incredulously at what was taking place, before lapsing back into an uneasy oblivion, but perhaps that was only a trick of the bright sunlight.

—Julia Blackburn, *The Emperor's Last Island*

The closeness in time of two regimes, authoritarianism and democracy, lends a clarifying simplicity to the analysis of political legitimacy. The decades of the seventies and the eighties provide a direct contrast for testing the degree to which Spaniards distinguish between these political systems.

The logic of the analysis can be applied to other instances of democratization as well. Regardless of possible dissimilarities to older, settled democracies in which research on legitimacy has been found wanting, Spain is no longer the rarity it once was in having a citizenry with firsthand experience of contrasting regimes. Since the 1970s, upwards of thirty countries have undergone transitions to democracy (Karatnycky 1995). The retrospective method also improves with age. The unfolding of time permits multiple soundings of public opinion from the beginning to the consolidation (or collapse) of democracy, which also generate information about the progressive attenuation of links between authoritarianism and democracy. So the retrospective method of estimating political legitimacy is workable in other new democracies, as long as a post-authoritarian time series is available and comparison with the pre-democratic regime is explicit.

However, whether the approach to legitimacy by way of regime comparison would work for long-standing democracies, where most citizens are out of touch with the terms of comparison, is doubtful. As a practical matter, attainment of the age of reason in studies of political legitimacy probably requires getting the analysis straight in one country, then worrying about cross-national generalization.

We proceed in four steps. First we review conventional measures of legitimacy. The standard approaches get at facets of political support or popularity but they don't tell us much, not much that is new anyway, about political legitimacy. If the distinction between generic regime and particular government is valid and comprehensible to academics, it is not easily amenable to measurement and it is not one that is transparent to ordinary citizens.

Next we prepare a testable model of legitimacy, which involves a consideration of the multiple criteria—political, economic, and social—by which governments are evaluated. The demonstration that authoritarian and democratic regimes are viewed as distinct entities, over and above whatever functional resemblance they share, and beyond their incarnations as particular governments, is a necessary but not a sufficient condition for establishing political legitimacy. It simply shows that the two systems are understood to be separate, not that one is more legitimate than the other.

Third, we examine how political legitimacy is shaped by demographic and cultural configurations that illuminate the contours of support for and opposition to Francoism and democracy. This procedure rounds out the analysis initiated in the preceding step, which verified the distinction between government and regime. Using orientations toward the democratic and authoritarian regimes as dependent variables, we examine how these rival legitimacies are spread or concentrated among major social groups—that is, across the political community (the third element in classic studies of legitimacy). Our thesis is straightforward. To the extent that the democratic regime, with support distributed fairly evenly across the community, is less polarizing than Francoism, it enjoys legitimacy of a kind—at least a negative consensus against the divisions left unreconciled by the authoritarian past.

Lastly, we refurbish some ideas—notably, trust and symbolic affection—that have long been thought to tie in with political legitimacy. We use the revamped measures to enhance our understanding of legitimacy as more than the expression of a functional calculus or the cultivation of temperateness and toleration.

OLD STANDARDS

Table 2.1 presents the univariate distributions of traditional indicators of system support at three points in the post-Franco period: 1978, during the first term of the center-right government led by Adolfo Suárez; 1980, during the second term of the Suárez government, when there was dissatisfaction with the state of the economy and talk of *desencanto* (disenchantment) with the democratic process; and 1984, two years into the socialist government headed by Felipe González.[1]

Popular consensus favoring democratic institutions—the need for elections and for the preservation of representative politics through the Cortes—looks overwhelming and steady. There is only the slightest hint of a fall-off, from the high to the low 80 percent range, in the belief that "Congress is needed." Yet fluctuations in political affect are appreciable. Trust in government and perceptions of its majoritarian versus elitist leanings shift over time. A sharp break occurs between 1980 and 1984, between the UCD and the PSOE governments. The jump in positive affect coincides with the incumbency of the socialists.

TABLE 2.1. Standard measures of political affect and institutional support: Marginal distributions, 1978–1984 (percent)

	Trust government?			Government favors:		Tax money is:		
Year	Yes	No		Many	Few	Spent Well	Partly Wasted	Wasted
1984	41%	59%		58%	42%	23%	48%	29%
1980	26	74		32	68	12	44	43
1978	27	73		35	65	12	47	41

Elections		Congress		Monarchy or republic?*		
Needed	Not needed	Needed	Not needed	Republic	Indifferent	Monarchy
91%	9%	81%	19%	—	—	—
94	6	86	14	23%	56%	21%
93	7	87	13	32	42	26

* Not asked in 1984.

These results reveal no crisp demacrations between government and regime or between popularity and legitimacy. Short-term shifts linking changes in conventional measures of legitimacy to alterations in government—changes that in theory should be practically nonexistent across particular governments—emerge when the indicators are aligned with variables such as party identification. The partisanship of Spaniards conditions their supposedly generic, relatively timeless political views.[2] With the socialists in power, 60 percent of the PSOE supporters indicated trust in government. When the socialists were in opposition, this figure among PSOE partisans was only about one-third as large. Conversely, under the reign of the UCD, about six out of ten UCD partisans said the government was "for the many," while only about one out of four socialists held the same opinion. Rather than signifying abiding dispositions, flurries in these indicators depend on change in incumbents.

However, another explanation is compatible with the evidence. The increase in esteem for the socialists may reflect a change in the bases of support from liberal-political to social-egalitarian values. The fact that commitment to the institutions of pluralism holds up at consistently high levels, while trust and other sentiments, such as judgments about whether government favors the few or the many, evidently tied to the fortunes of the socialists soar, controverts zero-sum interpretations of the trade offs between procedural and substantive readings of democracy. Whether support entails popularity, legitimacy, or some mixture of both remains to be determined. We have raised the possibility that the very criteria of support may be multiple and may change over time.

On the whole, however, the inferential ramifications of the conventional measures are clear enough. For example, the political orientations of those who identify with conservative parties—mainly, the Alianza Popular and later, in the nineties, its revivification as the Partido Popular—are quite stable relative to those of Spaniards in the center and toward the left. But it would be misleading to conclude that the Spanish right maintains a uniformly dim view of democratic institutions and values. It is closer to the mark to conclude that they just don't distinguish as finely as others between the center-right and the socialist left. Hence, their trust in and assessments of the government remain largely unaffected by the changes in governments that occurred in the seventies and eighties from the center-right to the center-left.

A REVISIONIST VIEW OF POLITICAL PERFORMANCE AND LEGITIMACY

The principal lesson of these first-cut results is that we aren't going to get very far with the analysis of system support by sticking to traditional

TABLE 2.2. Average scores on selected indicators of political orientation, 1978–1984

Indicators	1978	1980	1984
Satisfaction			
With democracy	4.5	4.2	5.5
With PSOE government[a]	—	—	5.0
With UCD government	4.5	4.2	4.4
With Franco government	3.6	3.7	4.1
Living standards			
Under PSOE government	—	—	5.0
Under UCD government	4.3	4.0	4.2
Under Franco government	3.9	4.3	4.5
Law and order			
Under PSOE government	—	—	4.7
Under UCD government	4.2	3.2	4.3
Under Franco government	4.9	5.2	5.3
Social equity			
Under PSOE government	—	—	5.0
Under UCD government	3.8	3.6	4.3
Under Franco government	2.8	2.9	3.8
Popularity			
King Juan Carlos	6.4	6.5	8.0
Pope John Paul II[b]	—	6.8	6.9
Felipe González	5.6	5.5	6.5
Adolfo Suárez	5.4	5.1	5.4
Santiago Carrillo	4.3	3.9	3.3
Gerardo Iglesias[c]	—	—	3.3
Manuel Fraga Iribarne[d]	3.3	2.9	3.7

Note: Responses were scored on a scale of 1 (lowest) to 10 (highest).
[a] The PSOE (Socialist party) did not assume power until 1982; its governmental ratings were therefore not elicited until the 1984 survey.
[b] Elected pope October 1978.
[c] Iglesias succeeded Carrillo as secretary general of the Communist party of Spain in 1984.
[d] Leader of conservative Alianza Popular.

measures or by leaving standard theories of legitimacy intact. Table 2.2 tracks the movement in alternative indicators, all of them scored between 1 and 10, across the same time points plotted earlier. We introduced a few of these measures in Chapter 1, in order to sketch in the decline of polarization. Here the full panoply is presented, for the purpose of documenting the growth of legitimacy.

The measures are of three types. Toward the top are global indicators like satisfaction "with the way democracy is working nowadays in Spain." The next set is made up of perceptions of how well different governments, including the Franco government "during its last ten years," did or have been doing along three dimensions: economic ("improving the standard of living"), social ("treating Spaniards from different social classes equally"), and political ("maintaining law and order"). A third group of indicators is composed of popularity ratings for major figures in Spanish politics, including the pope and the king.

The first trend to be noted involves the renewed favoring of democracy and the governments and leaders associated with it after a downturn at the beginning of the 1980s. Particularly striking is the recuperation in perceptions regarding how democracy has been working. These evaluations reached a high of 5.5 in 1984 after having fallen to 4.1 in 1980. A similar upswing marks the popularity of leaders associated with the new regime—notably, Suárez and González.

The bounce-back is not hard to explain. In the face of a deteriorating economy, mounting terrorism, and increasing crime, Spaniards betrayed a certain fatigue with democracy toward the beginning of the 1980s. Their spirits lifted with the advent of the socialists, with the hope of better economic as well as political times, and with signs that terrorism was waning.

A second set of trends—the decline in the popularity and the fortunes of the communist left—is linear but more complex. In 1984 Santiago Carrillo resigned as leader of the party, to be replaced by a younger militant, Gerardo Iglesias, whose following turned out to be no greater than that of his mentor (Paramio 1985). Despite its protestations of Eurocommunism, the Partido Comunista Español (PCE) was tainted by a simultaneously extremist and manipulative history, and was unable to shake its image as a repository of the antidemocratic left (Mujal-León 1983; Medhurst 1984). The communists were caught in a double bind. What they had to offer in the way of social and economic policy was seen as decreasingly appropriate to the new Spain, and the party was not trusted even when its members could get Spaniards to pay attention to their program. The Communist Party—the other church of Spanish politics—was, somewhat like Catholicism, losing it grip on the citizenry.

Third, in contrast to the fate of the communists, memories of Franco seem to become rosier the further he fades into the past. Much of this nostalgia is concentrated among older Spaniards, and the apparent rise in the popularity of Franco is largely a function of the remains of this conservative cohort, relative to the younger Spaniards who, as time advances, simply have no opinion about the caudillo.[3]

There is some substance to the warm memories of Franco, however. An absence-makes-the-heart-grow-fonder effect surfaces in evaluations of authoritarian as compared to democratic law and order. The Franco regime's low yet not quite abysmal grades with respect to social equity can be traced in part to the rudiments of the welfare state built during the last decade of authoritarianism (Castles 1995). For some Spaniards during the eighties the job tenure and modest medical benefits of the earlier period compared favorably to post-Franco unemployment rates and the hazards of the underground economy (Flora and Heidenheimer 1981; Lancaster 1979). When the difficult economic conditions that prevailed through the mid-eighties are set against the boom times of the later Franco period, the prosperity rating associated with the caudillo and his team—not so low as would appear in a black-vs.-white contrast between the old and new regimes—becomes understandable. This is the first of several clues we will encounter suggesting that security, rather than flat-out equity, were important public aspirations during the unsteady transitional days of democracy.

With the exception of the law-and-order area, the ratings of the socialists exceed those given to Franco. The two regimes are ranked differently, as are the center-right and center-left governments of the democratic regime itself. Still, creeping nostalgia for the good times of the Franco period and the vacillating esteem in which post-Franco governments have been held place the solidity of the new system at issue. The data warrant concern about the depth of support for the democratic system. Spaniards project a mixed endorsement of the new order, depending on the criteria employed to compare it with the old one.

At the heart of the notion of legitimacy is holistic judgment. Evaluation would be trivially simple if the political systems were completely discontinuous. But if the regimes are not seen by citizens as unitary composites, they cannot elicit political commitment. They may be considered transient assemblages à la carte, with superficial "democratic" or "authoritarian" labels. We need to estimate how the various indicators of political, economic, and social dimensions hang together in light of theoretical expectations about areas of governmental performance and the dimensions of regime legitimacy.

Consider the standards used for evaluating each of the governments—Franco's, the center-right UCD, and the center-left PSOE. Four outcomes of a data-reduction technique such as factor analysis are possible. The least likely is that no significant differences would emerge across either the three governments or the three criteria of evaluation. This blurred outcome is improbable in view of the evidence just presented, which shows that the governments and their functions are perceived differently. On the average the post-Franco governments receive higher ratings than the Franco regime, especially in such areas as social policy. These averages provide strong initial clues to the perceived differences between political systems.

Another pattern, more interesting and disturbing, would be reflected in the emergence of one or two functional factors that do not discriminate among the different governments. Such an outcome would indicate that while Spaniards may place greater or lesser emphasis on, say, social equity as compared to economic growth, they see virtually no difference between governments in the implementation of these goals or, more precisely, attach greater priority to the attainments of one or another such goal than to "procedural" differences between authoritarianism and democracy. Governments, not to mention regimes, would appear to be epiphenomenal, mere superstructures. Political systems would be neutral, merely the stages on which interests clash. Such results would highlight differences in the priority that the public gives to economic and social goals rather than to the democratic or not-so-democratic processes of decision making by which these goals might be reached. System support would appear to be driven by performance and effectiveness. In this case Spaniards would seem to be output-oriented and largely indifferent to matters of political form (Anderson 1970).

A third pattern would show Spaniards distinguishing sharply among the three governments, perceiving them serially as separate policy and leadership packages, while obliterating any significant separation between the two regimes. This pattern would demolish notions of regime legitimacy as something separable from support for particular governments, at least with the indicators at hand. Such results would reinforce the suspicion that the indicators are unlikely measures of system support but instead simply register perceptions of the efficiency of particular governments in different policy spheres.

By now the contours of the fourth outcome should be evident. This would entail a division not among the three governments, nor among the three criteria, but between the authoritarian and democratic systems, with the Franco regime on one side and the combined UCD/PSOE regime on the other. Only under this configuration would the typological separation of authoritarianism and democracy be substantiated.

Our data confirm the fourth outcome. Table 2.3 displays the results of a factor analysis of perceptions of economic, social, and political performance for the Franco regime and the post-Franco governments.[4]

Two, and only two, dimensions emerge: one for Franco and one for the combined democratic governments. What doesn't emerge is equally significant. Three separate factors for the different governments do not appear, nor do we pick up stray factors associated with one or another of the functional (social, economic, political) dimensions. The authoritarian and democratic regimes are viewed as separate blocs. Not only are they seen as more distinct from each other than particular governments might be; the perceived differences between them also dominate similarities in functions and policy areas.

The sensitivity of the quantitative results to the historical process of democratization adds nuance to the statistical summary. While the UCD government is tied, together with the PSOE government, to the democratic regime it is perceived as transitional. As the loadings of the UCD government on the Franco factor indicate, it leans toward the authoritarian dimension, despite the fact that its center of gravity is with democracy—in

TABLE 2.3. Oblique (promax) factor matrix with standardized loadings: Evaluations of Franco, UCD, and PSOE governments, 1984

	Factors[a]		
Evaluation indicators	Authoritarianism	Democracy	Communalities
Franco			
Standard of living	**1.01**	−.11	1.02
Social equity	**1.00**	−.05	1.01
Law and order	**1.01**	−.11	1.02
UCD			
Standard of living	.52	**.80**	.91
Social equity	.49	**.82**	.91
Law and Order	.39	**.88**	.92
PSOE			
Standard of living	−.24	**.96**	1.09
Social equity	−.25	**1.00**	1.05
Law and order	−.43	**−.95**	1.09

[a] Correlation between factors = .11.

effect, coalescing with the PSOE. Even though the political center as incarnated in the defunct UCD has disappeared in Spain, the public understands that the UCD carried out a crucial role in the early days of the transition.

The unfolding of the transition from the viewpoint of the Spanish public can also be followed more panoramically. Figure 2.1 shows the correlations between the authoritarian and democratic dimensions that emerge from factor analyses conducted on the 1978 and 1980 as well as the 1984 data (McDonough and López Pina 1984). The purpose is to see how separate or close the two dimensions become over time and to estimate the gradual differentiation of the two regimes in the eyes of the public.

The trend is striking. Orientations toward the regimes drift apart, without the two being seen, however, as diametric opposites. The decline in the correlations suggests (1) that, certainly in its initial stages, democratization was seen as genuinely continuous, even conservative, by many Spaniards, rather than as a sharp break with the past, and (2) that over time the democratic regime has taken on a life and imagery of its own, becoming gradually dissociated from the authoritarian past.

So Francoism and democracy are perceived not only as distinct regimes but, reflecting the fairly smooth transition, as regimes that grew progressively apart with the passage of time. Of course, the Spanish public distinguishes between actual governments—that is, between the center-right and socialist governments of the democratic era. Yet Spaniards also distinguish at a deeper level between the Franquist and democratic regimes.

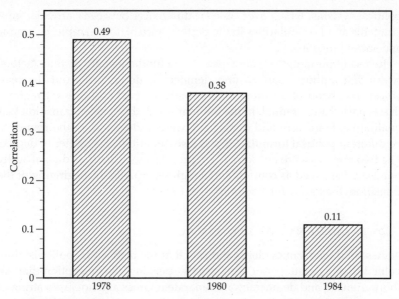

Figure 2.1 Correlations between authoritarianism and democracy factors, Spain, 1978–1984

This is what the factor analysis, which searches out underlying dimensions, demonstrates.

The historical proximity of the two regimes heightens the contrast between them and tends to submerge differences in governments within the democratic system that might otherwise be more prominent. In another setting—Spain twenty years hence perhaps, or any of the present-day polities of Western Europe that reestablished their democratic institutions after World War II—differences across governments based on the evaluation of performance would almost certainly come through. The appearance of differences between regimes, however, would be most improbable, for the contrast would be hypothetical. Such a possibility seems to require an experiential familiarity with alternative political systems prevalent in post-authoritarian and post-communist settings (Aumente 1985a).

We have stressed that the possibility of distinguishing between regimes doesn't guarantee that the distinction will be made. In the transition from Francoism to democracy, the separation, though real enough, seems to have been a close thing, less incontrovertible than categorical visions of democratic legitimacy would dictate. Our view conceives of political legitimacy as a *relational pattern*, one among many that can emerge from the contrast between successive governments across the multiple dimensions of political, economic, and social policy. The characteristically legitimizing pattern is one that reflects the emergence of perceived differences between political systems, which overcome (1) differences between particular governments and (2) similarities in the performance of, for example, economic and social functions.

Just as important, the emergence of two fundamentally distinct factors, separating authoritarianism and democracy, doesn't rule out the real-world likelihood of a differentiation between past and present regimes that is partial and gradual. In the popular mind, the Spanish transition was qualitative. Francoism and democracy were understood, in the round, to be different political formulae. It was also quantitative, a matter of degree. The two regimes were not seen as reciprocals of one another, diametrically opposed. Perceived as continuous though separate in the beginning of the transition, they grew further apart over time.[5]

DETERMINANTS OF LEGITIMACY

Assorted pieces of evidence indicate that the democratic polity is more valued than its predecessor. But, strictly speaking, the perception that authoritarianism and democracy are separate regimes and not just a string of discrete governments doesn't confirm the legitimacy of one system over another. It only indicates that they are seen as different systems; the question of better or worse, of legitimate versus illegitimate, is another matter. In order to specify the type and extent of support for the new system, we can start by comparing the social bases of the two regimes. The test is simple. The less polarizing the regime, the more autonomous and, by implication, the more consensual (or less controversial) it is likely to be across a broad band of the population.

Table 2.4 gives a preliminary diagnosis. It assembles the correlations, for three successive surveys, between the global indicators and personality ratings laid out in Table 2.2 and the factor scores tapping orientations toward the authoritarian and democratic regimes. The correlations convey a sense of the comparative polarization surrounding the two systems. For example, if religious practice correlates strongly with positive assessments of Francoism but only weakly with evaluations of the democratic regime, then one possibly crucial determinant of legitimacy, religious versus secular sentiment, can be said to be polarizing for the Franco system but probably irrelevant for the new regime.

This turns out to be consistently the case for the religious factor. Starting in 1978 the association between religiosity and Franco is .39, in 1980, .41, and in 1984, .38: steady as she goes. By contrast, the corresponding coefficients for the democratic regime are .19, .10, and .06: weak and getting weaker. Here, too, it is important to recognize what does *not* emerge. While the correlations of religiosity with Franco remain strongly positive (and the left-right/Franco associations even higher), the figures for UCD/PSOE regime are not reversed—that is, they are not strongly nega-

TABLE 2.4. Correlations between scores on democracy and authoritarianism factors and selected sociopolitical indicators, 1978–1984

Indicators	Authoritarianism			Democracy		
	1978	1980	1984	1978	1980	1984
Left/right placement	.60	.60	.57	.18	.13	−.12
Religiosity	.39	.41	.38	.19	.10	.06
Satisfaction						
With democracy	.13	.10	−.17	.81	.68	.57
With PSOE government	—	—	−.26	—	—	.68
With UCD government	.25	.22	.37	.91	.72	.57
With Franco government	.94	.80	.85	.21	.16	−.05
Popularity						
King Juan Carlos	.35	.33	.17	.37	.30	.31
Pope John Paul II	—	.46	.43	—	.17	.09
Felipe González	−.10	.01	−.25	.30	.32	.52
Adolfo Suárez	.32	.39	.14	.48	.42	.33
Santiago Carrillo	−.24	−.26	−.34	.15	.20	.18
Gerardo Iglesias	—	—	−.33	—	—	.19
Manuel Fraga Iribarne	.49	.51	.55	.14	.12	−.05

tive. They're simply washed out. Unlike the Second Republic, which Franco defeated in civil war, the democratic regime is viewed as less militantly anticlerical than indifferent to religion (Tusell and Queipo de Llano 1990).

The Franco regime elicits stronger passions, both positive and negative, than does the democratic system. This polarization has a historical rationale. Spanish authoritarianism was patently exclusionary. Although it may not have been ideological in the fullest sense, it did evoke powerful defensive loyalties from its adherents and hatred from those it had vanquished. Once the constitutional roadblocks to participation were overcome with the transition, overt political exclusion ceased to be a problem, and much of the combativeness of Spanish politics evaporated (Maravall 1984; compare Eckstein 1992: 343-77).

Public figures crystallize ideological *tendances* in Spain, and the correlations of their popularity ratings with summary evaluations of the authoritarian and democratic regimes reveal where the public locates them with respect to the past and the new system. The bridging roles of the king and of Adolfo Suárez show up in the positive correlations of their ratings with the Franquist *and* the democratic dimensions alike. The moderating functions of these men contrast with the polarizing figures of Santiago Carrillo, ex-leader of the communists, and on the right Manuel Fraga Iribarne, onetime leader of the conservative Alianza Popular and later governor of Galicia.[6]

One trend surpasses in importance those tied to individual public figures: the gradual dissociation of support for the democratic regime from satisfaction with mere effectiveness. The trend, first noted in Chapter 1, is worth highlighting here.

In 1978 the correlation between positive orientations toward the democratic government and satisfaction with "the way democracy is working in Spain" was a very impressive .81. In 1980 it dipped to .68, and by 1984 it had fallen to .57. It is unexceptionable that the two variables are positively related. What matters is that the strength of the correlation, though still impressive, has dropped over time. The victories and defeats experienced by any single government are less and less likely to touch off feelings of triumphalism or despair identified with the political system as a whole or with the fate of the nation.[7]

The statistics reported in Table 2.5 take the analysis past the presentation of bivariate correlations to an assessment of the relative impact of such factors as religion and region on regime support. The table summarizes the results of two multiple classification analyses—essentially, multiple regression in which nominal predictors such as region are permitted—for the factor scores measuring orientations toward the Franco and the democratic systems.[8]

The vastly greater percentage of variance accounted for in the Franco factor than in the democratic factor by the same set of standard predictors is significant. The Franco regime was tied closely to certain constituencies—to the culture of counterreformation Catholicism (Alvarez Bolado 1976; Payne 1984; Tusell 1984); to the Castillian zone much more than to regions on the periphery such as the Basque country and Catalonia (García Ferrando 1982); and to the upper class more than to workers (López Pina

TABLE 2.5. Multiple classification analyses:
Authoritarianism (Franco) and democracy (UCD/PSOE)
factors, 1984

Authoritarianism factor scores as dependent variable		Democracy factor scores as dependent variable	
Predictor	Beta	Predictor	Beta
Religiosity	.30	Political interest	.17
Region	.18	Size of city/town	.15
Political interest	.15	Region	.12
Class identification	.13	Education	.11
Age	.09	Age	.10
Size of city/town	.08	Income	.08
Education	.08	Religiosity	.06
Income	.05	Class identification	.02
R^2	.24	R^2	.05

and Aranguren 1976; Maddox 1991). The two classic cleavages of Spanish politics, religion and region, together with the sense of hierarchy embedded in class distinctions, delineate the mass foundations of the authoritarian state.

What is remarkable is not this confirmation of the social boundaries of the Franco system but the contrast with post-Franco governments. The constituencies of the democratic regime are much more heterogeneous, not to say amorphous. It is not region or religiosity that tops the list of predictors but "political interest" and the "small town/big city" (rural/urban) continuum. These are not the stuff of confrontation; they are not dividing lines that unequivocally demarcate political identities. Political interest and the like do not approach the primordial or preindustrial divisions in accounting for support for and opposition to the UCD/PSOE governments in the way that such forces operate with respect to Francoism.[9]

Again, it is the pattern of associations that matters more than changes in isolated indicators. The key point is the partial yet consistent nature of the contrast between the two regimes. By the transhistorical standards of legitimacy, a sharper division between authoritarianism and democracy might be expected. But this would fail to capture the continuities in the Spanish transition.

The results also provide promising though still provisional support for the significance of conflicts over identity, ideology, and interests. The gestalt of the correlates of support and opposition with respect to Francoism is fraught with polarization along numerous cleavages—by region, religion, and class, to cite the most conspicuous. Francoism evokes a clash of identities and ideologies. Even though conflicts of such severity did not disappear with the advent of democracy, the lightning rod metaphor is much less applicable to the new regime.

Lastly, no case has been made here that political legitimacy or the lack of it stabilizes or undoes democracy or any other regime. What the analysis does suggest is that the level of tension fell off with the coming of democracy. The inclusiveness that by definition came with democratization offset in some measure the unsettling features, the sheer uncertainty, of the process. Democratization did not assure a new stability but it offered a way out of the old equilibrium-as-impasse, the standoff between polar opposites. The outlines of this process are reflected in the attitudes of ordinary Spaniards. Some of the parameters of governability altered for the better.

A QUESTION OF TRUST

Spanish politics, then, is less polarized than it was during the days of Franco. The "spread" of the democratic system is wide compared to the sharply divided clients and dissidents underlying the old system. Furthermore, the Spanish public sees the two regimes as separate even as it recognizes the reformist, continuous nature of democratization. This fundamental distinction bolsters a sense of legitimacy that is broader than support for and opposition to particular governments.

But though the sparseness of the demographic and cultural matrix undergirding the democratic regime suggests societal depolarization and a certain autonomy on the part of the new state, the configuration might also be taken as a sign of shallowness in commitment to it. Whatever we have encountered until now in the way of support for the democratic dimension may not live up to what political analysts usually call legitimacy, which is supposed to reflect more than depolarization.

This brings us to the matter of trust. The phenomenon sounds more solid and positive than the somewhat pallid framework of support sketched so far. Trust, we have argued, is a continuum spanning private and public domains. Implicit in this differentiation is the idea that political legitimacy is enhanced by the sort of trust that extends to faith in democratic procedures and laws—the rules of the game that are distinguishable from the operations of particular governments.

This part of our theory, that trust in and respect for the rule of law feed into democratic legitimacy, and that they carry more weight than the popularity of governments, is a refinement of received wisdom, an amplification of the old standard of trust in government. We break new ground in situating this orientation toward the *state* alongside orientations toward *society*. Attitudes about the government exist in the context of comparable attitudes about various social groups. By bringing into view attitudes toward voluntary, autonomous groups, consideration of interpersonal trust—specifically, confidence in other persons and associations beyond immediate kin but short of the government itself—sets the stage for the examination of a component of *democratic* legitimacy, as compared to what might be little more than a study of compliance with an indeterminate species of rule.[10]

Figure 2.2 sorts out the first part of our reasoning about trust: its public-private makeup. In 1990 we asked Spaniards how much trust they placed in fifteen different things. The idea is to rough in a continuum, as a preliminary to possibly finer distinctions among types of private and public orientations. The chart plots the results from top to bottom in descending order of *confianza*.[11]

Objects close to home, starting with the self, inspire greater confidence than public figures and organizations, certainly more than "unions," "businessmen," "politicians," and "the government." These priorities seem obvious, even if a less democratic ordering, in which trust is ceded to agencies of government over associations closer to home, is conceivable (Cohen 1982).

Table 2.6 contains more interesting results. It displays the four dimen-

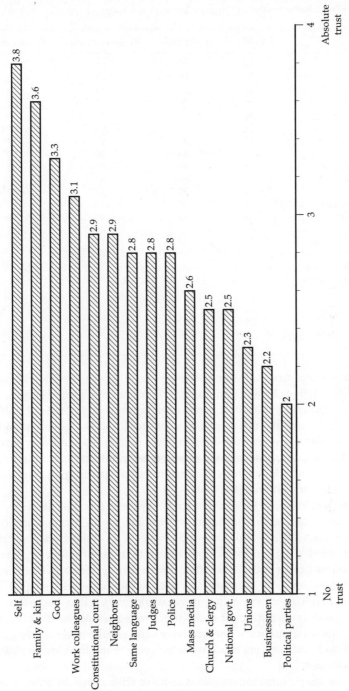

Figure 2.2 Average trust in 15 objects, 1990

TABLE 2.6. Factor analysis (oblique solution), trust, 1990

Trust in ...	I. Public	II. The law	III. Associations	IV. Religious
Politicians	**.80**	.20	.05	.01
Unions	**.77**	.07	−.01	−.12
Government	**.61**	.35	.07	.11
Businessmen	**.59**	.26	.13	.24
Media	**.56**	.15	.18	.15
Constitutional court	.24	**.85**	.09	.06
Judges	.23	**.85**	.15	.13
Police	.23	**.66**	.20	.27
Work colleagues	.18	.05	**.70**	−.03
Neighbors	.36	.00	**.59**	.33
Self	−.17	.22	**.54**	−.07
Same language	.46	−.06	**.51**	.24
Family and relatives	.04	.15	**.50**	.16
God	−.04	.13	.08	**.85**
Church and clergy	.21	.20	.12	**.81**
Correlation matrix, oblique solution				
I				
II	.25			
III	−.25	−.22		
IV	.22	.26	−.23	

sions that emerge from a factor analysis of trust across the fifteen items. The statistics define clusters or domains rather than rankings of trust.

The first grouping takes in concrete organizations and objects of public life: politicians, unions, the media, businessmen, and the government it-self. At the other extreme is the domain of the sacred: God and the church. One cluster includes the workaday public, mostly political sphere, and the other encompasses the religious dimension, which stands apart from and, to a degree, in opposition to the first.

It is the intermediate factors that lend nuance to the analysis. One di-mension taps trust not in quotidian government but in meta-institutions such as the congress, the judiciary, and organs of law enforcement. These are preeminently regime institutions rather than government organiza-tions (Toharia Cortés 1988). The other dimension gathers together senti-ments of confidence in primary and face-to-face networks shaped by neighbors, family members, colleagues at work, and the like. These are not formal organizations but rather social ties, proto-associations, that for the most part are separate from comparatively solid entities such as "the gov-ernment" and "unions" yet much more palpable than "the judiciary" and "the constitution."

What are the political ramifications of these affiliations? In order to an-swer the question it is necessary to realize that, across a basic private–public continuum, there exist subcultures or zones of trust that constitute variations on the private–public theme. Two of them are public, but in different ways, reflecting on the one hand contingent and concrete and on the other procedural and generic aspects of political institutions. Another pair is private. One centers on religious attachments and the other has a social component with an as yet undefined political content.

With these distinctions in mind, the probable connections between the pockets of trust and the political realm fall into place. It would hardly be surprising for public opinion to associate leaders of democratic governments such as Felipe González with the first, specifically political dimension of trust. Similarly, it goes without saying that the figure of the pope should be closely tied to sentiments of trust in religious authority. The important question is how the king is perceived. We need to know how he stands in the public mind relative to feelings about the meta-institutions of democracy.

Table 2.7 shows the correlations between each of the dimensions of trust and the popularity of Felipe González, John Paul II, and King Juan Carlos. Aside from the obvious associations of the political dimension with González and of the religious factor with the pope, two connections have substantive significance.

The figure of the king is associated not only with religion—that is, with tradition—but with positive sentiments toward the rules of the democratic game. At the same time, like the pope, he is perceived as independent from the government mechanics factor. Second, in contrast to all the other dimensions, the trust-in-personal-networks factor has no significant association with any of the public personalities. This cluster looks to be autonomous from politics conceived as policy-focused organizations.

The king brings three linkages to Spanish democracy which in combination fortify the new system. One is the tie-in with religious tradition, a connection that taken alone might be prejudicial to democracy but, in conjunction with the overall pattern of connections between the king and other public institutions, solidifies the continuity of democratization within Spanish political culture. Second, the king is seen as more or less neutral in respect to particular governments. Third, he is perceived positively in connection with confidence in and respect for the legal and au-

TABLE 2.7. Correlations between dimensions of trust and popularity of public figures, 1990

Public figures	Public	The law	Associations	Religious
King Juan Carlos	.01	**.23**	.08	**.29**
Pope John Paul II	.00	.18	.07	**.54**
Felipe González	**.25**	**.24**	− .01	.06

thority structures of democracy. This mixture of attributes makes for a remarkable conciliation of traditional and modern points of reference.[12]

There is an equally striking distance between trust in face-to-face associations and the political realm, regardless of whether the latter is defined as specific governments or as the democratic regime. This disjuncture appears to be a matter not of hostility toward but of independence on the part of immediate, relatively intimate social groupings. From one point of view, the remoteness of "the social factor" from formal political referents is healthy. It signifies the autonomy of the social, and the possible capacity of resistance against the state, as much as it suggests anything about the autonomy of the state.

In summary, the king is not just a celebrity; he is an institutional symbol, a cultural plumb line. Depolarization no doubt encouraged moderation. But it also created uncertainty and perhaps anxiety. The old patterns of conflict, whatever havoc they created, gave an implicit structure to Spanish mass politics. With these maps gone, and with a revival of maximalism ruled out, the vacuity of "moderation" and "pragmatism," essentially satisficing procedures, may generate some uneasiness.

Totemic figures—in the Spanish case, the monarch—are crucial and possibly essential trace elements in the popular symbolism surrounding democracy (Hunt 1984). They crystallize a shared commitment that neither institutions nor abstract formulas of legitimacy can articulate in the vernacular. In the absence of a civil religion, they become revered touch stones—sacraments—of political integration.

We have tried to convert political legitimacy from the invisible and perhaps nonexistent to the comprehensible and possibly consequential. If political legitimacy is a fiction, it is the kind of make-believe that persists in popular consciousness and not just as a cast in the academic eye. Moreover, we have begun to understand the components of political legitimacy both in functional terms, as a profile of evaluations of governmental performance, and as a selective confidence in public institutions.

Depolarization was once thought to be practically anti-Hispanic (Horowitz 1972). Now it is pretty much taken for granted in Spain. But just as it has prepared Spanish political culture for an extended run of tolerance and moderation, depolarization has also created a puzzle about the substance of political legitimacy.

On the one hand, legitimacy does seem to derive in part from commonsensical evaluations of what governments do. Clear-mindedness is no doubt abetted by historically vivid terms of comparison. Democratic legitimacy becomes less of a phantasm to the extent that fascism remained a vivid reality during the transition, near at hand. This temporal contrast enlivens what is otherwise little more than a speculative drill.

On the other hand, political legitimacy seems to have more to it than the decomposition of inherited antagonisms and a sense of what Spaniards dislike, heightened by a contrast with the immediate antidemocratic past. In the first place, the dissimilarity perceived in public opinion between authoritarianism and democracy is progressive and incremental rather than abrupt or radical. Fascism as a cultural commodity in Spain ended not with a bang but by attrition. From the perspective of the Spanish public, differences between the last decade of Francoism and the early years of democracy were evident but not overwhelming. It is only with the passage of time and, in particular, with the defense of the new regime by the king and the rise to power of the socialists, that the democratic system pulled further and further away, by degrees, from the modernizing authoritarianism of the sixties and the first half of the seventies. Initiation into democracy took time. As St. Augustine prayed to be free of impure thoughts, but not right away, Spaniards gave up authoritarianism decisively, at last, but not all of a sudden.

Second, something akin to a normative, positive orientation toward democracy emerges, taking the shape of trust in public institutions and political procedures. We don't have a series of comparable indicators going back to the start of the Spanish transition, so a reliable estimate of the evolution of this type of political norm is impossible to reconstruct. Besides, however suggestive the multidimensional configuration generated by the correlations between the diverse objects of trust might be, the fact remains that the level of trust in government, voluntary associations, and the like is low relative to the absolute confidence in private ties. And all of these evaluations are separate from the actual incidence of membership and participation in political parties, unions, and other associations, which we have yet to examine. Nevertheless, if the course of democratization was, as we have seen, accompanied by depolarization, then it is likely that it was accompanied as well by a growing confidence in the workings of newly created institutions.

Trust, like legitimacy itself, is a gradient rather than an either-or categorization. This gradient is shaded in recognizable ways. The public sphere is broken down into a *res publica* understood as (1) the state as a generic body of institutions, (2) concrete governmental agencies and political organizations, and (3) an assortment of ties going from the family to informal work and neighborhood linkages (these areas roughly parallel what analysts of legitimacy used to call "government," "regime," and "political community"). And variations in trust in these domains—specifically in law and the procedures of government—connect up with orientations toward the spanning figure of the king, the prince through whose image many Spaniards make intuitive sense of the grand abstraction of legitimacy in democratic guise.

Third, it is probably safe to say that nowhere, certainly not in Spain, does democratic legitimacy exist in unadulterated form, wholly separable

from the dynamics of governmental performance and the inflections of political culture. Confidence in institutional procedures is about as close to a
common denominator of democratic legitimacy as we are likely to find.
One-size-fits-all models of legitimacy are valid to the extent that they are
restricted to some such minimalist core. Around this nucleus a composite
of historically conditioned, variable norms and expectations tends to develop. In the Spanish experience this includes not only depolarization but
also the salience accorded to social fairness. The next two chapters give
particular attention to the role of social fairness in the consolidation of
democracy in Spain.

3

The Transformation of the
Agenda of Public Opinion

Few statistics express the release of Spanish political culture from authoritarianism so powerfully as the correlations, falling over the years, between popular orientations toward Francoism and the governments that followed. At the time of our first two surveys, in 1978 and 1980, the UCD was still in command, and Spaniards saw a modest, gradually dissolving continuity between the leadership of the transition and the government that had gone before. In 1978 the correlation between satisfaction with "the last ten years of the Franco government" and with the then-incumbent UCD government was a hefty .41. In 1980, still under the UCD, it was down to .30. By 1984, when the socialists had been in office for about two years, the Franco/post-Franco correlations had become mildly negative: −.15. The trend follows the calculated *reformismo* of the transition.

The UCD embodied partial continuity. After a few years, during which it succeeded in reconciling major players to new political rules, the conservative coalition had served its purpose in the public mind. Once political compromise had become the norm, the twin themes of economic competence and social fairness came to the fore, favoring the PSOE.

With the implosion of the UCD, the electoral center-right virtually disappeared. Under these circumstances, the received script of Spanish politics called for an escalation of hostilities between extremes. Yet no such thing happened. By the eighties the once-incendiary socialists had positioned themselves to fill most of the void left by the disappearance of the UCD. It was the adroitness of the socialists in economic management, following their strategic decision to back away from maximalism, that put the cap on the consolidation of Spanish democracy.

This chapter documents the transformation of public opinion leading to the ascent of the socialists in 1982, a trajectory that came to an end only in 1996. The analysis traces the mutations in public opinion that crystallized in a not wholly coherent mandate for economic performance and social distribution. In the earliest years of the transition, arranging a political settlement among the regions and between Francoists and democrats topped the agenda of public opinion. Once a working accord had been reached on these foundational issues, the agenda shifted toward economic demands and the provision of tangible benefits. It was this reformist gradualism that the socialists, through a strategy of enlightened clientelism, rode to power.

The analytical pitfall to avoid in light of this well-wrought outcome is that of missing the fluidity of the early days of the transition. Democracy ended up being consolidated but the course of democratization was full of uncertainties. The years from the late seventies, when the center-right UCD held office, to the early eighties, when its electoral collapse led to the coming to power of the socialists, were a period of economic recession, regional violence, military conspiracy, and political insecurity (Tezanos, Cotarelo, and de Blas 1989). Public opinion went through intricate changes. We focus on three of them.

One concerns the ways in which Spaniards understood the distinction between the *political* accomplishments of the transition and the *economic* tasks that lay ahead. This distinction entails an evolving agenda, the attainment of one set of goals setting the stage for the emergence of other priorities.

In hindsight the distinction looks crashingly obvious, but it was not so clear at the time. "Political" challenges encompassed not only fundamental questions of constitution-making but also regional and separatist pulls that were not quite eased by accommodations reached at the national level. At least some foundational issues spilled over, half-settled, still simmering, into the years when the resolution of economic problems could no longer be postponed. Nevertheless, unlike some attempts at democratization in post-communist societies, in the Spanish transition political and economic crises were played out seriatim rather than simultaneously (Encarnación 1996).

The sequence was a rough one. The politics of identity continued to flare up during the swift move toward economic pragmatism, and the government resorted to "special measures" to contain violence targeted at the center of the democratic system (Pérez Díaz 1996: 135ff.). The in-basket of the socialists was cluttered with the remains of understandings and truces that threatened to come undone. Eventually, in the mid-nineties, scandals surrounding the deployment of counterterrorist measures in the name of preserving democracy contributed to the downfall of the socialists. So estimating the weight of economic controversies in balance with extra-economic issues in mass politics during this transitional period is an important task.

A second focus of analysis is on a subtler division between problems which the government was expected to remedy and those deemed to be matters of personal responsibility or idiosyncratic chance and hence peripheral to the political domain. Although Spaniards rank quite high in cross-national comparisons of expectations regarding government action in economic affairs, state intervention is acknowledged to have limits. A culture that has fostered public-sector activism on both traditionally patrimonial and ideologically leftist grounds also harbors a streak of individualism.[1]

Great expectations of state protection from economic hazard and the pervasiveness of strong norms of privacy make for a seemingly contradictory but understandable combination. During the 1970s and through most of the eighties, norms favoring political intervention in economic affairs were so widespread they cut rather evenly across the populace. For this reason, it was difficult for any one party to stake out a class constituency on the grounds of social concern and activism. Even where expectations regarding the role of government dipped a bit, among younger and better-off Spaniards, they were still very high. Where the Spanish public most clearly drew a line between appropriate government intervention and a more or less off-limits private sphere was on the border between the economic realm in general and the "moral" or religious on the other. This separation of spheres was itself a sign of cultural depolarization.

In addition, the vast majority of Spaniards who favored state intervention to right social wrongs were not ideologues or radicals. For a long time the socialists were given the benefit of the doubt, and then some, against their neoconservative rivals, who suffered from a certain guilt by association with antediluvian reaction. Grievances and suspicions bred under the costive hierarchy of fascism still festered, and the state under Franco was thought to have committed as many sins of omission, particularly with regard to social policy, as it had crimes of repression. This resentment, however, was not undying, nor was it turned into incitement to revenge. If there was anything Spaniards had had enough of, more than hierarchy, it was maximalism.

By the nineties, after nearly a decade of developmental and distributive programs under the socialists, enthusiasm for state-sponsored initiatives began to cool. But during the eighties, poorer Spaniards were not alone in fixing responsibility on the government or in expecting the government to remedy their plight and the woes of the nation. Even many of the well-to-do, and a great many of the aged, expected the government to play a decisive if selective role in economic management. Economic issues were both highly salient and not terribly divisive. This functional consensus privileged administrative flair and material payoffs over ideological quarrels. Together with the fact that Spain simply had a long way to go to catch up with the modernized countries of Europe, the ethos favoring governmental action on behalf of economic problem-solving helps account for a growth in state capacity—notably in revenue extraction—that went largely uncontested until the beginning of the 1990s (Gunther 1996; Villaria 1995).

It is vital not only to remember how fitful economic growth was in the Spain of the late sixties and early seventies, in comparison with the rest of Europe, but also to recognize how underequipped was the bureaucratic apparatus bequeathed by the old regime. By the criterion of state strength, Spain barely ranked ahead of Portugal and Turkey, two other countries with authoritarian legacies, when its transition got started. Franco left his successors with a repressive but fiscally threadbare government; the machinery of state was only intermittently efficient (Gunther 1980). As democratization unfolded, the administrative capacity of the state grew (see Figure 3.1). Government solvency became a top priority under a socialist government committed to economic management and the extension of services (Comín 1992; Jiménez Fernández 1993; Maravall 1993). Whether associational life and political participation kept pace is another question, as we shall see.

In summary, the tendency of the Spanish public to accord the government a large role in economic management and social problem-solving has been only loosely related to class or other demarcators of social position. This disjuncture is an important element, we will argue, behind the slack association between the political parties and their socioeconomic bases. It has taken a good deal of the ideological sting out of economic policy-making in Spain.

Popular understanding of economic matters not only encompasses an

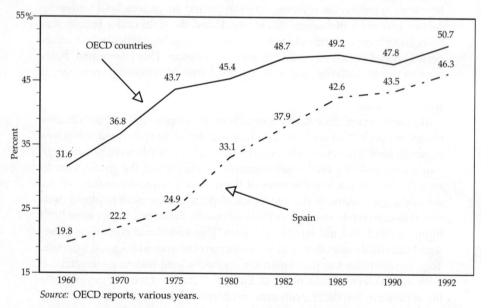

Source: OECD reports, various years.

Figure 3.1 Governmental expenditures as percent of GDP, Spain vs. other industrial societies, 1960–1992

ambiguous division between private striving and the government's role in fostering solutions as part of the public realm. Public opinion also takes shape around a distinction between distributive and more purely problem-solving, or growth-oriented, priorities regarding the economy. The rival cosmologies of capitalism and communism, or a market versus a command economy, were never seriously at issue during the transition in Spain. The ideological climate had cooled considerably. Still, Spaniards continued to differ about how much emphasis should be given to distributive and remedial programs, as compared to policies directed at aggregate growth—that is, roughly, to social democratization as compared to economic liberalization (Maravall 1997).

Issues like these tend not to be so inflammatory as grand debates over marketization or so abstract as the conflicts between alternative systems that once animated Spanish politics. Such tensions constitute the prose, rather than the confrontational drama, of ideological rivalry. They conjure up the currency of material gain and concrete loss. Interests are at stake more than ideologies and identities. By the beginning of the 1980s the Spanish public was primed for programs of economic restructuring cushioned by distributive compensation. The time had come not for the passions of redemption but for the politics of consumption. The fact that the package turned out not to be altogether coherent and possibly downright inconsistent (Argandoña et al. 1988; De la Dehesa 1991) was overcome by its appeal within a cultural context in which redistributive policies, far from being exclusively leftist, resonated with traditional paternalism (Buchanan and Conway 1997).

In fact Spanish social policy during the 1980s took on schizophrenic features. Even though unemployment was the highest in Western Europe, Spain was one of the very few countries to experience a progressive redistribution of income during the decade. This was not only because of ambivalence in domestic opinion. Democratization in Spain coincided with a worldwide decline in militant socialism and with the global vogue of economic neoliberalism (Bull 1993; Gillespie 1993; Kitschelt 1994; Kohli 1993). By the time the socialists were poised to come to power in 1982, the wind had gone out of the sails of socialism as the flagship of advanced democracy. This development undercut whatever triumphalist pretensions the socialists might have had, and it accelerated depolarization.

Yet ideological deflation and calls for economic stabilization did not square with the undercurrent of antihierarchical and distributive populism that had built up in the Spanish public during the Franco years. Expectations regarding the restitutive functions of democracy modified strictly procedural readings of democratic legitimacy, and much of the impetus for state expansion of social programs originated with older, fairly traditional sectors of the citizenry, as has been the case in some post-communist societies. For some time, the Spanish socialists handled the procedural and performance-oriented bases of regime support by casting the tension between the two as a series of variable-sum tradeoffs, at least as long as an economic boom and the infusion of European Community funds made such inclusionary expansion feasible (Bresser Pereira, Maravall, and Przeworski 1993).

Democratization took hold in Spain also at a time when the epistemic communities, the invisible colleges that shaped what constituted sound political economy, were undergoing realignment (Hall 1989, 1993, 1997; Sikkink 1991). The eclecticism of the democratizing project, as put in place by a center-conservative coalition and brought to fruition by the socialists, begins to make sense once this transnational transition in ideas is understood. The mix of innovation and opportunism, of neoliberalism and state-building, was made possible not only by the rejection of maximalism on the part of the Spanish public; revisionism was also a response to the international flux of ideas (Garton Ash 1995; Schmidt 1996b).

POLITICAL LIBERALIZATION AND ECONOMIC CONCERNS

"Mixed emotions" is as good a term as any to characterize the mood of the Spanish electorate during the late seventies and early eighties. Euphoria surrounding the transition had been replaced by disillusion with increasingly bleak economic prospects. Prices and unemployment were rising. Separatist-inspired violence persisted. There was a sense—a malaise, to use a buzzword of the period—that the new democracy had lost its bearings. "*Against* Franco," the madrileño wisecrack went, "we fared better."

Rather than being confused, however, popular assessments of the state of the country could more properly be described as ambivalent. In place of the black-and-white renderings that had been staple interpretations of the condition and destiny of Spain, the public recognized shadings. Perception of nuance was still another symptom of the decline of polarization and the emergence of a political culture geared toward compromise and tolerance. Messy as it might be, "confusion" was a step beyond a duel of absolutes.

In 1980, a few months before the brief takeover of the Cortes by disaffected elements of the military, a majority of Spaniards (56 percent) felt that "in some respects life in Spain has improved over the past two years," while in response to a follow-up question more than three out of four (77 percent) felt that things had gotten worse.[2] But the most representative evaluation was a combination of the positive and negative. Forty percent felt that in some respects Spain was doing better *and* that in other respects the country was worse off. Close behind were the 37 percent who claimed that things had simply deteriorated, followed by the few (15 percent) who judged that conditions had improved all around. The situation, though overcast, was not one of unrelieved gloom.

TABLE 3.1. Assessment of conditions in Spain by ideological, religious, and partisan orientation, 1980 (percent)

	Life in Spain has . . .				
	Gotten better *and* worse	Gotten worse	Gotten better	Stayed the same	Total
Ideological orientation					
Left	41%	26%	25%	8%	100%
Left-center	47	28	17	9	101
Center	42	35	14	9	100
Center-right	29	57	9	6	101
Right	17	70	7	6	100
Religiosity					
None	44	27	20	9	100
Little	46	30	16	8	100
Some	42	36	14	8	100
Frequent	35	44	12	9	100
Much	32	53	6	9	100
Partisanship					
PCE	46	22	25	7	100
Other	45	26	19	10	100
PSOE	45	30	19	7	101
Regional	58	28	9	5	100
UCD	42	38	12	8	100
None	38	40	13	9	100
Right	28	58	10	4	100

These judgments were distributed unevenly across social, cultural, and political sectors, as Table 3.1 shows. The left inclined more toward the affirmative than the right, which at the extreme shows a real distaste for the democratic order.[3] It is the emollient tenor of leftist opinion rather than the dismay of the far right that sounds a note of historical change. By the end of the seventies the rhetoric of politics as redemption and revolution had subsided. The ascent of reformism of the social democratic brand undid the symmetry between the fire-breathing left and the bunker right. Ideologically, reactionary forces were isolated; their mirror image had mostly faded away. The far right was stuck in unrequited enmity against a nemesis that no longer existed.[4]

Where disappointment seems to have set in, not as wholesale alienation but as demoralization in search of a promising exit, was among the adherents of the center-right and among Spaniards lacking partisan attachment. Without ideas, its capacity for improvisation gone, unable to lead, the

UCD, the holding company for the conservative center, looked frayed and exhausted.

A few years earlier such a pattern might have fueled polarization. Elements on the right—factions of the military and a few hard-liners in the church that composed the bunker—favored just such a confrontation. But the left failed to reciprocate. Now, instead of escalating hostilities, its leadership took the weakness of the moderate-conservative band of the ideological spectrum as an opportunity to build a majority out of variegated centrist opinions and interests. This was an iconoclastic but constructive maneuver, for the shibboleths that were demolished came as often from the left as from the right (Colomer 1991, 1995).

The left did not have a full-fledged program. Under González it, or a large part of it, stopped feeling guilty about this. In part because it lacked ideological certitude, the left was able to recognize and take advantage of an opening when it saw one. Its creative breakthrough was prompted by an awareness that, whatever rigidities persisted among ideological and partisan political groupings or in regional pockets, public opinion was labile. "When in doubt, do market research" is too glib a characterization of its resulting tactics. But the phrase does capture one American, Kennedy-style component of the new politics, which the Spanish right caught on to only later.[5]

In one crucial respect public opinion seemed unformed and up for grabs. Social class, the linchpin of orthodox analysis of Spanish reality, had been for some time a frail predictor of political leanings. The brittle emblem of mass ideology in Spain, class did have a role in fixing positions vis-à-vis Francoism. But its function as a guide to popular sentiment about the new regime and about the direction that economic policy should take was obscure. The uncertain center was very broad and unsettled territory, a frontier under the noses of Spanish elites. What was quickly to become known as *felipismo*, the pragmatism sponsored by Felipe Gonzáles, whose preeminent feature came to be skepticism of the socialist canon, was undefined, relative to the style cultivated under *franquismo*, which itself had favored triumphalistic opportunism over ideology (Sotelo 1992).

Because there isn't much to show, we do not break down here the worse–better assessments of conditions in Spain by social class. However, when we examine responses to the open-ended follow-up questions that asked *how* things had gotten worse and/or better, and when these responses are aligned according to ideological *tendance*, as in Figure 3.2, more interesting results turn up.

There is close to a consensus that the transition was a political triumph. The far right, where appreciation of the politics of the transition plummets, constitutes an exception. In 1980 only about one in five conservatives viewed political democratization with approval. But at this time very few Spaniards characterized themselves as of the right in the first place, so that

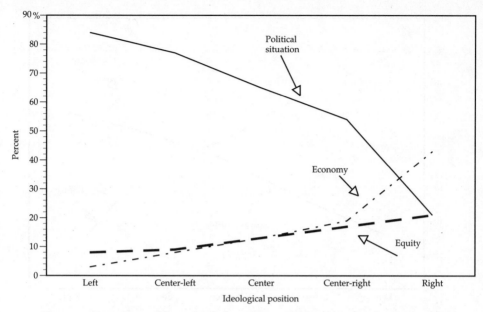

Figure 3.2 Perceptions of how things have improved, by left-right placement, 1980 (percent)

on the whole, nearly seven out of ten cite "politics"—political liberty, freedom of expression, and the like—when asked to explain how they feel the country has improved. The next most common category, "the economy," takes in only 11 percent of the responses, along with about 10 percent for whom the area of social equity tops the list of improvements.

No such unanimity exists on the debit side (see Figure 3.3). Still, it is clear that at the beginning of the eighties economic conditions of one sort or another bothered Spaniards far more than any other set of worries. One-third mentioned economic conditions in general—the cost of living, slumping productivity, and so forth—and one-quarter called attention to matters of equity and services: joblessness, wages and income distribution.

The right admits more frequently than the left to worrying about political order and stability. Conservatives tend to be down on "the political situation in general." Less obviously, it is Spaniards toward the middle, more than those on either side of them ideologically, for whom the mundane threat of crime in the streets poses a serious concern. They are exercised not about politics generally but about down-home matters like personal safety, just as those on the left tend to be concerned with economic security.[6]

Other familiar tendencies can be noted, even if they are not striking enough to warrant graphic presentation. The overriding concern of Spaniards is with the economy, but those who define themselves as devout care more about political order than social equity, and younger Spaniards

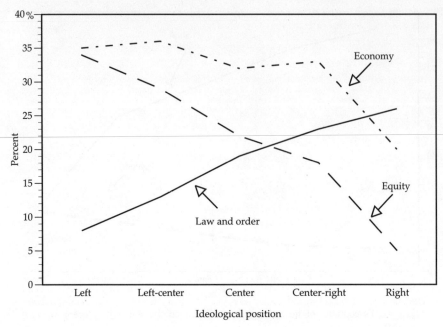

Figure 3.3 Perceptions of how things have gotten worse, by left-right placement, 1980 (percent)

show the reverse disposition, worrying about economic opportunity more than political stability. Along similar lines, lower-class Spaniards are twice as likely as their upper-middle-class counterparts (29 to 14 percent) to bring up questions of equity as the chief failing of the present system. But the sense of economic urgency is spread across classes, and comes close to being universal.

It is when we turn to variations in evaluations of how things have *improved* that departures from the commonplace begin to surface. Though overall satisfaction with the economy is low, ideological conservatives and the deeply religious are likelier than their opposites to claim that both the economy in general and social conditions have shown at least some improvement, just as they are less likely to think that political conditions have changed for the better.

Why were conservatives modestly generous in their evaluation of the economic situation associated with democracy? The transition was gradual. Economic shock treatment was not on the agenda; much less was social revolution. Although its capacity for political risk-taking alarmed some unreconstructed reactionaries, the UCD did not intend to perform radical surgery on Spanish capitalism or jeopardize the interests of the business class.

Members of the working class actually take a more sanguine view of conditions in matters of social fairness than those in the middle and upper classes. The same difference crops up in evaluations of the overall economy. Assessments of economic and social conditions do not follow class lines as might be predicted from romantic theories of class consciousness. Working-class Spaniards were not seething at their economic situation; and in fact, they were inclined to be optimistic about their prospects.

Working-class opinion was equivocal regarding the state of the economy and the movement (or lack of it) toward distributive social programs. At the beginning of the eighties, Spanish labor tended to be both critical and hopeful about the material promise of democracy. Their ambivalence suggests a willingness to wait and see, not flat-out militancy. It also indicates a politically significant gap between the sharper feelings of Spaniards when they are classified in ideological and partisan terms and the hazier, less fervid passions of broad social classes. If one remembers that leftist opinion is fairly moderate to be begin with, the profile of implicit expectations across the center-left zone of public opinion takes on a reformist tenor. This was the cast of mind that helped facilitate the series of economic pacts in which the Spanish unions agreed to "responsible" wage policies (Gunther 1992; Secretaría Confederal de Formación y Cultura 1989).

The overall configuration may look like nothing so much as the amorphous murk to be expected in the inchoate days of democratization, before parties and interest groups formulate strategic options and stakeout ideological alignments (Nelson 1993). This morass raised for purists the temptation and for pragmatists the possibility of building a movement around the majority position that encompassed the center-left. Instead of posing an obstacle to heightened political consciousness, the heterogeneous nature of public opinion represented an opportunity for putting together a broad-based coalition—in a favorite term of socialist politicians, a mass party rather than a class party. For this goal marketing could be just as powerful a strategy as mobilization (Geer 1996; Laufer and Paradeise 1990; Rosenstone and Hansen 1993; Schuessler 1995).

SOCIAL RESENTMENT AND ECONOMICS
PUBLIC AND PRIVATE

Ambivalence, tilted toward the left, was the hallmark of public opinion in Spain at the end of the seventies and the beginning of the eighties. The atmosphere of countervailing pulls was not at odds with the watershed events that were soon to take place: the aborted coup led by unreconstructed factions of the military in February 1981, and the electoral victory of the PSOE in October 1982, which enabled the socialists to form a majority government. Public opinion reflected the crosscurrents that surfaced in these events.

Most Spaniards took pride in the political sanity of the transition, having ratified the constitution of the parliamentary monarchy in 1978. Discontent centered on the economy and its social failures. Assessments of economic conditions were not bound up with ideological conviction, and differences between left and right corresponded to divisions between classes only in the loosest way. With the political gains of the transition locked in, the problem was how to put the democratic framework to work in overcoming severe economic challenges and to move Spain toward what came to be understood as convergence with Europe.

Though public opinion left room for policy maneuver, it was not completely formless. It exhibited three important patterns.

One was an expectation, high by cross-national standards, that it was the responsibility of the government to take on the economic crisis on several fronts. Such a posture was hard to categorize ideologically. Not reducible to purely left-vs.-right leanings, it bore strong traces of a statist tradition, together with an anxiety born of a lived experience of social hierarchies (compare Swank 1998; Veliz 1980). Social democratic urges were not impelled by hatred of Francoism alone; they also had roots in precapitalist tradition.

A second, related feature of Spanish public opinion was, and with some modification continues to be, its distributive-populist cast. The prevailing assumption was that social disparities were wide and that the government should assume a forceful role not only in boosting economic growth but in narrowing these disparities.

The egalitarian motif stops short of root-and-branch redistribution. Opinion on such matters borders on what used to be called petty bourgeois vacillation: a concern with fairness that also places a premium on the opportunity for individual achievement, the accumulation of comforts, and the guarding of selected privileges. It is not so much hierarchy per se that Spaniards oppose as impediments to getting a piece of the action. Conversely, the desire for strict egalitarianism does not appear to be nearly so powerful as a desire for protection against the vagaries of the market.

A third feature of opinion on socioeconomic issues is the tendency to compartmentalize private and public economics. Spaniards attribute a greater role to the public sector in economic performance than, say, citizens of the United States. They are hardly unique in this regard, since it is Americans who are chronic outliers in cross-national comparisons of welfare orientations (Pierson 1995). But the tendency of Spaniards to welcome state intervention in the economic arena, though substantial, is not all-encompassing.

The gap between private hardship and an expectation of public remedy holds pretty much regardless of partisan affiliation. A sense of individual hardship does not automatically or even usually translate into a demand that government assume responsibility for collective deprivation. This disjuncture can be traced to a respect for the adventitious in economic affairs, revealing an individualism opposite to the more celebrated state-centrism of the Hispanic heritage. Like citizens in other societies, Spaniards do not typically reduce their views of collective economic conditions to the state of their own pocketbooks (Kinder and Sears 1979). The tendency to separate personal hardships from collective hard times weakens connections across the classical fault lines of Spanish politics, such as class or partisan attachment and evaluations of government performance.

The distinction between the economic situation of individuals and assessments of economic conditions in the aggregate comes through in the responses to two roughly similar but substantively different questions from the first two surveys. In 1978 Spaniards were asked, "Taking into account the good and the bad, would you say that in comparison with the majority of persons in this country life has treated you better, the same, or worse?" The question elicits an interpersonal comparison, but the focus remains on the individual's situation rather than economic conditions generally. Then, in 1980, right after asking in what respects people felt Spain might have improved "in the last two years" and how it might have gotten worse, we posed a summary question whose connotations were collective rather than personal: "Taking into account the good and the bad, do you believe that in the last two years things have gotten better or worse?"

In 1978 three-quarters answered that life had treated them about the same as their peers, with about equal percentages saying they felt comparatively better (13 percent) and worse off (12 percent). Responses to the 1980, "public" economics question are much more negative. While a plurality (46 percent) believe that things are about the same, 35 percent assert that things have gotten worse, and fewer than one out of five feel that conditions have improved. "Public" economics generates a good deal more pessimism than "private" economics, and it is implausible that all or even most of this difference can be ascribed to deterioration in the economic climate from 1978 to 1980.

The systematic differences between the perceptions of collective and individual economic conditions include (1) a virtual lack of correspondence between assessments of individual economic circumstances and evaluations of economic conditions overall, and (2) a lack of connection between social class and judgments about the economy in general, together with (3) a close tie between social class and assessments of personal economic conditions.

It is natural to expect some division of opinion regarding personal and collective conditions. While ideology may color evaluations so that perceptions of the economic situation follow along partisan lines, there is no reason, short of attributing an exotic infantilism to the Spanish temper, to assume a direct link between the economic plight of this or that individual and his or her vision of the economy in general.

What is less evident is that there should be so little variation across so-cial classes in the way overall economic conditions are perceived. Class differences in perceptions of personal economic fortunes are impressive. So are differences in perceptions of the economy as a whole along partisan lines. But evaluations of the economy stay virtually invariant across social classes, and (as we will see in Chapter 4) it is these perceptions of eco-nomic conditions in the aggregate that carry political weight. Class posi-tion has a slight impact on economic opinion and, by extension, on perceptions of government performance. (Measures of "objective class po-sition," such as occupation, fare even worse than subjective class identifi-cation as correlates of economic judgments.)

Even the relatively clear connection between economic perceptions and partisan attachment has its surprising side. With the transition on its way to consolidation, the left might have been expected to vent its impatience with the pace of economic change. Yet, while only a small minority of Spaniards in 1980 claimed to be happy with the state of the economy, those on the left were actually somewhat more inclined to express contentment or at least less foreboding than centrist and conservative Spaniards. In con-trast to the fear and loathing displayed by the extreme right at the depre-dations of democracy, the left seemed cautiously upbeat. Such optimism deradicalized demands for social reform.

Besides putting into perspective the reformist expectations surrounding the ascendant popularity of the socialists, this gradualism helps explain the eventual disaffection of the center and the center-right from the UCD, whose economic imagination was unequal to its political skill during the transition. An important factor behind the willingness of conservative Spaniards to watch the UCD fade away was that they didn't consider the center-right coalition competent as a defender of their economic interests. Neither were conservatives unduly alarmed by the prospect of the coming to power of socialists, whose leadership preached the gospel of competi-tiveness. As irritation with the UCD grew, Spaniards were probably more anxious about the possible emergence of a minority coalitional govern-ment and about political paralysis than about the coming to power of a so-cialist majority.[7]

Two key points have been advanced so far. One is the distinction Spaniards made between the political glories and the economic loose ends of the transition. The other is the distinction between personal economic conditions and the state of the economy in the aggregate. It is this dissocia-tion that thwarts any one-to-one linkage between economic opinion, parti-san attachment, and social class. Working-class Spaniards are likelier than others to feel that things haven't gone well for them personally, but they don't ordinarily tie this evaluation to their perceptions of the economy as a whole.

A further twist must be added to the argument, however, lest we conclude that the Spanish working class not only violates images of radical-ism nurtured in idealized depictions of class consciousness but took leave of its senses in succumbing to a rosy view of the country's economic plight and lost whatever traces of egalitarian aspirations it might have had. Per-sonal pocketbooks are one thing; assessments of the economy in general are another. Still another—and here comes the twist—are perceptions of social differences based on implicit standards of fairness. The issue no longer entails a simple dichotomy between private and public economics; that is, a separation between individual gains and losses on the one hand and aggregate growth and recession on the other. Instead, it evokes norms of distributive justice, expectations of how people are treated relative to one another and, it may be suspected, of the role of government in correct-ing social inequities.

In 1978 we posed the following question: "Each of us has an idea about how things should be, according to what each of us is capable of. Would you say that the total amount that you and your family earn corresponds to what you should be earning?" Slightly more than six out of ten an-swered in the negative. Spaniards who feel economically disgruntled in these terms made up an impressive constituency for change. They are the core constituency that supported the socialists.

Responses vary sharply according to both social class and partisan affil-iation. Working-class Spaniards are about twice as likely to feel materially aggrieved than their upper-class and upper-middle-class peers (see Figure 3.4 The same goes for communists as compared to partisans of the right (see Figure 3.5). There is no mistaking the correspondence between the class and partisan referents of economic grievance.

To summarize: a three-tier distinction characterizes economic percep-tions in Spain. Evaluations of individual and collective economic condi-tions tend to be kept separate. Yet norms about the fairness of economic treatment are not reducible to this micro-macro division; they derive from a third, relational perspective. The political implications of this complex of perceptions involve, first and most clearly, the irreducibility of economic judgments to personal circumstance; second, close to a consensus on the centrality of "the economy" as a problem-solving venture in growth; and, third, a powerful current of egalitarianism and class resentment that hooks up with political preferences by way of class position. It is the third, dis-tributive theme that harbors the potential for partisan mobilization along class lines. Concern with economic growth is nearly consensual, cutting across social classes. But emphasis on fairness has an edge to it, a definite class bias.

The syndrome is one of patterned differentiation rather than total sepa-ration of the individual, collective, and distributive aspects of popular eco-nomics. Like citizens of other industrialized nations, Spaniards lean toward a "nothing personal, purely business" view of the economic condi-

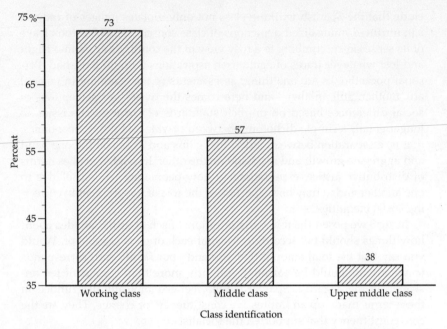

Figure 3.4 Percent who feel they fail to earn what they deserve, by class identification, 1978

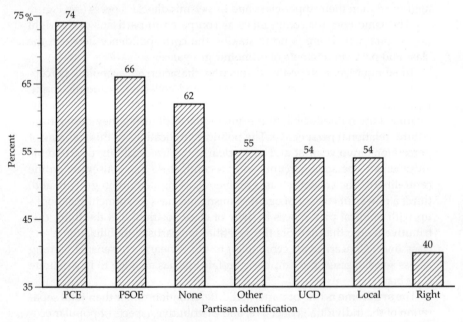

Figure 3.5 Percent who feel they fail to earn what they deserve, by partisan identification, 1978

tion of their country. In addition, while assessments of their individual situations change in expected ways according to their social status, perceptions of the entire economy hold steady across classes. On the other hand, on distributive matters—that is, regarding issues situated midway between mainly individualistic and collective understandings of a remote economy—a sense of class differences appears.

The mandate implicit in this configuration of opinion favors growth with equity. The slogan is not as anodyne as it may seem. What the latent platform joining growth and fairness avoids is the reduction of demands for equity to zero-sum retribution, in which economic reconstruction is sacrificed to distributive justice. The depiction of the state of public opinion as moderately distributive and reluctant to endanger the economic accomplishments of the recent past was reasonably accurate during the adolescence of the transition. The reformist interpretation gained momentum because of a peculiar conjunction of factors: among other things, vivid memories of the hideous consequences of "imprudence"—shared by older and younger Spaniards—together with the coming of age of a generation of political leaders with much to gain by moderation and little to lose from experimentation.

Hence, class consciousness of a kind, moderate and perhaps vaguely contradictory, came to the fore. Dissatisfaction with wages was much higher among poorer than better-off Spaniards, and this tendency fed directly into sympathy with leftist parties. Toward the end of the seventies and the beginning of the eighties, under the incumbency of the UCD, such conditions and opinions worked massively in favor of the PSOE. As Figure 3.5 reflects, in 1978 Spaniards without partisan affiliation—the modal category—joined adherents of the PSOE in their perceptions of unfairness regarding the distribution of economic rewards. For all this, it is important to remember what does *not* vary sharply by social class: the almost uniformly high level of priority given to the problem of restoring economic growth.

At least two variations on "class consciousness of a kind" can be discerned, depending on how responsibility for economic disparities is assigned. One perspective attributes a paramount role to the market. The other lays blame, and the burden of melioration, more squarely on the public sector.

In order to estimate the political repercussions of the sense of economic injustice, we questioned Spaniards who felt they were not getting their due (a sizable majority) as to "who was to blame" for their predicament. The follow-up probe read: "For you, who is responsible for your not earning what you think you really should earn?" We suspected that Spaniards' disappointment and resentment at their material conditions did not provide them a ready diagnosis of what lay behind those conditions. As it happens, most responses are spread across two categories: "the economy," "economic conditions generally," and so on (36 percent) and "the government," "the state," and the like (31 percent).

The difference between the two interpretations is a matter of degree. Even among working-class Spaniards, where the inclination to blame the government is highest (34 percent), the assignment of responsibility to "the economy" for one's financial woes reaches practically the same level (32 percent). Working-class Spaniards are only marginally more inclined to fix on the government rather than the economy. It is among the middle and upper-middle classes that the imputation of blame diverges, with the government receding and the economy—that is, the market—gaining in importance. Economic liberalism in the neoclassical mold is more respectable among middle-class and upper-middle-class Spaniards. The working class turns out to be a mushier constituency, its economic message more ambivalent. The appeal of a distributive populism is diluted by a respect for personal enterprise and individual mobility.

More forcefully than class identification, ideological placement separates Spaniards who fix the blame for economic conditions on the government from those who invoke the market or simply "the economy." Those toward the left are likelier to see the government as the culprit. However, opinion softens to the right of this extreme, yielding to the idea that the fault lies with the economy in general—until we get to the far right, where opposition to the government, and hence the inclination to blame the incumbents, picks up again.

Conservatives were reasonably content but extreme reactionaries felt betrayed by, or at least uneasy with, the center-right leaders of the transition not only because of the political rowdiness which they feared democratization would bring but also because of the threat that political disorder posed to the economy. Those on the left were more satisfied with the political opening; their complaint was with the economic mismanagement of the transitional coalition. The UCD was hemmed in on both sides. The center-left was encroaching on the increasingly impatient but unideological center whose main concern was economic growth with a modicum of equity. The far right was also concerned about the state of the economy, but paid less attention to questions of social fairness, and so remained on the electoral fringe.

To many Spaniards in the center—to those in other words who formed the majority of the electorate—the political faultfinding that ensued from economic deterioration was almost certainly thought to be less interesting than the imperative of economic problem-solving. The UCD government, it appears, was not so much blamed for economic stagnation as it was thought to be helpless to influence this reality. Politically successful, the party had become economically impotent. A rearrangement of the public agenda from the foundational to the pragmatic was taking place, and as this shift proceeded, the ramshackle coalition of the UCD slid closer and closer to disintegration. Increasingly, as the transition reached consolidation, the challenge facing Spain came to be understood as economic recuperation rather than constitution-building or the management of military peevishness. An agenda that gave priority to economic problem-solving, with an egalitarian slant, was taking shape in the public mind. The role assigned to the central government would probably be large. More important, the mandate was diffuse enough to provide considerable room for maneuver. No programmatic template shaped either public opinion or government policy (Cebrián 1984).

THE CORRELATES OF GOVERNMENT POPULARITY

As the UCD held the reins of government through the early eighties, public opinion whipsawed between two tendencies. One entailed pride in political freedoms and the consolidation of democracy, the other a concern with economic deterioration. Legitimacy ran one way, effectiveness another. In the long run, this divergence might undermine the viability of the regime. In the short term it proved to be the ruin of the UCD and a ticket to power for the PSOE. In the previous chapter we examined the determinants of the legitimacy of democracy. Here we examine the factors influencing the slide of the center-conservative government.

Our stripped-down approach to estimating the determinants of support for and dissatisfaction with the government distinguishes among three sets of factors. One set is composed of standard indicators such as class identification, income, age, and region. These measures cover the structural, baseline determinants of government popularity.

A second group is made up of primary cultural predictors such as ideology (left-right placement) and religiosity (reported degree of religious practice). Like their structural counterparts, the cultural indicators have a long-term slant. They tap the predispositions and biases that might carry or undercut governments regardless of their immediate performance. They are surrogates of "identities" and "ideologies."

The third array of predictors is circumstantial, directed at economic conditions here and now. For 1978 the principal measure of this kind comes from the "just deserts" question; for 1980 it is provided by perceptions of the overall state of the economy. These are rough-and-ready measures of "interests."

Table 3.2 summarizes the outcome of the multivariate analyses of government popularity for 1978 and 1980. The pair of analyses conveys the essential patterns, and the slightly different results succeed in capturing some evolutionary nuance.

What is striking about the outcome for 1978 is the primacy of religiosity and left-right placement in buttressing the popularity of the Suárez government. Support for the government on the part of religious, conserv-

TABLE 3.2. Multiple classification analyses, satisfaction
with UCD government, 1978 and 1980

1978		1980	
Predictor	Beta	Predictor	Beta
Left–right placement	.28	Economic situation	.31
Education	.16	Left–right placement	.27
Religiosity	.13	Region	.19
Just desserts	.10	Political interest	.11
Class identification	.08	Religiosity	.10
		Age	.10
R^2	.18	R^2	.29

ative Spaniards highlights the continuity between the cultural bases of
authoritarianism and the transitional government. The UCD government inherited some of the structural constituencies of the old regime.
Support crests among the better off though not-so-well educated strata of
the populace. The class bias of this support, though not overwhelming, is
incontrovertible.[8]

The sense of economic grievance turns out to be a significant predictor
of dissatisfaction with the government, close to but not quite matching the
force of religious sentiment and ideological leanings. This resentment ate
away at the popularity of the UCD; it represented a confining condition
which the party failed to overcome. The UCD was applauded for smooth-
ing the politics of the transition, for calming the right, and for giving reason for patience to the left and center-left. But the coalition had little
credibility, even among some of its followers, as an agent for redressing social disparities and as a promoter of economic growth.

By 1980 perceptions of economic decline take the lead in undermining
the popularity of the government. Left-right placement and religiosity still
count, and less politically tuned-in Spaniards furnish support through acquiescence and inertia. But with the democratic regime consolidated, cultural memory and historical attachment are no longer substitutes for
economic performance.

The judgment of economic incompetence is not especially partisan or
ideological or limited to distributive demands. It reflects widespread
recognition of the need for economic growth. The UCD was no longer
threatened mainly from the left; it was also being displaced from the center, where once it had been most popular. The role of social class as a determinant of political support had receded, but this didn't mean that
economic factors had disappeared from the political agenda. On the contrary, many well-off Spaniards had joined their working-class peers in dismay at the slow pace of recovery.

Another ominous sign for the UCD in 1980 was the prominence of the regional factor. The resurgence of separatist violence wore the government down. Relatively quiescent earlier, regional unrest began to look less tractable by the end of the seventies, at least under the management of the center-right coalition; dissatisfaction with the UCD government was acute in the Basque country and Catalonia.[9] The advent of the socialists would bring a fresh set of actors to center stage, with fewer scars and a different angle of vision. Besides permitting, under socialist auspices, an economic restructuring that could not be pushed forward by conservatives themselves, this changing of the guard reopened the possibility of advancing negotiations for the *Estado de las Autonomías*, the decentralized configuration of governance that signaled the consolidation of Spanish democracy.

Thus, as the first phase of the transition drew to a close, a confluence of two factors threatened the tenure of the UCD. The patience of the Spanish public with economic stagnation was evaporating. Dissatisfaction with economic conditions did not translate into a willingness to entertain ideological or ideological-sounding options. The keynote of public opinion on economic policy issues, insofar as it was scrutable at all, was problem-solving, with a bias toward fairness and security. Above all, public opinion in this area seems to have been indistinct and probably malleable, result-oriented instead of driven by principle with regard to policy implementation, but reasonably clear with respect to "growth with fairness." There is no evidence to suggest the Spanish public came to reject the UCD solely or even mainly out of class spite, and a good deal to indicate that managerial competence had become the dominant criterion.

But it would be a mistake to argue that the Spanish public was simply ready to move on from foundational to pragmatic politics or that a transition-within-the-transition, toward the politics of the functional, actually took place. Something close to this tendency was no doubt in the air. But regional enmities proved recalcitrant. The political capital of the UCD was drawn low. So much of it had gone into the bargaining over constitution-making and the ratification of pacts between economic interests that few ideas and little energy were left over for resolving regional tensions or overcoming "stagflation." As a center-right coalition, the UCD could not manage—more precisely, was never conceived as being able to manage—the passage toward the restoration of economic growth without veering in the direction of worsening social disparities. This transition required skills in problem-solving, which dealt in "flexibles"—mainly economic issues that were salient but with ill-defined alternatives—and sensitivity to popular norms of justice. Nor did the conservative elements in the UCD coalition permit the leadership much leeway in dealing with regional questions. When the PSOE came to power in 1982, its leadership was well along in the process of ideological revisionism and clear-eyed scrutiny of the polls. The party displayed a combination of imagination and realism, moving from political euphoria to the cultivation of economic hope. But it was not as if the potential for crisis embedded in regional identities had vanished, giving way to the "rational" quarrels of economic policy-making. Successful as they were, the socialists were never to operate with a slate uncluttered by obstinate localisms. The transition-within-the-transition, though real enough, never worked as if history had been consigned to oblivion.

By the 1970s the characterization of Spanish politics as a battleground of principles and a charnel house of visionaries had not only become wearisome; it was also recognized as a dangerous fiction, a self-fulfilling prophecy that might perpetuate the cycle of anarchy and despotism. Myth-shattering caution became all the more fashionable with the achievements of the political side of the transition. By the 1980s a subtransition was under way, evident in the desire of the Spanish public to move on from political engineering to economic problem-solving.

The horrors that an earlier generation had witnessed in the Civil War, together with reforms made elsewhere in Europe by revisionists on the left and pragmatists on the right, all served as a propaedeutic to a learning process favoring a moderation that did not jettison the past, especially the recent past. Negotiating the withdrawal from adherence to principle without being seen as promiscuous was probably less tortuous when one was dealing with economic issues than when one tried to finesse foundational conflicts. Most of the protagonists agreed that the costs of combat between visionaries and villains had proved too high, and fewer ordinary Spaniards than before seemed interested in this sort of adventurism. Even attendance at bullfights declined (Marvin 1988).[10]

The center-left socialists made do where the coalition of the center-right failed. Part of their ingenuity lay in perceiving and recognizing as appropriate the patterned ambivalence of the public regarding economic change, once political reform was in hand. This was close to but not quite an end-of-ideology condition. It was easier to discern what was ruled out—economic and social radicalism—and what remained extremely delicate—regional fission—than to fill in the script of mass politics during the immediate post-transition period. In place of polarization there was a certain puzzlement. Fading ideologies were not replaced by crisp blueprints. The mandate was for experimentation and the demand was for competence and the provision of public services. Just as Spaniards endorsed the procedural sanity of the democratic constitution, they embraced economic growth as the measure of public life. The pragmatic turn in Spain had two facets, one involving a relatively impartial appreciation of aggregate growth, and the other slanted in more partisan fashion to the distribution of compensatory benefits.

Viewed in the round, these departures from a messianic calculus constituted a paradigm shift, a new metabolism, for a perennially tragic mass politics. In a terrain burned over by phosphorescent ideologues, mystics, zealots, inquisitorial bullies, and assorted other zanies, the deep wells of pragmatism nourished the revival of a less pathological strain in Spanish political culture.

Such a denouement was not a sure thing, however, and it would be pressing the point to assume that struggles over material benefits are intrinsically more amenable to reasoned settlement than symbolic battles. After all, it is precisely when the agenda moves on to economic transformation from political emancipation that grand revolutionary coalitions, encompassing the diverse opponents of a common enemy, often fall apart (Shugart 1989). In Spain, even the rumble of mundane interests beneath the dimming clash of identities and ideologies aroused significant conflicts. It is to an examination of these tensions and their management by the socialists that we turn now.

4

The Golden Decade
of the Socialists

By the beginning of the 1980s Spain was ready for a change of leadership. Both prices and unemployment were soaring. Exasperation with the failure of the new democracy to deal with the economic difficulties of the country, now that its constitutional order had been put in place, was hard to ignore.

The shift in priorities from grappling with foundational dilemmas to managing the economy was rapid but not system-threatening. Severe as the economic problems facing Spain were, they did not challenge the constitutional settlement, as did the demands of separatist movements, nor did they throw into relief grand alternative designs, as between markets and planned economies. For the first time in a long while it was possible to contemplate a change of government that did not risk upheaval in the political system.

Stability beneath the shift in the policy agenda was not simply a spin-off of the institutional arrangement that elites had crafted so meticulously. Continuity registered in public opinion as well (Montero and Torcal 1990b). Figure 4.1 profiles left-right placement for each of our four surveys from 1978 to 1990. The distributions are practically identical, cleaving to the center-left from the outset; graphically, they are just about indistinguishable.

Important as it was to the electoral prospects of the socialists, the rise of economic issues on the popular agenda was not accompanied by a realignment from the right to the ideological left. The center of gravity of public opinion had favored the moderate left for some time. Had it been otherwise—had awareness of the urgency of the economic situation been confounded with an abrupt leftward transformation—the ascent of the socialists could not have been greeted with such equanimity or accepted as a venture in wait-and-see pragmatism. The socialists enveloped a majority of popular sentiment. In addition to the moderation of their appeal, the

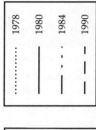

1978 ....
1980 ———————
1984 —·—·—·—
1990 — — — —

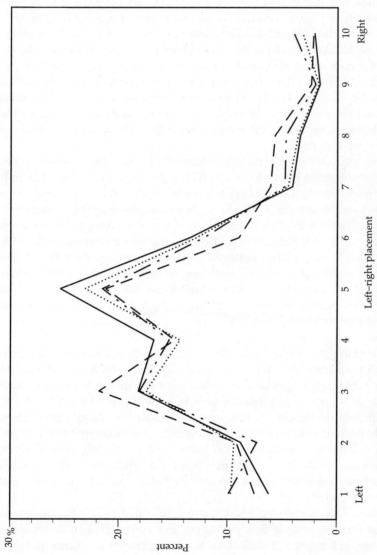

Figure 4.1 Frequency distributions, left–right placement, Spain, 1978–1990

probability of single-party, relatively efficacious government blunted the anxiety once associated with the prospect of socialist rule.

The leaders of the political transition now had a chance to catch up with public opinion and to do something about it. Decision-makers had been so consumed with getting Spain's constitutional house in order that most elites had little time to think through economic strategy. Insofar as it had an economic program at all, the UCD was out of step with the overarching tendency in the mass public: the tilt toward the center-left. The center-right coalition had abandoned much of the reactionary baggage of Francoism. Having done this, however, it seemed incapable of moving from political democratization toward the formulation of a plan for economic recovery. That the UCD did not have the electoral resources to move beyond the status of a minority government, skillful at reconciling various factions in a grand coalition for democracy, impeded decisiveness in economic and social policy-making. The UCD had steered the transition toward democracy without swerving abruptly away from the authoritarian past. Once this had been accomplished, the public was ready to get on with the job of economic reconstruction.

Like their adversaries on the center-right, the socialists, following their peers throughout Western Europe, had begun to abandon the wisdom of their past. They had started to convince themselves that the shibboleths of the left—nationalization of industry, for example—might be counterproductive. The vision of imposing a radical transformation on the economic system, once political power had been won, was dismissed as infantile. "Our task," one socialist strategist declared, "is to speed up the job that Spanish capitalists have taken so long to accomplish."[1] As the eighties opened, the socialists drew heterodox lessons from the fiasco of the first year of the Mitterand government, after which the French socialists recuperated by chucking many of the party's economic prescriptions (Schmidt 1996a).

Thinking the unthinkable, however, did not produce an alternative strategy. Like broad sectors of the Spanish public who were of the left but who might be hard-pressed to explain what this meant, the socialist leadership was open to suggestions, even to some that might violate conventional prescriptions of the left. And the fact that a majority government might be needed to push through economic reforms favored the socialists, who held sway in public opinion. But once the socialists came to power, memories of historical polarization, fears of a new inquisition, and ample documentation of the centrist mood of the public counseled prudence with regard to policy.

The indefiniteness of public opinion maintained a slight but discernible leftist cast, suggesting that packaging and labeling might be crucial in gaining endorsement, before the returns on performance came in. Figure

4.2 depicts the contours of partisan feeling that buoyed the socialists. It also captures the genuinely evolutionary nature of the movement from Francoism to the noncommunist left, by way of a pause at the center-right. Here are arrayed, for each point on the left-right scale, the average levels of satisfaction with "the last ten years of the Franco government," with the UCD government, and with the PSOE government.

The UCD covered a wider spectrum along the left-right continuum than the Franco government it succeeded. Franco's support was plainly concentrated in conservative quarters; the appeal of the UCD was more expansive. What is truly striking in the tilt of partisanship is the dominance of the socialists along the center-left of the ideological belt, where the bulk of public opinion lay. The PSOE had come close to being a catch-all party.

On October 22, 1982, the PSOE won a majority in the general elections. On December 10 of that year, the party was invested with the power of government. For the first time since the 1930s, the socialists ruled in Spain.

The PSOE was a party whose time had come. The organization had undergone a doctrinal makeover (García Santesmases 1993). A moderate leftism dominated the mainstream of public opinion. The PSOE took its electoral cues from this central fact, and the socialists came to power in a crescendo of common sense. Reform under socialist leadership was acceptable, at least insofar as the socialists did not inflict the hardship of industrial restructuring without preserving some forms of social compensation, while at the same time avoiding the climate of confiscation and revenge that had shrouded earlier clashes between left and right. Through the eighties and on into the early nineties, the socialists were hegemonic in the sense that they covered this spread in public opinion (De la Dehesa 1993). Rather than an exercise in squaring the circle, their program was possible as well as acceptable to a large extent because of infusions of foreign investment and European Community funds (Fishman 1990a; Geyer 1993; Guerra and Tezanos 1992).

This chapter examines the specific features of public opinion that went into the ascent of the PSOE and the consolidation of the party's hold on power. What we have seen so far is suggestive of the broad draw of the socialists. Much of their appeal lay in the tacit nature of their reform program. But there is more to the dominion of the socialists, and to the shape of public opinion, than deft sloganeering and mesmerized assent. Before we get into this story, however, another trend—one that we've glimpsed from a different perspective—needs to be stressed to round out the main lines of the moderation which the socialists helped usher in and which they benefited from. It involves not just the hegemony of the socialists but the longer-term movement toward the depolarization of Spanish politics.

Figure 4.3 teases out an important implication of Figure 4.2; it documents the decline of left-vs.-right divisiveness. The more evenly spread the

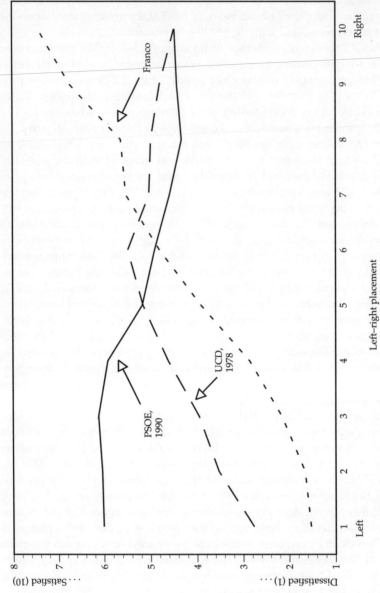

Figure 4.2 Mean satisfaction with three governments, by left–right placement, Spain, 1978–1990

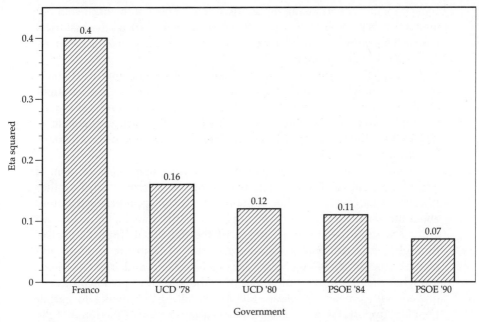

Figure 4.3 Measures of polarization (eta squared) between government satisfaction and left–right orientation

support for one or another partisan current across the left-right continuum, the less severe the polarization, at least along that line of division.
Flatter distributions of government satisfaction across the spectrum mean
shallower differences between points along the ideological space, and such
near-evenness is reflected in smaller "coefficients of between-group difference." This is what the etas squared, shrinking over time, express.

The series of coefficients traces the progressive fall in polarization not
only from authoritarian to democratic times but within the democratic period as well. "The last ten years of Francoism" fostered economic growth
but they were scarcely a decade of mass politics and catch-all parties. Figure 4.3 picks up the reaction of public opinion to the emergence of governments that lacked sharp ideological definition. To move away from the old
right was not to embrace an equivalently polarizing left. If this were the
case, the distribution of coefficients would be U-shaped, rising again with
the coming to power of the PSOE. But the ideological landscape seems to
have been transformed; inclusiveness withered the extremes.

This trend runs so squarely against expectations based on a legacy of
mutual intransigence that a weird serenity seems to enfold mass politics in
Spain. Agreement that the pacification of Spanish politics was by no means
inevitable is now so strong among analysts of democratization that there is

some danger of overlooking the genuine smoothness of the decline in polarization. Whatever its causes, depolarization is part of the historical record. This point established, it becomes important to probe the complexities of the broad development.

The depiction of the mellowing of Spanish politics in Figure 4.3 is unidimensional, hinging on a cleavage that is vital but limited. The left–right continuum touches on economic and social matters. We have yet to take systematic account of extra-economic lines of conflict, such as regionalism, and see how they might affect the popularity of governments and perhaps undermine their tenability.

Second, "economic and social matters" make up quite an assortment of issues and policies. There is a good deal of center-leftward drift, rather than dogmatic clarity, to public opinion. Yet it is still appropriate to inquire about the content and coherence of opinion in this domain. Otherwise we are left with an insubstantial image of the movement from Francoism through the transitional government of the UCD to the triumph and tenure of the socialists—with a mirage of labels ("left" and "right") obscuring what may look like little more than the appeal of personalities endowed with greater or lesser skill in exploiting the media to garner popular support. We need a clearer, less casual picture of the sense of the economic center-left.

This chapter focuses on the last pair of surveys, from 1986 and 1990, when the socialists were at the height of their power. We address three questions.

First, what mattered in determining support for the government? A distinguishing feature of the progressive dissociation of the political culture from Francoism, we've insisted, is depolarization. We estimate the relative contribution of "primordial" (religious, regional) versus "pragmatic" (economic) divisions in conditioning support for the socialists. The answer is a resounding vote in favor of pragmatism. The rhetoric of identities and ideologies gave way to attention to interests. Having discarded the Marxist label, the socialists became, in the words of a leading strategist, "a mass party rather than a class party" that corralled the vast center-left of public opinion. Performance counted for more than preferences on the issues, as studies of retrospective voting would lead us to expect (Fiorina 1981). Prosperity, enhanced by the infusion of funds from the European Community, buoyed the PSOE government. The trade off between growth and equity was eased. Social coverage underwent rapid expansion. A million new automobiles were sold in Spain in 1990. All this paid off in political popularity for the socialists.

Second, Spaniards turn out to be sociotropic voters—they take overall economic conditions into account, not just their own circumstances—with a twist. While their chief concerns have been economic, they are not pocketbook voters; they don't evaluate governments out of purely myopic self-interest. Instead, like voters in other advanced industrial democracies, Spaniards use the state of the economy in the aggregate as the point of reference for political judgment. Added to this sense of the collectivity are heightened expectations about the functions of government, compared to the modest vision of the role of the public sector in the United States, for example. The statist tradition continues strong in Spain.

Third, through the late seventies and into the eighties, the Spanish public displayed distributive, not to say populist, predilections. Powerful sentiments in favor of social fairness underlay the priority given to economic issues. By the end of the decade, Spain was one of the rare industrial societies—Portugal was another—to have undergone a redistribution of income in favor of the poorer strata (Braun 1997: 73–135). By the onset of the nineties, there were signs that this redistribution had reached the limits of political feasibility, and the stage was set for the eventual coming to power of the conservative opposition. But the industrial restructuring that exacerbated unemployment was not accompanied, under the socialists, by a retrenchment in social insurance programs. For a long time, the distributive agenda of the socialists corresponded, in very broad terms, to a motley majority of the Spanish electorate (Montero and Torcal 1990b).

OVERVIEW OF THE FORMATION OF ECONOMIC OPINION

Two explanations can be adduced for the sponginess of economic opinion in Spain. One is the mystification thesis: regional, religious, and other supposedly retrograde factors divert attention from the presumably core issues related to economic conditions and class rivalry. Although depictions of the Spanish citizenry as being peculiarly benighted by such elements are outdated, there are enough traces of archaic holdovers in contemporary Spain, and simply of noneconomic or preindustrial lines of contention, that interpretations of this sort cannot be dismissed out of hand (Weatherford 1983).

Still, a different argument fits the evidence better. Economic forces do in fact shape public opinion, but not in a neatly ideological way. This view highlights the ambiguity and confusion of the economic and political transitions that Spain has traversed (Aumente 1985b). The socialists reached power as socialist orthodoxy was falling out of fashion practically everywhere (Elorza 1985). Moreover, Spain made great economic progress during the last years of the Franco regime (Wright 1977). Even if the autocratic model that was applied in the late fifties and that held sway until the oil crisis of the early seventies came to be regarded as exhausted and nonrepeatable, the prosperity of that era was a tough act to follow.

The economic modernization launched under the auspices of the Franco regime meant that by the time the socialists were poised to assume power the strategic imperative was no longer one of wrenching Spain out of an agrarian morass toward an industrial future, as was the case around the time of Civil War. Much less was the challenge one of transforming a command economy into a market system, even if considerable restructuring of the industries and the financial apparatus of the country remained to be accomplished. This structural evolution had significant effects on support for the government; the choices were less stark.

The caution and eclecticism that typified economic policy under the socialists does not, however, mirror the inchoate nature of public opinion in popular democratic fashion. The mirror metaphor implies a sharp focus to the object being reflected, in this case, mass preferences. Such clarity was simply not out there. This muddle gave the socialists leeway, not a mandate.

With the experience of Francoist developmentalism and the decay of socialist dogma as backdrop, our argument can be extended to identify the contending elements in economic policy and public opinion. The socialists wanted to accelerate the process, initiated during the waning years of the Franco regime, of ridding Spain of precapitalism: the remnants of the fustian right and idle rich. The leadership of the PSOE also wanted to excise its own radical legacy. Socialists in power proved to be more pragmatic than socialists in opposition. As incumbents, they had to rationalize their heritage without quite demystifying it.

With a twist distinctive to Spain, this tension generated tradeoffs between policies geared toward growth and those aimed at distribution. The PSOE's leftist aura enabled it to enact policies in the area of industrial downsizing and restructuring that labor and its allies would almost certainly have contested more vigorously under a conservative government. Yet even had they desired to do so, the socialists could not forsake distributive commitments with impunity. The activist state was as much a legacy of the "paleo-corporatist" right (Pérez Díaz 1984; compare Brading 1991) as of socialist principle. The accent was on welfare and social protection more than radical redistribution (Castles 1994; Therborn 1994; Wilensky 1981). The technocratic temptation with which the younger generation of socialists linked to Felipe González were flirting threatened older cohorts on both the right and the left. Intergenerational strains between a paternalistic, autarchic past, and visions of a competitive future, with Spain integrated into a cosmopolitan Europe, blurred long-standing lines of ideological polarization and class conflict.

A confluence of two strains—old-fashioned social democracy, with an ideological edge, and the even more traditional norm of the curatorial state—built up support for the socialists and sustained them through the eighties (compare Lewis 1993). A third, technocratic current was more Eurocentric than peculiarly socialist (Altares 1985a)—neoliberalism in corporatist form. Impatient with archaic doctrines and ideologies, and silently embarrassed by the sentimentalism of old-line caretaking, it gained force from the replacement of polarization by the appeals of problem-solving (Encarnación 1997; compare Pierson 1996a, 1996b).

As the decade of the eighties opened, then, Spain was faced with the task of reforming rather than revolutionizing its economic policies. Maximalism was out of bounds in economics and politics alike. Policy-making through ideological deduction was rejected by almost all political actors. Yet this pragmatism was not completely open-ended. The economic program of the socialists was circumscribed by three considerations.

One was the need to continue the drive toward growth, which the country had savored during the salad days of Francoism, and to consolidate the ties of Spain with the rest of Western Europe. This factor favored competence over political correctness.

Another goal was to preserve the erstwhile constituencies of Spanish socialism among those dependent on routine welfare and social services— distributive instead of radically redistributive measures. Prominent among these constituencies were the elderly, a growing segment of the electorate in all industrial societies including Spain, and women. Members of these collectivities were at least as concerned about life after work, about security in old age, as about life after death and religious tradition.

A third, related factor reflected the expectations among ordinary Spaniards, and not the left alone, that the state had a major responsibility for promoting economic development and managing social programs. These were the components of a growth-with-equity ethos—"model" would ascribe too much system to the approach—that conceded a substantial role to the public sector (Mancha Navarro 1993).

THE CONTEXT OF PUBLIC OPINION

In order to envision the pushes and pulls that affect public opinion about economics in Spain, it helps to imagine three variations on the links between economic views and political support. One is the pocketbook model, where votes are thought to be determined by how well *individuals* or their families are doing. Another reflects a broader vision: political decisions are influenced by perceptions of *aggregate* prosperity—of how the economy as a whole seems to be doing (Kiewiet 1981; Kinder and Kiewiet 1981; compare Monroe 1979; Sniderman and Brody 1977); the focus is on collective prosperity and, eventually, on its trickle-down effect on personal well-being. A third variant, one that we stressed in Chapter 3, emphasizes *distributive* criteria. The standard here is social equity rather than either economic expansion or individual gain.

How does each of these factors affect support for and opposition to the government? Since extra-economic issue domains such as religion may also have a political impact, the question should be set in the broader context of multiple cleavages. Is it preindustrial ("symbolic") or industrial lines of conflict and allegiance that determine the popularity of governments in Spain (Lijphart 1992)? And, among economic considerations, is it primarily individual experiences and relatively idiosyncratic preferences that matter, or do perceptions of the state of the economy as a whole count for more?

Questions such as these and the reasoning behind them need to be adjusted to the Spanish setting. Whatever its psychological universality, the propensity to envision economic conditions in larger than immediate, personal terms gains a special inflection from the historical environment of Spanish politics. The Hispanic legacy of statism makes public, aggregate understandings of economic conditions fairly common. It is not that self-interest narrowly defined is absent from Spanish culture, or that the Spanish public is enamored of communitarianism or mutuality or is peculiarly altruistic. Rather, the very large role habitually granted to state intervention gives Spanish public opinion a collective cast as far as economic matters are concerned. Similarly, such divisiveness as obtains in the economic arena is less a matter of individualistic versus collective perspectives than of the clash between the priority given to economic growth and the need for socially meliorative, distributive policies.

In sum, the distinctiveness of Spanish public opinion on economic issues, vis-à-vis the cast of public opinion in the United States, is not that it is thoroughly collectivist. Spaniards regularly separate pocketbook and public economics. What stands out are the high expectations about the government's responsibilities for economic management. In Spain, a collectivist orientation more often implies reliance on governmental action, on the expansiveness of the public sector, than commitment to autonomous associations organized from the grass-roots up.[2]

Furthermore, we stress a distinction that is at most implicit in the sociotropic literature. Just as part of our analysis attends to the impact of identity factors such as religion in balance with the influence of ideological and interest considerations, we are also concerned with distinguishing between economic *preferences*, which may be more or less ideologically charged, and *perceptions* of economic conditions, which tend to be less polemically loaded. The historical antecedents of the rise of the socialists and the lessons learned from the pragmatic growth policies of the developmental authoritarianism of the previous regime suggest that the ideological component of public opinion is liable to be residual, relative to an instrumental calculus fixed on assessments of economic conditions and perceived interests. The impact of preferences on policy alternatives is likely to recede in the face of ideologically agnostic assessments of how the economy is doing.

Again, however, there is a characteristic tilt to such "objectivity." The realism of Spanish citizens is not dispassionate. Evaluations of the state of the economy are customarily enveloped within norms of government intervention that lean toward the compensatory—that is, toward the maintenance of social fairness. Spaniards are probably no more indulgent of radical redistributive ideologies than citizens of other industrial societies. But they do have their biases, and these are reflected in the distributive bent within the political culture. They are not ideologically finicky but they tend to be sensitive, after a populist fashion, about questions of fairness (Montero and Torcal 1990a).

Consider the data in Table 4.1. In their study of class awareness in the United States, the Jackmans (1983) inquired about the acceptability of differences in income. A breakdown of responses from their original study, arrayed by the social class of respondents, is given at the top of the table, followed by the results of our replications in 1984 and 1990 in Spain.[3]

In two respects the cross-national results are similar. The modal category in both countries is centrist: "some differences in income." In addition, within each country, the connection between class and preference follows an expected pattern. Lower-class respondents, both Spanish and American, express relatively egalitarian views. Otherwise the countries diverge markedly. "Large differences" are more acceptable in the United States; "practically no differences" are more apposite in Spain. The variation between countries with respect to appropriate income differences is greater than the variation between classes within countries.

A distributive discourse dominated political opinion in Spain throughout the eighties, even toward the end when evidence of corruption and

TABLE 4.1. Desired income differences, by social class: United States, 1975; Spain, 1984, 1990 (percent)

	Working-class	Middle-class	Upper-class
United States, 1975			
Great difference	26%	32%	49%
Some difference	56	58	42
Practically no difference	12	8	7
Don't know/no response	6	2	1
Spain, 1984			
Great difference	3%	4%	7%
Some difference	65	69	68
Practically no difference	31	26	24
Don't know/no response	2	1	1
Spain, 1990			
Great difference	7%	11%	17%
Some difference	60	63	64
Practically no difference	29	23	17
Don't know/no response	4	3	2

other scandals began to take its toll on the socialists. This inflection is understandable given the country's history of poverty and economic stratification and in light of the dirigiste tradition (Noya and Vallejos 1995). Note, however, that the distributive norm is not immutable. The populist orientation shifts between 1984 and 1990. There has been an increase in tolerance for "large differences" in income, though such differences do not approach the normative status they occupy in the United States.

One lesson here is that cross-nationally comparable regularities are filtered through cultural contexts developed out of distinctive histories. The cognitive maps by which Spaniards and Americans chart the paths between economics and politics are utilitarian in the sense that considerations of economic performance figure decisively in evaluations of the government—more so, as a rule, than symbolic issues (Lewis-Beck 1988). At the same time, the realm of the economic is itself enfolded within cultural norms (Wuthnow 1989). Just as the individualistic ethic tends to be hegemonic in the United States (Wilson 1997), the rhetoric of social egalitarianism and of governmental responsibility for economic management is more than a residual convention of Spanish political culture.[4]

Another lesson has to do with the nature of regime legitimacy in Spain. Egalitarianism may not be a principle in Spain—certainly not an immutable one—but it is clearly more than an opinion. It is a kind of demotic philosophy. Standards of "fairness" that in Anglo-American democracies reflect procedural impartiality (Hochschild 1981) carry an overlay of distributive justice in Spain. This strain appears to have evolved not just over the course of centuries as an antielitist streak in a hierarchical culture but more compellingly as pent-up populism during the Franco years. It corresponds to a profound distrust of oligarchic democracy. Its relevance to political legitimacy stems not only from the demand for material performance on the part of the government, although the notion of substantive justice is connected to this, but from the implication of social fairness, that is, of equal treatment across classes (Javier Noya and Vallejos 1993).[5]

Finally, we pay special attention to one aspect of public opinion that has no equivalent in advanced industrial societies: the comparison of the performance of democratic governments, along both economic and noneconomic lines, with that of their authoritarian predecessor.

EVALUATIONS OF THE GOVERNMENT

In 1984 (see Tables 4.2 and 4.3) our focus was on the effects of different levels of economic assessment—for example, evaluations of the performance of the economy as a whole, as compared to the ups-and-downs of individuals. In 1990 (see Table 4.4) we added several extra-economic dimensions: popular evaluations of the "morality of public life," of safety

TABLE 4.2. Perceptions of González's performance as president, 1984 (percent)

	Very good	Good	Not too good	Not good at all
Overall performance	13%	48%	30%	9%
Economic performance	10	42	34	14
Performance in foreign relations	23	49	19	9

from street crime, and the like. (Preferences on economic and noneconomic issues, introduced in the following section, were also elicited.)

Table 4.2 lays out the contours of the indicators at a time when the country was just beginning to pull out of a recession and two years after Felipe González, leader of the socialists, had been elected president.[6] Public opinion gave González reasonably good grades for his economic management and his conduct of foreign policy.[7] By contrast, impressions of the state of the economy, of family finances, and of the future of both were mixed. As Table 4.3 indicates, however, disappointment with the skimpiness of recent economic gains—about four out of ten Spaniards felt that economic conditions had deteriorated during the past year, and nearly as many felt the same way about their family situation—was tempered by optimism. Almost a third of the respondents expected things to pick up in the future.[8]

By 1990, as Table 4.4 shows, assessments of the economic situation had improved. A solid majority now believed that the economy of the country was on the mend and more than a third expected it to get even better during the next year. This bolstered the already positive image of the PSOE as the party of responsible reform. Three-quarters of the respondents asserted that the economic situation of the country had improved since the days of Franco. The socialist government and the democratic system had both gained from their association with prosperity.[9]

TABLE 4.3. Perceptions of Spain's economic performance, 1984 (percent)

	Better	About the same	Worse
Family economics, past year	12%	51%	37%
Family economics, expectations for next year	21	50	29
Government's effect on family economics	11	60	29
Whole economy, past year	22	37	41
Whole economy, expectations for next year	30	41	29
Government's effect on whole economy	29	38	34

TABLE 4.4. Perceptions of Spain's economic, political, and cultural situation, 1990 (percent)

	Better	Same	Worse
Country's economy since 1982	57%	25%	19%
Country's economy since Franco	77	11	12
Country's economy next year	35	31	34
Country's economy compared to rest of Western Europe	16	45	40
Corruption under socialists	7	37	56
Street crime under socialists	7	25	68
Public morals under socialists	36	22	42
Family as an institution since Franco	25	31	44
Own situation compared to peers'	18	76	7
Own situation compared to parents'	82	10	8

The interpretive key to the tabulations lies in the multiple frames of comparison which the questions elicit. One type of comparison is short-term or virtually cross-sectional—for example, the estimate of how the economy had been doing since the socialists came to power or of Spain's economic performance vis-à-vis that imputed to the countries of Western Europe. Responses along these lines run from the positive, when the terms of comparison are internal to Spain, to the not so favorable, when the contrast shifts to the continental setting.

Another type of comparison is longer-term, contrasting the democratic system with the Franco regime or educing estimates of social mobility across generations, with perceptions of the previous generations' economic fortunes as the baseline. When the long-term comparisons are restricted to economic conditions, the democratic present comes up looking unequivocally better than the authoritarian past. This bonus to the democratic regime should be set against the fact that for most of the last decade of Francoism the Spanish economy grew rapidly. The performance of post-authoritarian governments, especially that of the socialists, was therefore all the more impressive.[10]

In addition to the temporal dimension, the terms of comparison are divided topically between the economic and the para-economic or the symbolic and moral. We asked how people felt about public safety ("crime in the streets") under the socialist government. We also asked whether they felt the family "as an institution" was better off, worse off, or in about the same condition since the days of Franco.

The socialists fare less well in the moral than in the economic domain. Yet as happened in the economic sphere, the inclination to connect moral decay with the leadership of the socialists softens when memories of Francoism are brought up. Fewer than ten percent of the respondents felt that corruption had actually declined under the socialists, but one-quarter felt that the family has improved "as an institution" and more than a third claim that the state of "public morals" has gotten better since Franco died. The latter estimates do not outweigh negative assessments of family life and civic probity, but evaluations shaped by comparisons with the prior regime are consistently more positive than evaluations that refer to the socialists alone.

In the nineties, as comparisons with the old regime became less and less vivid, economic corruption and political scandals would cause the popularity of the socialists to plummet (Jiménez 1994). But through most of the eighties the party could count on a boost from the retrospective contrast with Francoism on economic as well as political fronts. During this time memories of the old regime functioned like the reputation of a ne'er-do-well neighbor, making the failures of those closer to home tolerable by comparison.

These patterns set the stage for testing the idea that surplus approval that comes from pitting the new against the old regime constitutes legitimacy of a kind, in excess of what might be expected for democracy or the socialist government on their own, torn from historical context. Retrospective comparison reinforces the unattractiveness of antidemocratic alternatives.[11]

Economic growth was in fact vital to generating support for the socialists. The trend had several components. The most obvious was its size and rapidity. In addition, during the eighties in Spain, in contrast to what happened in almost every other industrial society, growth was associated with an impression of fairness—with a sense of justice stemming from Spaniards' perceptions when they compared themselves with one another. The terms of reference are interpersonal. Still another element involves the evaluations of present conditions in the light of recollections of or attributions about the Franco regime. Here the basis of comparison is intertemporal.

The impression was not illusory. Despite record unemployment, a genuine redistribution of income took place in Spain, redressing some of the concentration of the Franco years and resulting in a dramatic contrast with increasing inequality in the United States and other industrial societies (see Figure 4.4).[12]

Table 4.5 summarizes perceptions regarding all these facets of economic growth. Spaniards were asked whether they felt economic conditions had improved, stayed about the same, or gotten worse for the working class, the middle class, and the upper class. Identical questions were posed in 1984 and 1990. Responses were first elicited for "the years since 1982" and then "in comparison with the last ten years of the Franco government." The same dual time frame as before was used, with the focus kept on eco-

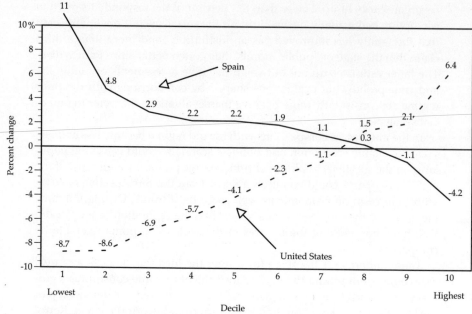

Source: Moreno 1993a, 1993b.

Figure 4.4 Change in income share, by income decile, Spain and United States, 1980–1990

nomics. Now, however, comparisons were elicited across classes as well as across time. In this way, looking at impressions of fairness as well as growth, we can examine changes in perceptions of social equity.[13]

The first-round results were promising but not spectacular for the PSOE government. In 1984 few Spaniards felt that the situation of any class, with the partial exception of the upper strata, had improved much under the socialists when the comparison was limited to the immediate past. This was

TABLE 4.5. Perceptions of economic improvement since 1982 and in comparison with Franco regime, by class, 1984 and 1990 (percent)

	1984	1990
Since 1982		
Working class	18%	62%
Middle class	13	56
Upper class	32	72
In comparison with Franco regime		
Working class	47	73
Middle class	34	65
Upper class	33	72

a realistic judgment, since the country was then at the tail end of a recession. But in contrast to the situation under Franco, many more felt that economic conditions had improved, especially for the working class. Once again, amplifying the frame of reference to establish a contrast between the two regimes works in favor of the democratic leadership and shows that despite all the grumbling, the new system had a reservoir of legitimacy. Even so, favorable responses were in the minority.

By 1990, after eight years of PSOE rule, the most recent five of which recorded impressive rates of economic growth, the political weather had lifted. Confining the terms of comparison to the years since 1982 no longer produces a sense of jejune improvement or none at all. On the contrary, substantial majorities contended that all classes had done better. When the comparison is set against the Franco years, the perceived improvement becomes even greater. It would be hard to imagine a more ample base of support for the socialist government, and for Spanish democracy, than the political credit built up out of economic performance. Two elements were crucial: the perception that economic growth proceeded with a degree of social fairness and that such redistribution as occurred was not zero-sum.[14]

PREFERENCES ON ECONOMIC POLICY

The rhythm of the transition in Spain was such that the settlement of foundational, political conflicts (identity and ideology) took precedence over functional, economic, and social issues (interest). When management-labor issues did come to the fore in the bargaining over wage increases during the early days of the transition, "responsibility"—moderation for the sake of protecting democracy—was the overriding posture on all sides (Lancaster 1984).

Statesmanship was facilitated by the structural transformation of the Spanish economy that had gained momentum under Franco. Recollections of prosperity and the promise of more in the offing helped avert an escalation of hostilities. Economic growth and long-term demographic shifts had undercut agrarianism, illiteracy, social stasis, and the other pinions of the divisions between classes, between religion and secularism, and to some extent between the regions of the country and Madrid (Djurfeldt 1993; Shubert 1990). Political moderation in Spain no longer bore the stigma of mediocrity it had in the days of the pitiless divisions between sacerdotal triumphalism and secular maximalism. The aspiration to get on with material advancement joined with ideological ambivalence induced by the achievements of authoritarian-sponsored growth. For younger generations of Spaniards, the lessons of recent history relegated maximalism to a formulaic gesture mismatched to the times. Illustrated serial histories of the Civil War were newsstand bestsellers and commemorative medallions of Franco and his more notorious generals were peddled on the streets of Madrid, but these were echoes of combat, not the thing itself.

With the electoral victory of the socialists in 1982 economic problems rose to the top of the policy agenda. The challenges of unemployment and industrial upgrading were pressing, along with efforts to expand the fiscal base of the government by increasing the collection of personal income taxes.

Implicit in this sequence of issues, then, is a movement from the more to the less ideological or foundational and, within what is left of the ideological, from the redistributive to the infrastructural and neoliberal. The socialists did not hesitate to confront traditional conservative interests—for example, the church on moral issues—and they were firm in combating regional separatism and street crime (Hernández 1984). But they dropped the Marxist label from their economic platform. The PSOE government adopted a stance that, although not free of ideological signals, was predominantly technocratic or, less harshly, problem-solving (Altares 1985b). The common thread in socialist policy through the eighties was disdain for what party leaders viewed as the irrelevant archaisms of the left and the right (Sotelo 1984).

To what extent did the newfound economism of the socialists correspond to the preferences of ordinary Spaniards? A few hints can be gathered from Table 4.6, where the responses to over a dozen questions about economic and social concerns in 1984 are displayed.[15]

The tilt is in a populist, statist direction. Nearly nine out of ten Spaniards endorse the idea that the country would have fewer problems if people were treated more equally; nearly eight out of ten disagree with the notion that business should have greater freedom to fire employees; nearly seven out of ten claim that the government should intervene more in the economy—yet nearly half deny that higher taxes are needed to pay for more public services. Unscientific as it may be, this is socialism of sorts, of the grass roots or rather of the pavements and tenements of Barcelona and Madrid, and it attributes to government a major role in promoting social welfare.

It is equally plain, however, that public opinion does not provide a mandate for social redistribution at the expense of business interests. In apparent contradiction to the 87 percent who sympathize with an egalitarian stance ("We would have fewer problems if people were treated more equally"), fully 45 percent agree with the opposite contention, that "Spain would be better off if we worried less about everybody being equal." Such discrepancies indicate that Spaniards have reservations about egalitarianism in the sense of social leveling.

Furthermore, half of those who had an opinion on the question agreed that government taxes and regulations prevent companies from making the profits they deserve. Equally suggestive is that "Don't know" re-

TABLE 4.6. Responses to economic and social statements, 1984 (percent)

Survey statement	Agree	Neither agree nor disagree	Disagree	Don't know
1. In general, most people pay the taxes they should.	37%	6%	51%	5%
2. The laws and taxes of the government prevent businesses from making the profits they need.	40	12	27	21
3. People who work hard almost always wind up getting what they want.	50	8	41	1
4. We would have fewer problems in Spain if people were treated more equally.	87	6	4	3
5. Many people who don't get ahead probably work as hard as those who succeed.	83	5	9	2
6. If we want more services like education and health care, we will have to pay higher taxes.	38	8	49	5
7. Spain would be better off if we worried less about being equal.	45	13	33	9
8. In order for the country to grow, the government should intervene more in the economy.	68	8	12	12
9. Greater freedom has to be given to companies to lay off workers.	14	6	76	5
10. There are too many people in this country who don't pay the taxes they owe.	78	5	10	8
11. The government should offer fewer services, including such things as health and education, in order to reduce taxes.	13	6	74	7
12. Cheating on your income tax is all right, if you don't get caught.	12	5	80	3
13. Profits should be taxed more than salaries.	59	9	15	26

sponses soar on issues that require judgments about relatively technical means (fiscal policy) toward economic ends (growth), as opposed to statements about preferred goals or results (growth as compared to equity). Popular culture in Spain does not fixate on principle, nor is the public well informed about economic strategy.

Two patterns may be gleaned from the evidence on preferences presented so far. First, public opinion was skewed to the left—more accurately, in a populist direction—as far as economic and social policy goes. These preference distributions hew closely to the center-left cast of the left-right continuum documented earlier. Second, however, there seems to have been considerable shallowness and softness to the opinions themselves. They do not make up a particularly coherent message for policy-makers.[16]

Table 4.7 delineates the boundaries of this uncertainty. It summarizes a factor analysis of the thirteen economic and social items displayed in Table 4.6. Of the thirteen items only eight hang together in something approaching a consistent policy space. The remaining five—for example, items gauging orientations toward presumably basic values such as hard work, individual initiative, and so forth—do not join with one another or with the dimensions that finally emerge.

The eight items fall along three dimensions: one tapping a free-enterprise, small-government mentality; another favoring a service-oriented, socially distributive state; and a third that concerns evaluations of the honesty of Spanish taxpayers and probably of the fairness of the tax system.[17] The sheer number of dimensions is important. Three factors are required to make sense of eight economic and social items. This is not a configuration redolent of overarching polarization. Besides, the fact that the first two dimensions are separate, rather than opposite poles of a single continuum, indicates that conservative and progressive attitudes with re-

TABLE 4.7. Varimax rotation, economic and social statements, 1984

	Free enterprise	Welfare populism	Taxes	Communalities
7. Less equality	**.54**	.11	−.01	.31
2. Business taxes	**.42**	−.10	.05	.19
9. Freedom to fire	**.37**	−.33	.01	.25
11. Fewer services	**.31**	.00	.10	.10
8. Government intervention	.09	**.60**	.03	.37
4. Greater equality	−.07	**.42**	−.11	.19
1. Taxpayer honesty	.20	.05	**.56**	.36
12. Tax cheats	.04	.17	**−.67**	.47
Percent variance explained	9.5%	8.8%	9.8%	

TABLE 4.8. Correlations between factor scores and selected attitudinal/demographic indicators, 1984

Attitudinal/demographic indicator	Factor score		
	Free enterprise	Welfare populism	Taxes
Left–right placement	**.33**	− .19	.07
Religiosity	**.26**	− .03	.06
Age	**.19**	− .08	− .08
Political interest	− .08	− **.21**	− .06
Education	− .15	− **.30**	.00
Family income	− .08	− **.21**	− .02
Class identification	.08	− **.25**	.03

gard to economic policy are not pitted diametrically against one another. Instead of being in contradiction, they are compartmentalized.

The absence of polarization does not imply a complete mushiness to economic and social preferences. Table 4.8 presents the correlations of the factor scores for the "progressive," "conservative," and "tax" dimensions with a set of standard demographic and generic attitudinal indicators. The dimension related to honesty in payment of taxes fails to correlate with anything—an unsurprising result since it is based mainly on perceptions of behavior rather than preferences about policy alternatives.[18]

What matters are the correlations with the conservative and progressive factor scores. They run from the mild to the modestly strong, and they are distributed in straightforward ways. For example, Spaniards higher up the income scale are not enamored of socialist-populist economics; neither are the deeply religious.

Perhaps more important is the asymmetrical nature of the correlations. While those toward the ideological right tend to approve of the "conservative" cluster of economic options, they are not vigorously opposed to "progressive" opinions. Conversely, although Spaniards who identify themselves as belonging to the working class favor welfare measures and a degree of state intervention, they cannot be depicted as holding firm views one way or the other regarding capitalist economics of the free-enterprise variety.

Finally, the progressive orientation tends to be associated with *structural* demarcators, such as low education and income, rather than with ideological conviction or cultural dispositions, such as left-right placement and religiosity.[19] The opposite holds true for the conservative stance on economic issues, which is more clearly tied to broad *cultural* orientations.

The contrast between the "structural" left and the "ideological" right is

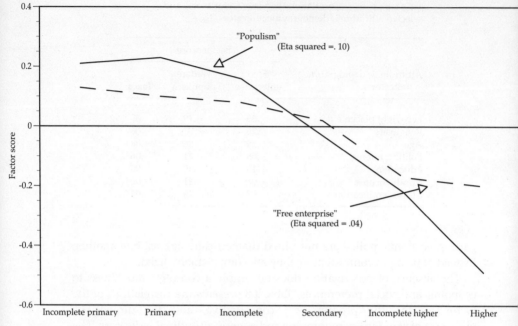

Figure 4.5 "Populism" and "free enterprise" factor scores, by education, 1984

illustrated in Figures 4.5 and 4.6. This contrast is diagnostic of the cultural differences between the constituencies of the prosaic left and the "principled" right in Spain.[20] Although the relationship is not nearly so acute as to suggest polarization, sentiments in favor of free enterprise vary linearly along the ideological continuum. Populist-distributive sentiments are more evenly spread along this dimension. Indeed, they show a slight resurgence toward the extreme right, where the ideals of reactionary paternalism and paleocorporatism kick in. The patterns confirm the idea that movement away from the conservatism of the ancien régime right did not correspond to an acceptance of the watchwords of the left.

In summary, the constellation of beliefs about economic and social policy in Spain is patterned but not polarized. During the eighties there was a socialist-populist ethos more than a clear-cut mandate for rigorous socialism. It had a hold on the lower class, on those with lower levels of education, on the elderly, and on the less politically involved. It resonated more to structural conditions than to ideological refinement. There is also a free-enterprise, antistatist orientation. It appealed to ideologically conservative, comparatively religious Spaniards. But its appeal spread as well across class and income groups. Mass leftism in Spain was not a crisply defined ideological package but rather a diffuse disposition that favored some measure of economic reform and social fairness, and it was hedged around

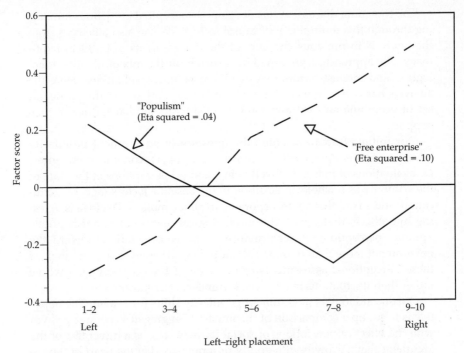

Figure 4.6 "Populism" and "free enterprise" factor scores, by left–right placement, 1984

by prudent, respectable prescriptions concerning individual enterprise and the attractions of the market.

Does this complex of preferences jibe with socialist economic policy? A more precise if clumsier way of phrasing the question may be: was public opinion sufficiently undefined so as to be compatible with a variety of economic alternatives that might be implemented by a socialist government, even if the policies themselves departed from socialist orthodoxy? The query is virtually untestable if what we are looking for are standards of internal consistency and intellectual coherence. But it begins to make sense once we ask what attitudes on economic issues might have to do with the practical politics of support for and opposition to the socialist government.

THE DETERMINANTS OF GOVERNMENT SUPPORT

In considering the factors that might affect orientations toward the socialist government of the eighties, we are faced with an embarrassment of riches. Religion and regional attachments, opinion on economic issues, and estimates of the performance of government, and such baseline indicators as sex, age, and class position can all be expected to have some influence.

The foregoing discussion has developed conceptual guidelines for sorting through this multiplicity of causal factors. We can also take cues from the analysis in previous chapters of the determinants of political legitimacy. The approach is governed by a search for the mix of identity, ideological, and interest factors that condition political evaluations. Here the analysis narrows to a focus on government support and to the particular set of economic and extra-economic considerations that influence such support.

Our initial effort to examine the question of government popularity takes into account primarily the contributions of (1) economic preferences, (2) evaluations of individual well-being, and (3) perceptions of the state of the economy as a whole, in addition to the baseline factors (age, sex, education, and so on) that are incorporated in all the models. The idea is to test the hypothesis that, given the unideological texture of Spanish public opinion, perceptions of performance influence orientations toward the government more than opinions about policy alternatives do, and that, of these perceptions, assessments of the state of the economy as a whole rather than fluctuations in personal fortunes matter most of all.

Our second look at government popularity shifts focus a bit. The objective is to set up a comparison of the impact of aggregate economic growth with the effect of perceptions of social fairness. This is a direct test of the argument that a growth-with-equity program stood at the heart of the socialists' success, and it introduces an emphasis on collective sentiment regarding distribution that is for the most part absent in explanations of governmental popularity that give priority to the role of collective views of economic performance, over and above the situation of individuals.

Third, we examine the regional factor. While preindustrial cleavages—notably, religion—have run through the analysis up to this point, regionalism has been relegated to the margins. Unlike left-right placement or religiosity, it is "lumpy," that is, difficult to conceptualize as a continuum, and for this reason awkward to deal with by conventional methods. Yet it remains an important element in Spanish politics. Our goal is to estimate its importance relative to other powerful determinants of government support.

Finally, we alter the dependent variable, introducing a factor that has no equivalent in long-standing democracies. Our interest turns to the retrospective comparison of the socialist government with the Franco regime. This strategy rounds out the analysis of political legitimacy begun in previous chapters.

PREFERENCES AND PERCEPTIONS

We have laid a profile of public opinion against a sketch of government-policy and have suggested that the two are not wildly at odds. Within broad but discernible boundaries, the socialist government had room to innovate. Our task is to assess the relative impact on support for the government of economic and extra-economic cleavages in opinion, and to do so while retaining distinctions within as well as between these factors. We want to estimate the effect of personal economic situation as compared to perceptions of the economy as a whole, while holding the effect of religiosity, for example, constant.

The data in Table 4.9 make a first pass at this goal. The dependent variable is satisfaction/dissatisfaction with the socialist government.[21] The left-hand panel contains the results of Model 1, which regresses the dependent variable on the set of generic indicators (age, class identification, religiosity, and so on), together with the factor scores for the laissez-faire ("business") and progressive ("populist") dimensions. These scores provide indicators of opinion on economic issues.

Model 2, on the right, keeps the factor scores but drops the generic indicators. Instead it incorporates measures tapping (1) personal/family economic conditions, (2) perceptions of aggregate economic performance, (3) evaluations of how government economic policy affects personal/family fortunes, and (4) assessments of how the government has been managing the economy as a whole.[22]

The results of Model 1 are suggestive but not very robust. The populist-

TABLE 4.9. Explaining satisfaction with socialist government, 1984: Multiple regression analysis, preliminary models

	Model 1		Model 2	
Predictors	b	T-value	b	T-value
"Business" factor	−.04	−.47	.01	.12
"Populist" factor	.27*	3.17	.22	3.36*
Age	.02	.01		
Class identification	−.10	−1.04		
Religiosity	.18*	3.23		
Left–right placement	−.33*	−10.47		
Education	−.16*	−2.71		
Political interest	.24*	4.03		
Family income	−.02	−.42		
Family economy, past year			.13*	1.86
Family economy, next year			.20*	2.60
Government's effect on family			.16*	1.85
Spanish economy, past year			.21*	3.06
Spanish economy, next year			.39*	4.82
Government's effect on economy			.43*	6.02
González's economic management			1.02*	15.34
R^2	.12		.46	

* $p < .01$.

distributive factor has a significant impact on support for the González government. The business factor does not—a nonevent of some importance. Evidently, Spaniards who favor a capitalist ethic saw little contradiction between their views and those of the incumbent socialists. Unlike populist sentiments, which cluster toward the lower end of the social hierarchy but don't link up with a distinctive ideological package, positive feelings toward policies favoring business have, as we've seen, something of an ideological tinge. But since the beginning of the eighties the socialists assiduously cultivated a pragmatic image, and so amid the public at large there doesn't appear to be much connection one way or the other between preferences regarding business, as a set of ideological convictions, and government popularity.

Most of the stock demographics do not correlate with support for the government. Schooling is an important exception: less-educated Spaniards are actually a bit more likely to support the socialists. The positive connection of religiosity with support for the government is more surprising. The more devout tend to give the socialist government greater approval, and the suspicion arises that religious Spaniards might be inclined to support *any* government, so long as it wasn't outrageously of the left. In addition, age does not have any significant net influence on orientations toward the government.[23] For now, at any rate, it suffices to note the chief characteristic of Model 1: all of the predictors combined fail to account for much of the variation in approval of the government.

On this score, Model 2 is much more successful. While the populist factor remains significant, the other original predictors drop out. What boosts the explanatory power of the model is the series of economic indicators. Perceptions of the economy a whole, together with evaluations of the effect of government policy on families' economic situation and on the economy in the aggregate, all have impressive effects on the popularity of the government.

So the simple demographics-plus-*preferences* model seems less promising than the demographics-plus-*perceptions* model. The comparison, however, has been rudimentary. We can now combine the two models. The procedure is not as haphazard as it may sound. Unless something very untoward happens, the perceptual indicators will probably remain significant. Their immediacy and concreteness give them an edge. The fate of softer indicators such as religiosity and populist orientation is more doubtful. But the real question concerns the fate of some of the perceptual measures themselves. Will assessments of the government's and the economy's impact at the micro level—that is, among individual families—be sustained, relative to evaluations of the state of the economy as a whole and the government's role in managing it?

Table 4.10 presents, first, in Model 3, the results of the crude contest between all the significant predictors from Models 1 and 2. Model 4 is a re-

TABLE 4.10. Explaining satisfaction with socialist government, 1984: Multiple regression analysis, adjusted models

Predictor	Model 3		Model 4	
	b	T-value	b	T-value
"Populist" factor	.08	1.16		
Religiosity	.04	0.81		
Left-right placement	−.13*	−4.90	−.13*	−6.40
Education	−.16*	−4.12	−.19*	−6.29
Political interest	.10	1.91		
Family economy, past year	.17	2.35		
Family economy, next year	.19	2.30		
Government's effect on family	.13	1.48		
Spanish economy, past year	.20*	2.86	.24*	3.90
Spanish economy, next year	.35*	4.17	.33*	4.69
Government's effect on economy	.43*	5.89	.52*	8.06
González's economic management	.94*	13.61	1.05*	17.99
R^2	.47		.46	

* $p < .01$.

fined version of this "smash them together and see what hangs on" tactic. It incorporates the significant predictors from Model 3 and estimates the regression once more in order to determine whether an equally satisfactory accounting of government support can be obtained with a smaller number of independent variables.

The most striking alterations are negative. The populist factor vanishes as a determinant of political support, as does religiosity. The implication, especially of the disappearance of the populist factor, is that explicit economic preferences have little effect on the popularity of government. Whether this also signals a decline of the distributive impulse is a question we will take up below. For now it is the decline in the influence of individual, family considerations, compared to perceptions of the economy in the aggregate as well as of the government's handling of it, that is the major news.

The gist of the analysis is that perceptions of the state of the economy powerfully affect support for the government, more so than economic conditions viewed in individual terms and more so than certain extra-economic factors, such as religious sentiment, which have been thought to exercise great influence on political approval (and legitimacy) in the past. While assessments of personal economic circumstances retain a role at the margin, their omission from Model 4, along with the omission of factors like religiosity, is no great loss; their deletion reduces the proportion of variance explained by an exiguous one percent. Moreover, ideological prescriptions for or against capitalism do not affect attitudes toward the PSOE government; these seem to be separate from perceptions of economic growth.[24] The bottom line is a combination of perceived economic rejuvenation and of the association of government policy with this improvement.

GROWTH VS. DISTRIBUTION, DEVOLUTION VS. FRAGMENTATION

The model just presented establishes the point that at least some "passions" give way to "interests" as determinants of government popularity, and that these interests encompass a perception of the economy as a collective entity. Still, the explanation suffers from a serious deficiency. It has a made-in-the-U.S.A. flavor that ignores potentially critical factors that are likely to have been salient around the time of the transition in Spain. One of these is the distributive agenda usually associated with post-authoritarian capitalism; another concerns regional sentiment.

Insofar as they are assessed by the compilation of economic preferences that we have called "the populist factor," distributive considerations appear to have had no net effect on support for the socialists during the eighties. Yet by now we should also be mindful of the probability that economic *opinions* of any sort, regardless of their "populist" or "business" bent, exert little impact.

Perceptions of economic performance tell another story. We know that evaluations of how different social classes were thought to have fared economically under the socialists, as compared to their situation under Franco, are promising correlates of support for the PSOE government. Now we can marshal these indicators to estimate their relative effect on political popularity. The class-perception measures get at the key distributive dimension: a sense of social fairness.

Coming to grips with the role of regionalism is difficult not just because the raw variable is sticky but also because "regionalism" is an opaque attribute. Even if it turns out to be statistically weighty, we need to know what it is about regionalism that might affect the popularity of the government. Here it is helpful to recall the devolutionary as well as the distributive connotations of democratization. In Spain and other countries, democratization has promoted the diffusion of power along subnational lines. Thes result has been the *Estado de las Autonomías*, a quasi-federal decentralization of the state, in which separate territorial units enjoy a real measure of self-government. Expenditures on local and regional governments have grown faster than those at the center (Dirección General de Coordinación . . . 1991). If such a process is to occur without fragmenting the polity, however, decentralization cannot be purely zero-sum, working itself out implacably at the expense of the central government.

In order to get a systematic view of the ramifications of this aspect of post-authoritarian politics, we posed three parallel sets of questions. "How do you think the decisions or measures adopted by the central government have affected the living conditions of you and those of your family? Has the central government made things better, made things worse, or hasn't it affected you and your family at all?" The series was repeated for the regional and local levels of government as well.

Of the numerous outcomes conceivable from correlating the responses to these questions with orientations toward the government, one has great importance. It emerges when favorable assessments of the central government's actions are positively associated with the popularity of the socialist government. The two would seem to go together naturally. And this is, of course, a wholly routine occurrence except when set against the *absence of a negative correlation* between evaluations of, for example, local government and national government popularity. An inverse relationship between satisfaction with local and subnational levels of government and satisfaction with the central administration would indicate a zero-sum mentality, with different levels of government pitted against one another in the public mind. The underlying relation between orientations toward the central and subnational authorities would be centrifugal.

Table 4.11 summarizes the results of including the distributive and devolutionary measures in our model of government popularity. The outcome restores some elegance to the proceedings: an improvement in parsimony without a loss of predictive power. Perceptions of the government's handling of the economy prove to be unshakably decisive as determinants of its popularity. Yet growth is not quite everything. Insofar as the popularity of the socialists is concerned, a positive image of the workings of the central government counts even more than equivalent evaluations of regional or local government, and this non-zero-sum vision of the regional factor is followed in importance by a sense of distributive justice regarding the working-class constituents of the PSOE. Above all, it is perceptions of growth and a sense of equity that count, rather than clear-cut or ideologically framed opinions about policy tradeoffs.

TABLE 4.11. Explaining satisfaction with socialist government, 1984: multiple regression analysis, reduced model

Predictor	b	T-value
González's economic management	1.04*	19.62
Government's effect on economy	.57*	11.88
Improvement due to central government	.63*	9.97
Workers' situation under PSOE	.48*	8.10
R^2		.47

* $p < .01$.

Equally important is that region—that is, the bare indicator of latent localist division signaled by "province of residence"—no longer has a direct impact on the popularity of the government, as it did during the earlier days of the transition under the UCD government. This is not to say that subnational attachments are without effect on the political fortunes of the government in Madrid. The finding does suggest, however, that the regional factor receded in the face of the economic prosperity of the eighties and the sense of social fairness that went with it. For a time, interests, not identities or ideologies, were in the saddle.

THE SOCIALISTS VIS-À-VIS FRANCO

The socialists benefited not only from the boom times of the eighties, fueled by foreign investment and boosted by the incorporation of Spain into the European Community, but from the contrast, fresh enough to carry weight, with the Franco regime. Two sets of forces were at work. Changing the frame of reference from the immediate present to the authoritarian past boosts the popularity of the socialist government. A factor that may not be obvious here is the prosperity that characterized the last decade or so of Franco's rule. At least some nostalgia for that slice of the old days could be expected even among Spaniards loath to say anything positive about "that bloodthirsty son of a bitch." Since the terms of comparison are not entirely invidious, any net positive evaluation of post-Franco governments represents a genuine bonus.

Second, and a bit more subtly, the mix of factors that determines attitudes toward the socialists differs from those underlying orientations toward Franco. Like the democratic regime itself, the socialist government arouses less passion, pro and con, than the system identified with Franco. In Table 4.12 the sense of polarization surrounding the Franco government comes through clearly, as it did in our analysis of political legitimacy.

The substantive interest of the results comes from the makeup of the predictors. In contrast to what holds for the socialists, practically none of the determinants of support for and opposition to Francoism are narrowly economic. They revolve instead around attachments to hierarchy versus egalitarianism (left-right placement, the rise of the working class since Franco) or symbolic battles centering on opinions about social and gender order (the role of women, the legalization of abortion, piety).[25]

Francoism was the embodiment not only of economic privilege but also of a welter of cultural prerogatives and codes—of exclusive identities and intolerant ideologies. It incarnated a way of life, encompassing multiple, reinforcing domains of stratification (De Miguel 1975). In this respect the films of Buñuel, Saura, and Almodóvar furnish better diagnoses of Francoism and its outpatients than strictly economic models (Evans 1995).

Retrospective comparison lent the new regime a modest but still sub-

TABLE 4.12. Explaining satisfaction
with "last ten years of Franco government," multiple
classification analysis, 1984

Predictor	Beta
Left-right placement	.38
Working class since Franco	.18
Women's place is in the home	.14
Religiosity	.13
Region	.13
Political interest	.09
Legalization of abortion	.09
R^2	.47

stantial boost. On the other hand, most of the political support garnered by the socialists was just that: government popularity ensuing from their economic performance, irrespective of legitimation through hindsight.

What was legitimized in the eighties in Spain was not democracy in general—that had already happened—but a variant of democracy based on a modicum of social as well as procedural fairness. Consumer socialism for the cynical perhaps, driven as much by the imperative of bringing Spain up to speed with the European Community as by ideological precept, but probably an irreversible accomplishment nonetheless. This was not a transition to democracy but a metamorphosis of democracy, analogous to a compressed evolution from one permutation of capitalism to another. During the eighties, in the midst of regional pulls and excesses that rivaled the vulgarities of the Gilded Age, the socialists seemed to be genial equilibrists, able to reconcile what had torn Spain apart half a century earlier (Boix 1995).

After 1990 the Spanish economy entered into recession and so did the popularity of the socialists. But the democratic system did not collapse, and the socialists hung on to power through the middle of the decade (Craig 1994). If nothing else, democracy enjoyed legitimacy by retrospection, and the socialists kept support by default. The political alternatives were looked upon as unpalatable and infeasible (compare De Miguel 1992). There was more to the mass politics of democratic consolidation and the durability of the socialists, however, than popular acquiescence faute de mieux. A handy way of gathering up these elements is through the mnemonic of the "three Ds": *differentiation, decentralization,* and *distribution.*

The demise of authoritarian politics in industrial societies typically encourages a differentiation—a growing complexity—of governmental structures, not their downsizing. Elites are replaced, but the machinery of administration takes on new functions, while abandoning few of the old ones. As an ensemble of problem-solving agencies, the Spanish state under Franco, while more than passingly repressive and certainly more capable than an agrarian bureaucracy, was underfunctional. Not many taxes were collected. The capacity of the government to deliver services was low.[26]

In Spain democratization picked up where the authoritarian order left off, expanding and refurbishing the apparatus of government and, eventually, contributing to the acceleration of economic growth. The differentiation of government accentuated the corporatist tenor of policy-making. Increased participation—more precisely, access to participation—did not automatically cut through the complexities of economic management. "Elitism" was now democratic rather than authoritarian. Political leaders could now be held to account. But the standards of accountability not only entailed upholding democratic procedures; they also involved material performance. If we are to judge from the moderation of public opinion, there was no groundswell of discontent at this delegation of authority so long as it produced results. Administrative differentiation meant both governmental expansion and organizational rearrangement, and the delegation of authority that it entailed helps account for the perceptions of gradually, rather than brusquely, diminishing continuity between the Franco regime and democracy. The socialists proved themselves as problem-solvers, as politicians who used the state-centric traditions of the country to rationalize its economic system and to amplify the delivery of services (Maravall 1993).

Democratization in Spain also meant the decentralization of authority. The expansion of government capacity was not synonymous with political centralization. The *Estado de las Autonomías* worked out in the grueling late seventies and early eighties of the transition proved to be a serviceable formula for absorbing demands for self-determination at the grass roots, while providing a buffer against political instability at the national level. The institutional wisdom of the design paid off in public opinion. The decentralization of authority and of problem-solving resources made for political flexibility that helped to offset some of the bureaucratization that came with governmental differentiation. Devolution created government jobs in the regions, even as unemployment outside the public sector got worse.

Distribution was also on the agenda of Spanish democratization. The maintenance of trust in democratic institutions, reflected through the prism of the king, has its social analog in the sense of economic fairness that the socialists cultivated and built on. It is as much a feeling as a demand, and much less a radical program than a broad but insistent parameter of opinion—a norm—that helped keep the socialists in power for more than a decade in the face of economic reversals and the recrudescence of neoconservative organizations such as the Partido Popular. Democratization in Spain made the perception of unfairness and a restoration of the airs of hierarchy impermissible, even if social equity in the egalitarian mold stayed beyond reach. Though economic growth stalled with the advent of the nineties, the socialists still commanded the rhetoric of social justice.

The 1980s were truly a golden decade for the socialists. There were, to be sure, clouds on the horizon. One prefigured the onset of an economic slowdown which lent credibility to criticisms that the dominant economic model was perilously dependent on foreign inputs (López Pina 1994). An equally serious but less evident problem, which would become obvious only in the mid-nineties, was that the socialists were about to become victims of their own success. The gross national product per capita had doubled in one decade (García Delgado 1990). And, in contrast to the performance of governments run by their neoconservative peers in Britain, the United States, and elsewhere, the Spanish socialists managed to guide social payoffs in a direction that benefited the disadvantaged. But as the decade of the nineties dawned, the socialists had probably reached the limits of their redistributive accomplishments, and they had yet to bring down unemployment. In addition, with the growth and reforms of the eighties in place, segments of the electorate began to move on to somewhat different concerns and slightly different views about the distributive agenda than those they had favored during the boom years of socialist government (Valenzuela 1995).

5

Identities, Ideologies, and Interests

Spaniards don't have political opinions, so the folklore used to go; they nurse ferocious, dysfunctional passions instead. The consolidation of democracy in Spain, its ordinariness, the uncanny fit with the happy teleology of modernization theory have so discredited children-of-the-sun caricatures and stereotypes of collective dyspepsia and exotic improvidence (Pritchett 1954) that depictions of the political culture of the country now run the risk of portraying it as a venture in sweet reason. Demystification of "the Spanish fury", "the black legend", and the overall bad craziness that made Spain notorious may overlook the landmarks of social identity that continue to shape the popular culture and politics of the country.[1]

Region, religion, and class have been the master divisions of Spanish politics. To them can be added age, or rather the battles over historical changes that generational differences represent. The hold of these signs of social partisanship is slipping. They may nonetheless anchor political loyalties more firmly than identification with political parties. Social partisanship is not unique to Spain; class and other social bonds have counted for more than conventional political partisanship in other settings as well (Shively 1972). Yet the phenomenon may be accentuated in Spain because of the weakness of the customary institutions of political organization, especially political parties.

Cultural bonds such as regional attachment may provide subcultures with "organic nuclei" that rally political movements. The implication is not that primordial ties are peculiarly intense or inherently atavistic but that they furnish a handy basis for collective action, compared to the debility of the formal, supposedly instrumental paraphernalia of modern mass politics. The costs of organizing around cultural identities are low when most vehicles of participation in civil society have been dormant under decades of antidemocratic rule (Díez Medrano 1994a; Nielsen 1985; Taggart 1995).

During the early stages of democratization, experience with secular, nonparochial vehicles of political participation tends to be scanty, and the start-up hurdles for political parties, labor unions, and other voluntary associations tend to be correspondingly high. Getting them going requires networking and logistical know-how. As the experience of several post-communist countries testifies (Ignatieff 1995), identity conflicts may gather momentum as they build on preexisting enmities. Ascriptive ties facilitate mobilization not only because they provide flash points for rival and possibly regressive identities; they may also serve as surrogates for economic resentment and ideological quarrels. They are at hand.

The basic idea behind our analysis of political subcultures is the notion of a hierarchy of divisiveness between relatively conflict-ridden identities or ideologies, on the one hand, and comparatively manageable interests on the other. As a rule, political identities forged around region and religion have an either-or tenor that is lacking in the more-or-less controversies engendered by the clash of material interests.[2]

A second idea is one that grows out of the analysis of depolarization in the preceding chapters. Regardless of whatever gradient of divisiveness may exist across identities, ideologies, and interests, all such cleavages seem to have attenuated with the structural transformation of Spain (Beltrán Villalba 1992) and during the course of democratization itself, through skillful political management.

Consider the declensions illustrated in Figure 5.1. In defiance of scenarios associated with mechanistic theories of secularization, affiliation with the working class is much lower in the younger cohorts than among their elders, together with religious devotion. In round numbers both have been halved (Bayón 1995a, 1995b; Fishman 1990b; compare Lemke and Marks 1992). Figures like these do not sustain a vision of Spanish politics as inveterately polarized.

Figure 5.2. documents an equally significant change. It traces the withering of parent-child linkages in both cultural (ideological leanings, religious devotion) and structural (educational attainment) domains. The correlation between the left-right placement of respondents and the ideological position that they attribute to their fathers is highest among the oldest Spaniards and falls off regularly from that peak. A similar loosening occurs with religiosity and education. All of the associations are strong, indicating that the pull of the past is far from trivial. Still, cultural slippage and structural mobility look to be irresistible. The gradualness of the erosion across generations reflects some continuity in Spanish political culture, but the erosion is real nonetheless (compare Beltrán Villalba et al. 1984).

The third idea touches on the political expression of cleavages. Neither identities nor ideologies nor for that matter interests are disembodied. Their capacity for generating conflict is aggravated or offset by organizational reinforcement or the lack of it. Here we encounter a significant asymmetry.

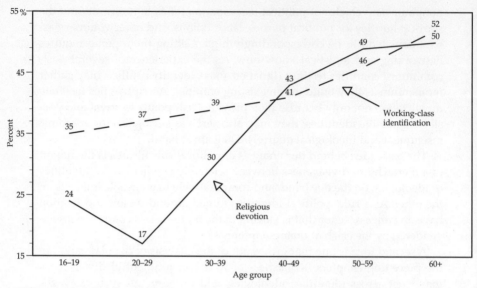

Figure 5.1 Working-class identification and religious devotion, by age group, 1984

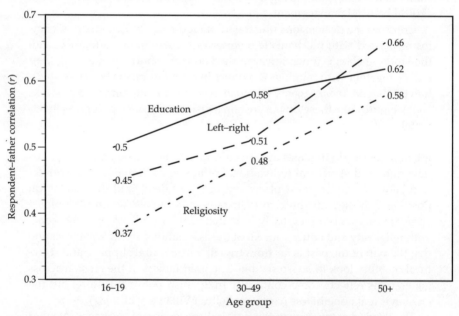

Figure 5.2 Correlations between respondents' and their fathers' left–right placement, religiosity, and educational attainment, by age group, 1978

In Spain, the conflict between religiosity and militant secularism has generally involved weightier intellectual content than that between center and periphery. Historically the fortunes of religion have been bound up with a discourse couched in terms of right versus left, between tradition and the party of human welfare. Detested as it was by many intellectuals, Catholism was nonetheless seen as an ideational force, capable of dealing in abstractions and fine feeling, that had contributed to a national, indeed cosmopolitan ethos, fostering a high culture that promoted esthetic achievement in the midst of superstition (Maravall 1986). As Antonio Gramsci and a few others on the left conceded, the appeal of Catholicism ran from popular devotions to creative expression with a certain intellectual cachet, and this range made it a formidable presence (Cruz and Perry 1992; Pagden 1995).

The programmatic rationale of localist sentiment—of attachment to the *patria chica*—has been harder to make out. "Parochialism" has traditionally had only pejorative currency in intellectual circles, connoting little or low culture and blind attachment to the tribe. During its ascendancy in the Spanish intelligentsia, leftist theory dismissed localism and its works as so much retrograde sentimentality or, worse, brute tribalism and prescribed an enlightened centralism as the antidote. Parochialism was not an idea but a congeries of particularisms, an anti-universalism. Ideologically it was opaque (Díez Medrano 1994b).[3]

The fact that over the past few decades the Spanish left has modified—indeed, practically reversed—its centralist ambitions and that it is now commonplace to speak of a "Europe of the regions" has not added to the consistency with which this complex of issues is viewed. In the end, "inconsistency" has made for flexibility in dealing with center-periphery divisions. The result is that this domain of conflict is less ideologically loaded than the classic split between left and right. It was the regional party of Catalonia that lent coalitional support to the PSOE when the socialists lost their absolute majority with the evaporation of the Spanish miracle in the early nineties, and it was regional parties, led by a coalition of Catalan nationalists, that provided the parliamentary resources for the Partido Popular to form a government when the thirteen-year tenure of the socialists came to an end (Simons 1996). Whatever intransigence has marked regional and micronationalist quarrels in Spain has come from the fusion of cultural, identity politics with the *organizational* resources of local resistance, and much less from ideological polarization per se.

There is also an asymmetry within the ideological sphere itself. For all their intellectual coherence, political currents on the right have probably not had as much of a mass base as those on the left. Both the socialists and the communists maintained an organizational presence during the years of dictatorship, while the Falange was primarily ornamental even under the auspices of Franco (Payne 1987, 1995). Also, during most of the twenti-eth century, conservatives have not been favored with the "natural" orga-nizational resources of regional and separatist sentiments.[4] As suggested in Chapter 4, the articulation of principles on the part of the Spanish right has not quite made up for its organizational weakness.

A political consequences of these ideological cross-currents and organi-zational imbalances is a reduction in the explosiveness of left-vs. right an-tagonisms. While adherence to political parties of any stripe is pretty thin throughout Spain, the organizational—that is, partisan—resources of the right have been still weaker than the coverage of the left. By the same token, the sway of organizational over ideological resources implies an irre-ducibility to regional divisions that is difficult to account for if the rhetoric of localism is viewed in isolation from its institutional reinforcement.

So, especially on the right, ideological convictions have a Platonic air that has generally lacked organizational embodiment at the mass level. In Spain, religious devotion has only infrequently sparked political activism. Reaction has ordinarily meant depoliticization and demobilization, not fundamentalist activism. On the left, which has a more successful record of mass organization, political demands are not typically suffused with ideo-logical passion. Members of the Spanish working class can still be ex-pected to favor redistributive policies, but this inclination is not identical to radicalism. And identities subsumed under "region" are not undifferen-tiated blocs. Collective identities lend themselves to oversimplification in part because they really do evoke us-vs.-them feelings that often leave lit-tle room for fine discriminations. Still, regionalism is not routinely re-ducible to separatism, much less fanaticism (compare Laitin, Solé, and Kalyvas 1994).

The differential volatility of identities, ideologies, and interests, the par-tial decline in the salience of identity and ideological distinctions during the course of democratization, and the uneven organizational expression of these distinctions raise important questions about the institutionaliza-tion of mass politics under Spanish democracy. On the one hand, regional and micronational organizations founded on pride in local identities can flourish by default, in view of their modest costs of entry. They don't have to gain national stature for their presence to be felt in the main arena of Spanish politics, and they may act as conduits to participation, benign or otherwise. On the other hand, the rebirth of democracy in Spain has coin-cided with the expansion of the mass media, with their capacity to dis-place the "normal" agencies of mass mobilization (compare Bennett 1993). These forces, one traditional, the other modern, in conjunction with the managerial bent of corporatist democracy, may augment the fragmenta-tion and the chronically surrealistic air of mass politics in Spain.

The net effect of such developments on political participation is unclear. In this chapter we explore some of the factors that may impede consolidation of and identification with political parties. Chapter 6 extends the analysis to other forms of mobilization and civic engagement.

THE CONTOURS OF SOCIAL IDENTITY

In contrast to the pre–Civil War period, Spain is now predominantly urban, industrial, and educated. Such changes are reflected not only in a thinning religiosity and in the declining number of younger Spaniards who identity themselves as working-class. As geographic mobility has increased, there are now fewer natives in previously isolated regions of Spain, and fewer still in cosmopolitan areas. Moreover, the migration of labor to the industrial democracies of Europe and back again during the sixties and seventies and increasing exposure to the transnational consumer norms of television have contributed to the decay of parochialism in Spain. Demographic heterogeneity may create problems of its own, sparking an insecurity that may lead to cultural revivalism (Lash and Friedman 1992). But it is important to understand that the bases of whatever parochialism remains—in particular, sheer isolation—have been undercut and that the structural preconditions for a modest cosmopolitanism have increased.[5] The tyranny of distance has succumbed to modern means of transportation and communication (Malefakis 1992).

How intense are regional, religious, and class divisions in Spain? A revealing way to approach this question is to estimate how close or far apart Spaniards belonging to one social class, for example, or locating themselves along a continuum of religiosity, feel toward those of another social class or religious conviction.

Figures 5.3 and 5.4 lay out the rudimentary patterns for class and religious identification. Figure 5.3 shows the average difference between scores on the sense of distance from closeness on a scale from 1 to 10, to the upper and working classes, and Figure 5.4 shows the equivalent differences between scores on feelings about practicing Catholics and people without religion. The differences are broken down, respectively, according to Spaniards' own class and religious position. Table 5.1. does the same for differences between scores of natives and migrants on orientation toward Spain and province of residence.[6]

A curious result emerges. The religious cleavage appears to be strong compared to the muted divisions by class and region. Though the split between classes is significant, as are the regional differences, they do not approach the perceived distance separating devout Catholics from Spaniards without religious affiliation. Some of this polarization faded in the mid-sixties with the Second Vatican Council, but the division lingers in the minds of many Spaniards.

On the basis of sentiment alone, then, religiosity appears to have greater potential for conflict than class or region. However, feelings, pro and con,

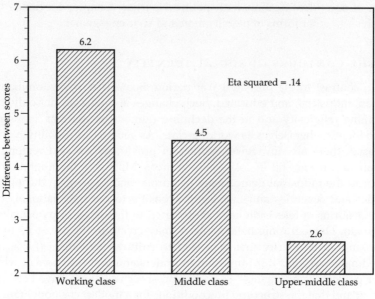

Eta squared = .14

Class identification

Note: Numeric values represent the average numeric indicators of feelings toward the working class minus those of feelings toward the upper class on the part of respondents who identify with the three classes. The higher the score, the closer the orientation toward the working class.

Figure 5.3 Average differences between feelings of distance-closeness toward working class and toward upper class, by class identification, 1984 (1 = distant . . . 10 = close)

turn out to be stronger among "practicing Catholics" than among "nominal Catholics" and much stronger than among Spaniards without religious affiliation. Catholicism generates stronger passions than secularism. This asymmetry regarding Catholics and secularists recalls the difference between the strong passions surrounding the Franco regime and the cooler attitudes toward democracy.

Whereas the Catholic church, though weakened, is still a significant corporate actor in Spanish public life, nominal and nonpracticing Catholics are a heterogeneous, diffuse collectivity. A gelatinous secularism doesn't provide unequivocal clues to the political leanings of Spaniards, but "Catholicism" still broadcasts something of a politically—in particular, morally—conservative edge. In contrast to the days of the Second Republic, which saw the expulsion of religious congregations, the confiscation of church properties, and similar acts of anticlericalism, nowadays secularization has come to be associated more with a pliant pluralism than with ideological aggression and revolutionary retribution (Paramio 1982).

The difficulty lies with devout Catholics, who feel a wide gap between themselves and nonpracticing Spaniards, not to mention the professedly

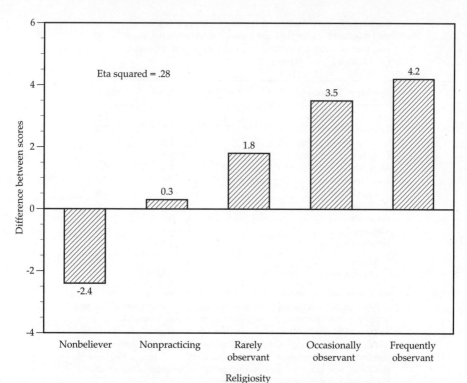

Eta squared = .28

Figure 5.4 Average differences between feelings of distance-closeness toward practicing Catholics and toward nonreligious Spaniards, by religiosity, 1984 (1 = distant . . . 10 = close)

irreligious. Religious Spaniards care more about this division than do their secular counterparts.

Part of the reason for the apparent relaxation of center-periphery tensions emerges when the sample is divided between natives and migrants (Table 5.1). Movers are more positive toward Spain than are stayers, even in separatist strongholds like the Basque country. On the average, migrants are less parochial.

Feelings of closeness to the working class are strong among members of other strata. Indeed, middle-and upper-class people claim to have warmer feelings toward the working class than they admit to having toward their own class. There is doubtless much sentimentality here. But the skepticism that such views elicit should not obscure the power of distributive expectations and populist appeals after nearly forty years of enforced deference. Invocations of a "natural," "organic," and quasi-permanent system of

TABLE 5.1. Average differences between natives'
and migrants' feelings of distance–closeness toward Spain
and toward local community, 1984, by region of residence
(1 = distant . . . 10 = close)

Region of residence	Natives	Migrants
Castille-Cantabria	2.0	2.6
Levante-Murcia	1.7	2.2
Castille–La Mancha	1.6	2.9
Galicia	1.5	2.8
Madrid	1.5	2.4
Estremadura	0.7	1.8
Aragón-Rioja	0.5	0.8
Andalucía	0.3	1.2
Asturias	0.0	0.0
Catalonia	−0.9	0.8
Basque country	−2.2	0.1
Mean	0.6	1.5
Eta squared	.14	.07

Note: Figures represent the average algebraic differences that result when numerical indicators of feelings toward respondents' own
community are subtracted from those of feelings of closeness toward Spain. The larger the positive difference, the closer the feelings
toward Spain in relation to feelings toward the locality. Regions of
residence are listed in descending order of feelings of closeness to
Spain among natives (i.e., nonmigrants).

stratification have lost such legitimacy as they once had; meritocratic hierarchies are less repugnant to Spaniards than castelike, ascriptive divisions.
It is diagnostic of the mildness of the class cleavage that on the average,
Spaniards of *no* class, whether self-proclaimed working, middle, or upper
middle, actually assign a negative score to the working class in comparison with the upper class. Perceptually the class cleavage is less sharp than
either the religious-secularism or the center-regional split.

The elevated regard in which the working class is held in Spain has a
whiff of the formulaic, just as invocations of individual initiative have in
the United States. Nevertheless, this partiality sets the tone and boundaries of political discourse in Spain. It reflects a collective norm, a rhetori-
cal code biased toward the egalitarian, which even conservative parties
hesitate to transgress.

The differences between orientations toward Spain and region of residence pose a puzzle. The ordering of the differences from top to bottom in
Table 5.1 matches what observers of Spanish politics would expect. On the
average, Catalans and Basques feel alienated from Spain whereas
Spaniards at the traditional center of the country (Castille, Madrid) and in
generally conservative areas (Galicia to the north, for example) feel liter-

ally at home in Spain. All the same, the inter-community differences are weaker than religious ones and virtually as weak as those engendered by class. They do not appear to be as sharp as might be supposed from inferences drawn about the turmoil based on regional grievances.

The puzzle stems in part from the limitations of the evidence considered so far.[7] It is time now to view the class, religious, and regional differences from a more genuinely multivariate perspective, and in their institutional context.

THE IMPACT OF TIME

Spanish generations, from "the generation of 1898," which came to maturity during the conflict with the United States over Cuba and the Philippines, to the fortyish "generation of the king" that gained ascendancy with democratization, demarcate political boundaries (Rivière 1984). Especially since the early 1960s, social change has been rapid, and Spaniards who were in their twenties, thirties, and forties around the time of the transition came to adulthood in a less restrictive and more prosperous climate than their older peers. This transformation sets up a simple hypothesis: over time, with the structural modernization of Spanish society, and in line with what is known about the depolarization of Spanish politics, the strength of the canonical cleavages should have diminished.

Table 5.2 reflects the pace of change in tensions based on region, class, and religion. It portrays shifts in relational identities, once again defined as differences between orientations toward Spain and toward the community of residence, between orientations toward working- as compared to upper-class Spaniards, and so on, across age cohorts.

All of the differences get smaller among younger Spaniards. Older cohorts are likelier to give precedence to Spain over the localities, just as they are more inclined to see a greater distance between the working class and the upper class. But the most vivid pattern emerges in the steep decline not just of professed religiosity but of perceptions of vast differences between practicing Catholics and nonbelievers. The younger, post-Vatican II cohorts have become more secular and religiously indifferent, less concerned about the gulf between religion and unbelief.

This transformation is sharper than the fairly mild loosening up of class and regional distinctions across age cohorts. The tendency of young Spaniards to be less religious than older cohorts is one piece of a larger pattern. Among younger cohorts the cleavage itself, between religion and irreligion, is simply not very important, where elderly Spaniards are both more devout and more divided among themselves about religion.

The analysis of change in regional, class, and religious identities implies that age itself is a cleavage. However, younger and older Spaniards do not

TABLE 5.2. Average differences between feelings of distance–closeness toward Spain and local community, toward working class and upper class, and toward Catholics and nonreligious Spaniards, 1984, by age group (1 = distant . . . 10 = close)

Age group	Spain–local community	Working–upper class	Catholics–nonreligious
16–19	0.28	4.59	0.53
20–29	0.46	5.05	−0.26
30–39	1.07	5.28	1.02
40–49	1.18	5.38	2.05
50–59	1.08	5.44	2.41
60+	1.13	5.17	3.20
Mean	0.90	5.18	1.55
Eta squared	.01	.01	.10

Note: Numbers in the left column represent, as in Table 5.1, the average algebraic differences that result when numerical indicators of feeling toward respondents' own community are subtracted from those of feelings of closeness toward Spain. Similarly, numbers in the middle column represent the average numerical indicators of feelings toward the working class minus those of feelings toward the upper class. The larger the score, the closer the orientation toward the working class. The right column gives the scores that signify feelings of closeness toward Catholics minus those that signify feelings toward nonreligious Spaniards.

line up against one another on all dimensions. It is the religious factor that divides cohorts.

Thus all the classic dividing lines of Spanish politics have faded to some extent, and religion has faded faster than others. Concentrating on the simplest difference between economic and extra-economic domains helps pinpoint the key trends. While perceptions of class differences have eroded only a bit among the young, these perceptions do not appear to vary strongly across social classes. Regardless of the changes that class distinctions have undergone in the eyes of the young as compared to the old, they are not terribly divisive in the first place.

Religion may retain a sharper edge. Although religious practice shows signs of erosion among younger Spaniards, it is unclear whether the slippage signifies a waning of interest in the antinomy between clericalism and secularism or a shifting of conviction from the religious to the secular side of the debate.

What seems to have happened is that the contents—or better, the connotations—of the left-vs.-right dimension, with which both economic and extra-economic domains have long been associated, have altered. Cohorts are only mildly divided along class lines and on economic issues.[8] They are more sharply divided along religious and, more broadly, cultural lines. The new left is separated from the old more markedly on moral and life-

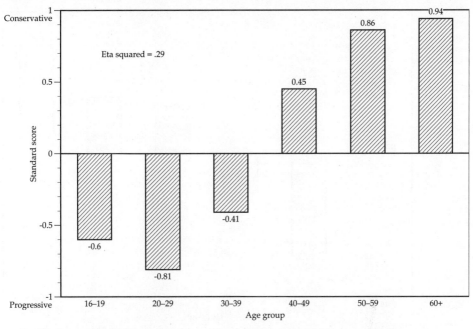

Figure 5.5 Attitudes toward women's role (standard scores), by age group, 1984

style issues than on matters of economic and social policy (Montero and Torcal 1994; compare Abramson and Inglehart 1995).

Figures 5.5 and 5.6 lay out the contrast. Figure 5.5. traces the age-specific changes in attitudes toward the role of women.[9] Figure 5.6 does the same for progressive ("populist") as compared to conservative ("laissez-faire") economic orientations.[10] The liberalism of the young and the traditionalism of the old are accentuated in the first graph and less pronounced in the second. The intergenerational chasm is much wider on moral issues than on matters of social and economic policy. Younger leftists in Spain are as divided from the old left, when it comes to moral issues, as they are from the right, regardless of generation, on economic controversies.

The generational split, then, is selective. Although the numerical balance of power has shifted toward the secular camp, the polarization implicit in the religious-vs.-secularist tension retains some importance. Just as significant, however, is the fact that cross-generational differences are not all-encompassing. The fire that can be ignited by issues such as the legalization of abortion or the reduction of government support for private, largely Catholic schools does not spread to differences over fiscal or monetary policy. A global radicalism is not pitted against a holistic revanchism. Pragmatism and a propensity to bargain have penetrated the system of cleavages. Left-right *tendance* divides generations, but in a limited way.

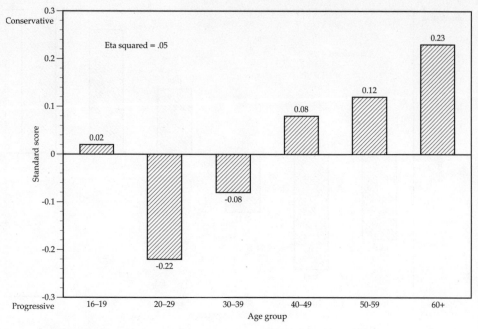

Figure 5.6 Economic conservatism (standard scores), by age group, 1984

THE POLITICAL CONSEQUENCES OF SOCIAL IDENTITY

There are multiple identity-based subcultures in Spain, of varying significance. Some erosion has taken place in the previously dominant categories. The working class has shrunk. So has the number of practicing Catholics. Geographic mobility has increased, cutting into the homogeneity of peripheral and center areas alike. As a consequence, while religious and regional distinctions persist, their center of gravity has shifted toward the "modern" side. Each of these distinctions is a fading tradition, powerful among older Spaniards and attenuated among the young.

All this is true enough as long as the discussion is confined to latent or potential conflicts. How these shifting identities might be expressed politically remains uncertain. It is hard to tell to what degree the polarization "inherent" in the religious identity, for example, takes on political form.

To answer this question, we examine how social identities link up with or diverge from political partisanship. Attachments to one or another social or symbolic collectivity may as well be fictions, politically innocuous, unless they combine with some institutional vehicle of mobilization. Table 5.3 reports the connections of partisan identification with the three indicators of social identity (nation–community, lower class–upper class, and practicing Catholic–irreligious), as well as with left–right placement.

Aside from left-right orientation, none of the distinctions lines up

TABLE 5.3. Average differences between feelings of distance–closeness toward working class and upper class, toward Catholics and nonreligious Spaniards, and toward Spain and local community, and average left–right orientation, 1984, by partisan identification

Partisan identification	Working–upper class[a]	Catholics–nonreligious[a]	Spain–local community[a]	Left–right[b]
Local parties	4.88	0.58	−2.34	4.49
Communists	6.42	−1.92	−0.22	2.50
Others	4.80	−0.25	0.08	3.76
Socialists	5.67	1.40	0.97	3.52
None	5.13	1.87	1.08	4.90
Center–right	4.71	2.60	2.06	5.58
Right	3.49	3.22	2.25	7.57
Mean	5.18	1.56	0.90	4.50
Eta squared	.04	.06	.09	.34

Note: Numbers in the first three columns represent the average algebraic differences explained in Table 5.2. Figures in the right column represent the average placement on a scale of left–right political orientation.

[a] 1 = distant . . . 10 = close.
[b] 1 = left . . . 10 = right.

closely with partisan identification. The social partisanship–political partisanship link is weak. The national–community contrast is a partial exception, and the salience of this cleavage in Spanish mass politics stems from an institutional fact: elites succeeded in organizing regionally defined parties for which single-issue supporters could vote.

By contrast, although religious and politically conservative Spaniards (who are not quite the same group) favor parties of the right and center-right, the religious cleavage doesn't find direct, institutional expression in the party system. A religious–secular division that retains emotional charge has lost much of its explosive potential because political parties have not organized around that division. Notwithstanding predictions of the rise of a Christian Democratic force after the Italian example (Linz 1978), no major religious or confessional parties emerged in post-Franco Spain. The ecumenical climate of the years after Vatican II discouraged the formation of a Catholic party in Spain.[11]

The logistics of organizing a confessional party were more daunting than the obstacles against the creation of local and regional parties. Regional parties do not have to be national in scope to be counted as successful. The barriers to entry faced by incipient confessional parties, however, are formidable. Unless religious affiliation and practice are highly concentrated in geographic terms, a national or nearly national presence is required to give a confessional party political weight.[12]

Class identities fail to come across strongly in the party system for a variety of reasons. The socialists succeeded in cultivating an interclass image, but Eurocommunism was never a convincing platform for the Spanish communists, with their history of fealty to Moscow during the Civil War and their long record of clandestine militancy (Caciagli 1984; Sotelo 1985). And behind the triumph of the socialists and the failure of the communists is the opening up of the class structure itself.[13]

The party system is most directly organized on the basis of neither region, religion, nor class but of left–right *tendance*. This traditional Spanish framework proved hardy enough to survive the long hiatus in party politics during the reign of Franco and the modernization of the Spanish social structure.

Left–right *tendance* is tied, loosely and unevenly, to region, religion, and class. The disjuncture between partisan identification and these major areas of contention derives in the first place from the slippage in the social bases of the three categories. Left–right leanings are a set of symbolic cues whose meaning has softened with the crumbling of their structural underpinnings.

Furthermore, the cleavages do not overlap very tightly even on the ideational or symbolic level. Religiosity is not a close reflection of class identification, and neither of them is intimately associated with particular regions. Partisan identificaton, in turn, is a two-dimensional composite, derived from region on the one hand and, on the other, class and religiosity by way of left–right *tendance*. A handy way to gauge the differential links between the cleavages and the party system is through the associations between the indicators of social identity and left-right orientation. The correlations between left–right placement and the pertinent social-cultural dimensions are: Catholic–secular, .33; working class–upper class, –.27; and Spain–local, –.19.

While all the coefficients are significant, it is the gradient on which they are aligned that counts. In Spain, as in many other Latin polities, religion and class were for a long time the defining referents of left–right orientation. Nowadays much of the ideological charge has drained out of class antagonisms and out of religion as well. The nation–region split is not so neatly matched with progressive and conservative options, even though the centrist balance tilts in a conservative direction. It was not so long ago, as recently as the sixties and early seventies, that the Spanish left was synonymous with the advocacy of central planning, and in the nineteenth century Spanish reactionaries—for example, the Carlists—flirted with ultramontane causes that had a decidedly anti-Madrid bent (Carr 1980; Coverdale 1984). By the eighties there was a direct though modest connection between sympathy for devolutionary and separatist causes and a generally leftist *tendance*. But the links between regional versus national loyalties to policies that are unabashedly of the left or right are muddled.

The regional cleavage has less ideological crackle than the division between religion and secularism.

The Spanish party system cannot be arrayed along a continuum. The reason is not only the persistence of the regional cleavage, which is separate from the antagonism between left and right. The structural bases of left-right polarization, associated with the harsh days of Spain's transition to capitalism, have also come undone, creating a social heterogeneity that helped make the pragmatism of the socialists an electorally successful strategy. While the left-right cleavage is more than just a symbolic remnant, its salience has been diluted by organizational weakness and ideological revisionism on the left and the right, as well as by demographic and economic change.

PARTISANSHIP AND *TENDANCE*

The wisdom of political science regarding the blossoming of partisan allegiance boils down to two ideas. One emphasizes the influence of traditional loyalties, established during earlier democratic periods, on the present. It is not uncommon to encounter significant continuity between pre-and post-authoritarian political loyalties. José María Maravall (1984), for example, has documented the geographic carryover in the distribution of partisanship across the authoritarian hiatus that separated the Second Republic from the constitutional monarchy of the post-Franco era. Provinces that voted socialist in the thirties give an edge to the left nowadays. A good measure of political continuity stems from partisan inertia, from the transmission of loyalties among the mass public that resist antidemocratic interruptions.[14] The resilience of partisanship reflects a kind of cultural torpor.

The second idea emphasizes the forward movement of partisanship. It stresses the social-psychological momentum that evolves from a baseline of low and weak adherence in the aftermath of authoritarian systems toward broader and more abiding affinities as democracy matures. More of a predictive theory than the first, it stresses the passage from a practically shapeless present to a future of ample partisanship (Converse 1969).

This is a learning theory of partisanship. As experience with democracy builds over the years, so should loyalty to political parties; the binding in of partisanship becomes largely a function of time. Political systems that in their early days are subject to the quick proliferation and disappearance of parties settle down, if not to a reduced number of parties, then to a steadier adherence to a few main parties. Not only is there thought to be a strong, almost inexorable connection between the passage of time and the consolidation of partisan loyalties, but attachment to parties in general expands; the ratio of people who identify with political parties to those who don't increases. "Macropartisanship"—party allegiance in the aggregate—grows. Insofar as parties are crucial armatures of representation, the consolidation of democracy grows apace. Presumably the stabilization of the party system aids accountability (Converse and Pierce 1992; MacKuen 1989).

How much these theories tell us about the evolution of partisan loyalties and the consolidation of the Spanish party system is uncertain. Franco nearly obliterated autonomous political organizations. Repression virtually smothered their institutional bases, yet it could not expunge ideological leanings or extirpate cultural memories. Similarly, the accelerating social changes that the country underwent toward the end of the Franco period and on into the democratic era cut the ground from under many organizations, the church as well as the parties. But lines of partisanship hung on as cultural templates, as loyalties, as perceptual maps and memories of hatred and affection, in a political afterlife whose organizational format was indeterminate.

So we have some slippage between the two types of partisanship: one from the smithereens of the old party organizations and another from the remnants of the ideological currents, cultural ties, and emotional ghosts they embodied. To be sure, there is bound to be some similarity between the institutional connotations of party identification and the more psychological bonds implied by ideological disposition. As the party system emerged, one factor that worked in favor of the socialists (and against the communists) was that their acronyms were widely recognized from pre-authoritarian days and were readily associated with ideological positions. Such brand-name recognition was much lower, practically nonexistent, toward the right. Thus the coming of democracy helped resuscitate the left, albeit a domesticated left; the right had no such advantage. The demise of authoritarianism made party labeling a matter of some delicacy: tags reminiscent of fascism or of blatantly clerical interests were to be avoided.[15]

Furthermore, the institutional repertoire that prevailed at the time democracy returned to Spain differed from the pluralistic ambiance in which Western Europe redemocratized after World War II. No longer the undisputed agents of mass politics, Spanish parties shared the stage with business groups, labor unions, and the expanding media as transmitters of opinion and vehicles of policy negotiation (Barnes, McDonough and López Pina 1986; Padgett and Patterson 1991; Paramio 1988; compare Wattenberg 1995).

An irony of the political transition in Spain, and indeed of all recent instances of democratization, is that by the 1970s political parties of the textbook variety, of the sort once thought to dominate the mobilizational alternatives of mass politics, were no longer a growth industry. Spain democratized just as the institutional paraphernalia of pluralist democracy were on the wane. Parties began to look like the husks of once-vibrant organizations. According to this reading, it is not just political repression at the hands of authoritarian regimes but the obsolescence of a political form within democracies that accounts for the low levels and possible withering away of partisanship. Neocorporatist scenarios would have it that the partial vacuum created by the decline of political parties has been filled by an ensemble of interest groups and government agencies whose job it is to do the real work of jockeying for power and implementing policy. The grind of governing is punctuated only intermittently by the need to deal with electoral politics and public opinion.[16]

The historical timing of democratization, then, may undercut the tendency for party identification to solidify with the passing of the years. Even durable loyalties may shrink in the absence of organizational reinforcement. In Spain, parties resurfaced in an institutional and cultural marketplace where their competitive advantage with the mass public had dwindled (Mainwaring 1992–93; Mainwaring and Scully 1995). Adapted to competition in an earlier era, they face bleak evolutionary prospects.

Table 5.4 tracks partisan identification across the four surveys from 1978 to 1990. "Evolution" is too charitable a word for the pattern. A majority of Spaniards—in fact, the same high percentage in 1990 as in 1978—claim *not* to identify with any political party. This finding offers no encouragement to the momentum model of partisan growth. As we noted in the opening pages of this book, partisan identification, more than a decade after the breakthrough to democracy, is lower in Spain than in Brazil and Korea, where democratization got under way later, and at about the same low levels as partisanship in Eastern Europe.

Among those who count themselves as partisans, trajectories of growth and decline can be detected. The collapse of the center-right that first went under the label of the UCD, which guided the transition, and later the Centro Democrático y Social (CDS), registers clearly. What is revealing is not so much the decline, which closely reflects the electoral record, as the fact that even during its tenure in office the UCD had few partisans. Many more Spaniards voted for the UCD than felt obligated to it as a coalition that in-

TABLE 5.4. Partisan identification, 1978–1990 (percent)

Partisan identification	1978	1980	1984	1990
None	54%	62%	40%	54%
UCD/CDS	10	9	3	2
PSOE	21	15	34	26
PCE	6	7	4	5
Right (AP/PP)	3	2	9	7
Other	5	4	9	7
Total	99%	99%	99%	101%

1978	1980						
	None	PCE	PSOE	Right	Others	UCD	Total
None	**72%**	2%	12%	1%	3%	11%	101%
N							796
PCE	39	**42**	14	—	3	2	100
N							93
PSOE	46	6	**41**	1	2	5	101
N							316
Right	44	2	—	**37**	2	15	100
N							41
Others	39	4	14	2	**36**	5	100
N							56
UCD	59	—	7	2	1	**31**	100
N							165
Total	61%	5%	18%	2%	4%	11%	100%
N	889	73	258	28	56	163	1,467

corporated their social and political agendas. A less drastic but nonetheless marked drop, also from a low base, is evident for the Communist party.

The series of snapshots in Table 5.4, based on panel data, gives an overview of the contours of partisanship. Table 5.5 provides finer-grained evidence of stability and shifting in partisanship during the early days of democratization. It shows the balance of continuity and turnover from 1978 to 1980.

The parties are arrayed along the main diagonal, from top left to bottom right, in descending order of continuity. The ranking brings out the asymmetrical axis of the party system. Not only is the largest grouping "the party of those without any party"; nonpartisans are also the steadiest segment of the Spanish public. The big divide comes between partisans and nonpartisans.

Next in strength of continuity are organizations with some ideological heft: in descending order, the communists; the socialists; the assortment of groups on the right, principally the Alianza Popular and its latter-day offshoot, the Partido Popular; and a medley of mostly regional and subregional parties labeled as "others." Ideological identity and sheer brand-name recognition reinforce partisan loyalty. Then there is the UCD, unable to consolidate its space on the center-right—a narrow and precarious zone in public opinion, at least during the opening of the eighties.

The lack of partisan adherence was probably not just a passing symptom of the shakedown phase of mass politics, naturally given to fluctuations during the transition to democracy. Many tiny parties fell by the wayside, and the total number of parties dropped. But as Table 5.4 shows, total nonpartisanship had not declined by the beginning of the nineties. Attachments to party organizations of any sort are weak.

Does this situation make for instability in the party system? The disintegration of the UCD indicates a localized instability and the comparative steadfastness of nonpartisans in their lack of affiliation argues for a stability of sorts. But those who started out as partisans in 1978 were more likely to pass into nonpartisanship by 1980 than to retain their original partisan identification and were, indeed, more likely to lapse into this option than to identity with *any* party. Some of this early decay can be attributed to an unsteadiness of the shakedown phase of the system, and—as will be demonstrated below—the adherents of parties that can be located on the left-right spectrum are somewhat less skittish than those whose loyalties, such as they are, lie elsewhere.

Nevertheless, the volume of switching, together with the magnitude of persistent nonpartisanship, is so large that to speak of the evolution of partisanship, as a path leading toward a reasonably predictable distribution of shares across the electorate, is riskier than to forecast low partisanship, period. One can imagine a random scenario in which nonpartisans at time 1 fly all over the lot at time 2, then back to their nonpartisan ways or to another choice of parties at time 3. But the political leanings of nonpartisans seem to be guided mostly by inertia. They constitute a very large sludge factor, which, we suggest, has a steadying influence on the party system.

By way of interim summary: even though more recent data are not available to generate matrices for tracing shifts from nonpartisanship to partisanship and from one party to another, the fact is that through 1990 the absolute level of partisan attachment had not grown. Thus there is little reason to expect a crystallization or tightening of party loyalty over time. This stagnation is almost certainly a special case of a shortfall in political involvement of other kinds, as we will see in Chapter 6.

The frailty of partisan affiliation, however, needs to be set alongside the carryover in cultural attachments. Decades of authoritarianism, together with the altered configuration of the institutional landscape when democracy returned to Spain, suggest that while loyalty to party organizations is apt to be slight, adherence to *tendances* that represent partisan and ideological currents will be relatively persistent. This is the case. Table 5.6 arrays the distribution of Spaniards who in 1980 declared themselves at various points along the left-right continuum against those who gave their positions along the same dimension in 1978.[17]

The temporal correlation with respect to left-right placement (.53) is appreciable.[18] Continuity is enhanced by the fact that switching generally takes place among neighboring cells rather than randomly across the ideo-

TABLE 5.6. Left–right placement in 1980 by placement in 1978 (percent)

1978	1980					
	1–2	3–4	5–6	7–8	9–10	Total
1–2	29%	50%	19%	2%	1%	101%
N						167
3–4	14	48	34	4	1	101
N						259
5–6	5	27	60	6	3	101
N						268
7–8	5	14	46	27	8	100
N						78
9–10	—	5	41	26	29	101
N						42
Total	12%	36%	41%	8%	4%	101%
N	100	291	333	61	29	814

Note: 1 = left . . . 10 = right.
Correlation (r), 1978/1980 = .53.

logical scale. Continuity is imperfect but change is far from haphazard. Crudely put, centrists are more loyal than extremists.

This tendency appears to contradict the link between ideological conviction and partisan persistence suggested earlier. But that connection, though consequential, is mild rather than determinative. In fact, temporal connections and discontinuities are partially dependent on the absolute numbers of centrists (large) and "extremists" (small). In addition, the concentration of those who stay toward the center might be characterized more appropriately as a regression toward the mean than as loyalty pure and simple.

These technical questions aside, the sheer number of nonpartisans lends them a kind of magnetism. This condition contrasts with that of the UCD, which always had far fewer partisans than actual votes. Even more important, nonpartisans tilt heavily toward the ideological center, when they can be said to have any ideological leanings at all. This massive demographic fact did not go unnoticed by political strategists, certainly not by the pragmatists ("What we need is a mass party, not a class party!") who charted the PSOE's electoral campaigns.

Most important of all, the drift of nonpartisans toward the center suggests avoidance of sweeping transformations and a move toward tactical attachments on the center-left and possibly center-right in an effort to minimize losses. The party system may lack evolutionary direction, but the pattern of cultural dispositions that lies behind it drifts in increments rather than swinging from peak to trough and back again. In this overall sense the tenor of politically relevant attachments in the mass public seems conservative, even stable, holding to memories and inclined to small adjustments, even as the substantive mode of the mass political culture during the 1980s clung to the center-left. Instability *in* the party system (common) is one thing; instability *of* the party system (much less likely) is another.

Whether because of inertia, or belief, or by reason of the costs of commitment to minor parties, or some mixture of all these considerations, adherents of the center-left are more inclined to be tenacious than their counterparts on the center-right. The PSOE started out with name recognition on the respectable left, and by cultivating a large, variegated constituency that favored social reform and intuited where the main chance lay, the party parlayed it into a core of partisan loyalty. The base of conservatism in the sense of right-wing leanings was not only smaller but also less secure than the constituency of the left defined in terms of *tendance*. Certainly in the early days of democratization and probably through the eighties, the center of gravity of the party system tilted toward the left.

We now have a picture of partisan attachments that are flightier than nonpartisanship itself, when partisanship is treated as loyalty cued to organizations, but that exhibit some consistency along the lines of left versus right. Partisan *mentalité* appears to be comparatively durable and partisan institutional identification comparatively unstable, for a couple of interconnected reasons. By the time autonomous political organizations were allowed to function again after the Franco years, political parties were probably not so important as they had been during the redemocratization of post-fascist Europe a few decades earlier. After their prolonged repression, political organizations resurfaced, like Rip Van Winkle, in an institutional world that had been transformed and had begun to pass them by (Luttwak 1995). Organizational suppression and demobilization, however, could not curb cultural and political undercurrents so tightly. Over the long haul, *tendances* survived better than organizations. Awareness of left-vs.-right terminology is higher and steadier than identification with specific parties.

Political repression was responsible for an unanticipated irony as parties reestablished themselves. Franco had eliminated autonomy for parties on the right as well as the left. With democratization, communists and socialists enjoyed legal status, but no serious party could carry the banner of the Falange—the fascist "movement." Once democracy returned, the short-term effects of authoritarian demobilization were nearly fatal for the Spanish right. At a minimum, conservative parties were disadvantaged in public opinion. The UCD that led the transition was a baggy coalition, not a single party. It was not until the mid-1990s that a conservative party, the PP, could come within reach of power.

Other factors may be taken into account when one considers the turnover in attachment among Spaniards who identify with one party or another. Imagine a simple divide between partisan loyalists and switchers. A dichotomy can be formed separating those who identify with the same party over time from all the rest (e.g., those without partisan identification from 1978 to 1980; those with partisan identification in 1978 but a different one or none in 1980; and so forth). The question then becomes: What is the origin not of high or low partisanship but of constancy and switching in partisan identification?[19]

Two different answers can be imagined. One would explain constancy and turnover by the characteristics of individual Spaniards. The less educated, for example, should evince less constancy; in general, partisan constancy and change should be a function of standard demographics. The theoretical significance of this line of reasoning lies in its emphasis on long-term transformations in the socioeconomic makeup and cultural memories of the Spanish electorate.

The alternative explanation emphasizes the shorter term. It attributes partisan constancy or change to the muted and uncertain signals sent by almost all of the parties during the transition. Aside from the fact that they all "stood for democracy," at the time most of the parties were more given to compromise than to staking out clear positions. Moderation was in vogue, and depolarization was its watchword. In this interpretation the reason for instability lies with institutions—with the parties themselves, because of their failure to provide consistent policy cues. The center-right in particular had difficulty in keeping up the appearance of consistency. However crucial a symbol of continuity-in-transition it made itself out to be, "enlightened Francoism" or democratic conservatism was not electorally successful once the transition had been effected (Maxwell and Spiegel 1994).

It is hard to come up with a precise test for either hypothesis. Nevertheless, it is clear that the effects of socioeconomic transformation on partisan continuity cannot be dismissed. While partisan persistence is not the general norm, college-educated Spaniards were about twice as likely as those without formal education—23 versus 12 percent—to have persisted in their partisanship from 1978 to 1980. The impact of such structural forces is significant though not very forceful.

The modesty of these background effects also indicates that circumstantial factors must be responsible for some of the inconstancy in partisanship. Figure 5.7 pulls together clues to this process. It arrays along the left-right continuum the percentages of Spaniards reporting the same

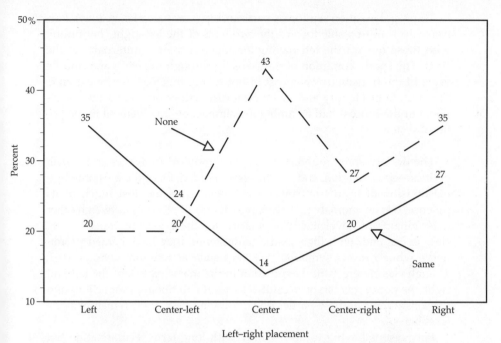

Figure 5.7 Percent with same partisan identification and without partisan identification in 1978 and 1980, by left–right placement

party identification in 1980 as in 1978 and the percentage disavowing partisanship at both times.

Three patterns are noteworthy. The right had a harder time keeping adherents than did the left. Neither side was brilliantly consistent during the 1970s and '80s but the left had brand recognition going for it. Although the Spanish right can pride itself on an intellectual tradition, the penetration of conservative parties in the mass public has generally been shallow. This flawed legacy combined with the virtual nonexistence of traditional right-wing parties around the time of the transition tended to thwart the right's ambitions in the party system.

Second, those toward the center are far and away the likeliest to declare themselves nonpartisan or to switch from one party to another. This finding, together with the penchant among centrists for prudent moves toward the near periphery rather than the poles of the system, provides strong support for the argument that nonpartisanship itself is no symptom of instability of the party system. It may lumber on in a low-grade equilibrium, with nonpartisanship outranking partisanship and with small, sometimes electorally decisive shifts in loyalty from one party to another.

Third, polarization reinforces partisanship (compare Hazan 1995). Partisanship is most stable toward the two ends of the left–right continuum, with those toward the left having an edge on their counterparts to the right. The spotty condition of partisanship through the early and middle years of the transition was a cost of not taking this logic to the extreme. The decline of identity and ideological distinctions smoothed the transition, but the process had an ambiguous impact on involvement in the political system.

The demographic foundations of the canonical cleavages of Spanish politics—class, religion, and region—have eroded. Once the most intelligible division of industrializing Spain, social class has lost much of its salience. It is no anomaly that economic-distributive issues outweigh other determinants of government popularity, for these are not equivalent to class issues and, with their instrumental tenor, they have gained prominence while heavily symbolic cleavages such as religion have receded. Though class interests find expression in the major parties of the left and right, the policy mix has been diluted to nonrevolutionary proportions and the constituents of these parties do not divide solely or even mainly along class lines.

For reasons having to do not only with long-term secularization but also with the timing of democratization (after Vatican II and before the emergence of the ecclesiastical counterreaction under John Paul II), Catholic interests do not have their own vehicle in the party system and they are weak outside this orbit, because of the traditional association between religious devotion and political quietism. Regional and separatist pulls have also lost demographic ground. To the extent that geographic mobility has increased, the narrowest parochialism has faded. Insecurity induced by such modernization—by a reduction in nativist homogeneity within provinces—may have contributed to secessionist appeals, and the fact that regional parties do not have to be organized on a national scale has given them greater leverage than political interests structured along other lines might have. But the containment of regional parties within the party system, off on an axis separate from the divide between left and right, testifies to a genuine distinction between support for the devolutionary politics of local government, astutely designed within the *Estado de las Autonomías*, and popular ambivalence about outright separatism.

Aside from the attenuation of all of these fault lines, the big change has been the disentangling of once-overlapping ones. The differentiation of left-vs.-right from secular-vs.-religious feeling has been devastating to the ideological intensity of class. On its own, without sharp class content to it, the division between left and right now constitutes a useful but less than vivid guide to a political landscape virtually devoid of heroes and evildo-

ers. Moral and cultural differences in lifestyle preferences between generations—permissiveness versus piety—seem more important than economic
struggles between classes that stand for alternative ways of life. The politics of identity in Spain—mostly the politics of micronationalism—never
had much ideological heft, and many of its protagonists and interlocutors
have settled for a provisional and profitable domestication.

There is a further sense in which depolarization has been benign in
Spain. Moderation has not come about at the cost of political exclusion—
that is, by stigmatizing minority interests. Militants, who are more apt to
organize than the great mass of moderates, may be frustrated by the snip-
pets of power they are able to attain, but they are not forced beyond the
pale, outside the competitive system. The combination of centrist lethargy
and institutional amplitude, fueled by material payoffs, has helped consolidate a movement toward depolarization that might just as well as have
terminated in fragmentation.

Arguably, the drawback of depolarization has been apathy that shows
up in the stability-as-stagnation that characterizes the system of party allegiances. Ideological moderation and the containment of identity divisions
have brought political relaxation to the point of organizational lassitude.
The manic style that used to plague Spanish politics was so discredited
among the reformers and revisionists who gained power in the seventies
and eighties that depolarization came to be viewed as the sovereign
attribute, probably a precondition, of viable democracy. The triumph
of devotion to strategic pragmatism was the crafting of flexible
meta-institutions—the *Estado de las Autonomías*, and the constitution itself.
The cost may have been the atrophy of line organizations, most prominent
among them political parties.

Three emendations need to be made to this diagnosis. The new Spain is
not quite the land of bland antagonisms. Conservatism is on the rise. The
ideological climate of the transition and its aftermath delayed the emergence and consolidation of right-wing parties that were disengaged from
religious tradition. The possibility of a national conservative party called
forth images of reaction and obscurantism. By the 1990s, with the gradual
passing of old points of reference, the Partido Popular had surfaced on the
center-right as an enterprising, morally tolerant alternative to the exhausted socialists. The close association between conservatism and scanty
political involvement may be severed.[20]

Second, "depolarization" (or its partial reversal) cannot bear all the responsibility for low participation (and possible recovery from it). The phenomenon, however real, does not constitute a single-factor explanation of
levels of political involvement. The boredom thesis is as simplistic as its
overheated opposite, based on the imagery of *España atormentada*. The trail
from depolarization to such pathologies as apathy and anomie is vague. It

is time to consider other, specific causes for the participatory deficit in Spain.

Third, "participation" itself needs to be disaggregated. It is likely that depolarization does in fact depress overall rates of political partisanship and it probably contributes to a shopping around from party to party; that is, to instability in the configuration of partisan identification. But partisanship is only one, rather indirect form of participation. One can imagine others—for example, membership in voluntary organizations—where activity is conditioned by a different set of structural, cultural, and political factors.

Finally, questions about levels of participation have no definitive answers, as if an absolute scale designating the range of high and low rates existed regardless of national context. Chapter 6 takes up these questions from a cross-national perspective.

6

The Puzzle of Participation

The price of depolarization in Spain, so it seems, has been a certain weakness in political involvement. The low level and the lability of partisan loyalties suggest some such tradeoff. But what exactly is it about moderation, aside from a general lack of excitement, that might discourage Spaniards from taking part in politics?

Cultural explanations risk a diagnostic style that is both deterministic and diffuse. It is not as if depolarization and thin legitimacy are unique to Spain. Public opinion in several countries that have democratized recently can be characterized as temperate, yet participation has not been reported to be extraordinarily low in these places. A generic "depolarization," torn from historical context, cannot be the villain of the piece. If boredom with politics were the problem, the club of weary democrats to which Spain appears to belong would not be nearly so exclusive.

Our answer to the puzzle runs along the following lines. Among third-wave democratizers, Spain is singular in the intensity associated with the religion-secularism split that destroyed its earlier forays in democratization. Spaniards may have come to dread the escalation of conflict the way Germans learned to dread inflation after the legendary Weimar currency collapse. The consolidation of democracy in Spain during the seventies and eighties involved, among other things, playing down the potentially traumatic religious-secular cleavage. A side effect of the strategy of forbearance was the loss of church sponsorship, a vital stimulus to mobilization.

It was not a woolly moderation, then, that lowered participation. Nor did "cultural factors" in the shape of a lethargic tradition simply retard participation. Rather, the outcome resulted from a specific organizational strategy of "active neutrality." The Spanish church consciously stayed on the sidelines during the transition, refraining from mobilizing its followers on a large scale in support of democratization. To be sure, the strategy would not have produced such lethargy had an inertia toward political passivity, rooted in the religious conservatism of the Franco years (Gunther 1980:36), not been present in the first place. The church's inaction reinforced rather than instigated low participation.

There is some irony to the manner in which this process played out in Spain. Just as churches elsewhere were rediscovering their capacity as a mobilizational resource, institutional Catholicism in Spain cut against the grain and held back, in some measure because it got want it wanted—a privileged position in the democratic constitution—without rallying the faithful and also because it feared the uncontrollable consequences of inciting participation (compare Hehir 1993). Then, too, the influence of the church had receded so far by the time Franco passed from the scene, and its leadership was so divided, that the outcome of a decision to pursue a mobilizational strategy was doubtful (Callahan 1992).

As explanation, the religious factor has limitations. For one thing, there is an indeterminacy about the length of its impact. What rings true as a causal agency during the eighties, when memories of the Civil War lingered and there was still some uncertainty about whether Spain would go berserk yet again, may become less forceful a determinant of participation as time goes by and as the editorial pages of Spanish newspapers express concern not about an excess but about a deficit in civic engagement.[1] And, apart from the durability of its effect, the religious factor alone cannot explain the shortfall in participation.

What else might help account for this deficit? We have identified two prime candidates: unemployment and the exceptionally low level of women's participation in the work force. The reasoning here is not very complicated. These factors are known to depress political participation everywhere. To some extent, the parlous state of participation reflects a global downturn in various types of civic behavior; partisan attachment, for example, has fallen off in Europe generally and in other advanced industrial societies (Franklin et al. 1992). But Spain respresents an acute case, brought on by special conditions. The country has been an outlier on employment and female participation in the labor force precisely during the years when political participation and other forms of civic engagement have been very low. The parallel is not coincidental, and the effects of these chronic structural conditions are likely to continue as long as the conditions themselves persist.

Thus our model of political participation: Levels of civic involvement and conventional political participation have been low to modest in Spain because of a confluence of factors—very high unemployment, exceptionally low female participation in the work force, and mobilizational abstinence on the part of the church—that have not been matched elsewhere.

In effect, we have three classes of predictors. One set is made up of the usual suspects, the standard socioeconomic variables such as education and class, which operate in the same way no matter what the country and therefore give us no leverage in our efforts to account for cross-national differences in participation (Inkeles and Smith 1974).[2]

A second type of predictor, employment status, has virtually the same form of association with participation, one that is well documented in numerous countries. But its absolute level varies markedly from country to country; in Spain it is out of line with comparable conditions in Brazil, Korea, and for that matter the rest of Western Europe.[3]

Religiosity—or rather, the mobilizational strategy channeled through religion—represents a third type of predictor. It is the direction of its association with participation that matters, differing for political reasons between Brazil and Korea on the one hand and Spain on the other.

The diagnosis, however, runs a bit ahead of the disease. A review of the varieties of participation is in order before we try to figure out why the amount of participation varies from country to country.

MODES OF PARTICIPATION

Civic engagement varies along a gradient from neighborliness through membership in secondary associations to expressly political participation. Consider first the political realm, measured by self-reports of engagement in half a dozen "conventional" activities. In Spain participation of this sort stands at about half of what it is in Korea and Brazil, and it is very low compared to rates in the peer democracies of Western Europe, even though participation has declined there as well.[4] We will return to the question whether emphasis on indicators of orthodox types of participation creates a false impression of civic anemia in Spain by neglecting newer, more spontaneous forms of public involvement. For the moment it suffices to note that by ordinary standards political participation in Spain is low.

At the other end of the continuum are neighborhood ties. Earlier we noted that the level of neighborliness is practically uniform across Spain, Korea, and Brazil. Between one-fifth and one-quarter of the citizens of each of these countries report "very close ties" with their neighbors. Because there are no cross-national differences in neighborliness to account for, these relations seem quite unproblematic. Nevertheless, neighborliness bears watching on three counts.

First, neighborhood ties are much thinner among the young than the old, regardless of country. Demographic transformations—in particular, the varieties of mobility—are the principal reasons for the passing of local familiarity. So powerful is this movement away from a sense of attachment to a small local world, from the intimacies of the front porch, the corner store, and the back fence, that it is probably a major factor behind the impression that "social capital" has eroded, even if other types of association are growing.[5]

The other cross-nationally uniform property of neighborliness is that it is bound up with religiosity. On the whole, the more religious people are, the closer they feel to their neighbors. What is striking is how widespread the link between localism and religion, in the sense of frequency of attendance at religious services, seems to be. In addition, even in Spain, where women are supposed to be more devout than men, the tie-in between religion and neighborliness is for the most part independent of gender. Women are slightly, but not significantly, closer than men to their neighbors.

Third, two things happen once we get beyond neighborhood ties. Not only are there differences between countries in levels of the less private types of interaction, but the determinants of these forms of participation change, and their causal influence varies from country to country. In general, as we move toward the public and political side of the continuum, variables that have practically no impact on neighborhood interaction, such as gender and employment, become significant predictors of participation.

The cross-national constancy of neighborhood ties doesn't hold for more public forms of sociability. As we've noted, nearly 60 percent of Koreans report high political participation, and nearly 50 percent of Brazilians do so. The corresponding figure for Spaniards is under 30 percent.

A similar discrepancy between Spain and the other two countries obtains for affiliation with voluntary organizations. Figures 6.1, 6.2, and 6.3 document membership rates in different types of organizations in each of the three countries, breaking the figures down—to anticipate a key variable—by gender. The paramount fact is the imbalance in membership across countries, regardless of gender. In Korean it is twice the magnitude of membership in Brazil, which in turn is over twice that in Spain.

Membership in religious organizations contributes significantly to associational life in both Brazil and Korea; it plays a minor role in Spain. In all three countries, on the average, more men than women are involved in voluntary groups. It is equally clear, however, that women take the numerical lead in religious organizations and, less consistently, in charitable associations and the like (compare Schlozman et al. 1995; Verba, Burns, and Schlozman 1997). Spain falls behind across the board in particular with regard to the channeling of social involvement through religious organizations. This evidence gives a foretaste of the role of religion and gender in accounting for uneven participation across countries.

To summarize: as we consider different types of social and political interaction—in particular, as we move from the private to the public—significant differences emerge between Spain and the other countries, with Spain consistently coming up short. In addition, within each country the

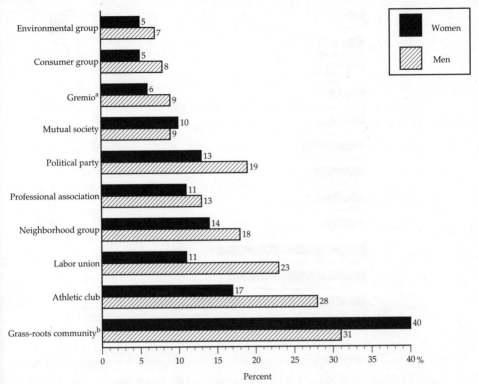

Environmental group — Women 5, Men 7
Consumer group — Women 5, Men 8
Gremio[a] — Women 6, Men 9
Mutual society — Women 10, Men 9
Political party — Women 13, Men 19
Professional association — Women 11, Men 13
Neighborhood group — Women 14, Men 18
Labor union — Women 11, Men 23
Athletic club — Women 17, Men 28
Grass-roots community[b] — Women 40, Men 31

Percent (0 to 40%)

[a] Corporatist term for professional association. In distinction to the professional associations listed separately, *gremios* have official state recognition.
[b] *Communidades de base* (literally, "base communities"), usually church-related, identified with the liberation theology movement.

Figure 6.1 Membership in voluntary associations, by gender, Brazil, 1993

varieties of participation differ, correlating only imperfectly with one another. The three types of participation—neighborhood ties, membership in voluntary associations, and conventional political participation—are distinct enough empirically to warrant separate analyses, and there is no theoretical rationale for lumping them together in a global index of participation, especially since there is reason to believe that causal patterns vary from one type of participation to the other.

What's been left out? Perhaps measures of some of the newer forms of political participation variously termed "unconventional," "protest," "direct action," "grass-roots," and "elite-challenging." Such indicators might restore estimates of political participation to their true, presumably higher level.[6] From this perspective, Spain may matter less because it is on the low side in modes of participation inherited from the pluralist era than because it represents the future of mass behavior in neocorporatist democra-

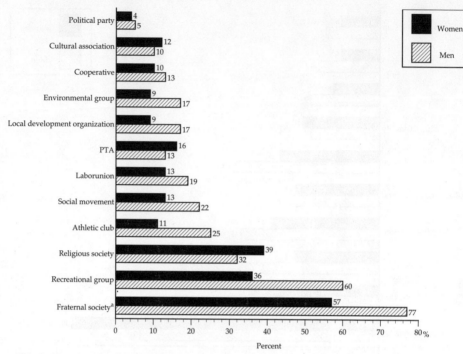

Political party — Women 4, Men 5
Cultural association — Women 12, Men 10
Cooperative — Women 10, Men 13
Environmental group — Women 9, Men 17
Local development organization — Women 9, Men 17
PTA — Women 16, Men 13
Labor union — Women 13, Men 19
Social movement — Women 13, Men 22
Athletic club — Women 11, Men 25
Religious society — Women 39, Men 32
Recreational group — Women 36, Men 60
Fraternal society[a] — Women 57, Men 77

Percent

[a] Alumni association, clan, hometown organization, other than an informal bank that lends money to members.

Figure 6.2 Membership in voluntary associations, by gender, Korea, 1991

cies, where outlets for political expression are fluid and intermittent (compare Maier 1987).

Evidence in support of the rebirth of participation in Spain under new guise is sparse, and some of it contradicts the hypothesis of a surge in novel modes of participation. Almost all of the countries that Ronald Inglehart and his colleagues monitored from the beginning to the end of the eighties showed movement toward increases in protest behavior, and among the very few exceptions is Spain, where the contrary trend prevails: a flattening and in fact a reversal in both conventional and protest behavior from 1980 through 1990 (Inglehart 1997: 307–15). Some political deflation might be expected after the euphoria of the early days of the democratic transition. But downward drift does not appear in the other new democracies sampled in the World Values Survey. By this evidence, Spain continues to be a deviant case.

Similarly, Peter Gundelach (1995) reports such low levels of "grass-roots activity" in Spain that he suspects there may be "something wrong with the Spanish data." He estimates the percentage of Spaniards who have engaged in two or more types of grass-roots activity (signing a peti-

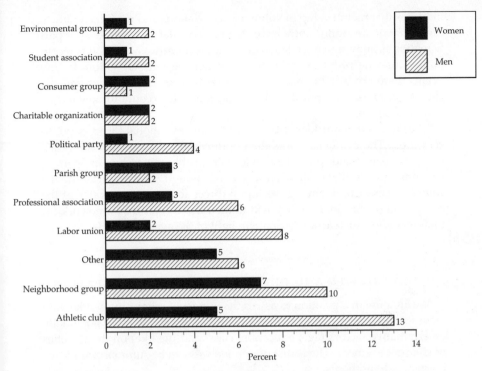

Figure 6.3 Membership in voluntary associations, by gender, Spain, 1990

tion, attending lawful demonstrations, joining boycotts, occupying buildings or factories) to be 14 percent in 1981 and 11 percent in 1990, placing Spain last among twelve European countries.

When we calculated the incidence of such activity from our 1990 data, using the same four indicators, we came up with a figure of 20 percent. This still places Spain at the bottom in Europe. Still, our estimate nearly doubles Gundelach's. Furthermore, the range of this sort of activity appears to be modest across Europe. France, at 31 percent, stands at the top (ibid.: 422).

In addition, protest activity appears to be no lower in Spain than in Brazil.[7] And in an earlier look at attitudes toward collective action, we discovered that Spaniards stood near the top among Europeans, close to Italians, in their *approval* of protest behavior (McDonough, Barnes and López Pina 1984). The political culture of Spanish democracy may indulge protest, even if Spaniards themselves are cautious, even retiring, in their habitual political behavior. The gap between beliefs and behavior, to the extent that it exists, is an interesting and possibly consequential feature of Spanish political culture.[8]

What can be said so far about participation in Spain? All the evidence indicates that membership in voluntary associations and mainline political involvement are significantly lower than in peer democracies, even if participation is known to have fallen off in those countries as well. It is worth noting that the problem in Spain is not decline but stagnation. In any event, there are testable reasons—among them unemployment and the church's hesitancy to spur the faithful to action—to account for low participation in Spain.

The situation is murkier with regard to unconventional forms of political action. The evidence is less than optimal and occasionally, contradictory. This being said, protest behavior is probably not so low in Spain as conventional political participation, even though, almost certainly, the country doesn't rank among the top in direct action politics. Later, at the conclusion of this analysis, we will tighten the theoretical framework for understanding such action in Spain in light of the available evidence.[9]

THE VARIETIES AND DETERMINANTS OF PARTICIPATION

We are now in a position to assess the impact of religiosity, gender, and labor force participation in relation to one another and to other potentially determinative factors (age, education, class, and the like) on the varieties of civic engagement. The thrust of our analysis can be summarized in two clusters of hypotheses.

On the one hand, we are interested in *differences among modes of participation*—neighborliness, membership in voluntary associations, and political activity. Not only gender but also participation in the work force and more specifically employment take on causal weight as we move from the private sphere to the public. The participatory gap between men and women widens in those domains where broadly collective, as contrasted to largely domestic, benefits and sanctions are at stake. In general, "women's importance declines," as Vicki Randall puts it, "the nearer to the real locus of political power one goes" (1982: 69).

Our second set of hypotheses concerns *differences across countries* as well as among modes of participation. The effect of work-force participation and employment varies in extent rather than direction. The impact of religion varies in direction from country to country. Religiosity drives down participation where tradition has associated commitment to an established religion with quietism punctuated by eruptions of "enthusiasm," as in Spain (Mardones 1995; Sánchez 1964). It amplifies participation where the church-state nexus is fragile or absent and, as in Brazil and Korea, where the churches helped rally the mass public against authoritarianism (Bedeski 1994; Gomes Consorte and Da Costa 1988; Juergensmeyer 1995; Park 1992; compare Leighley 1996).

We test these hypotheses by nine regression analyses, one for each

TABLE 6.1. Regression analyses, dependent variable = closeness of ties with neighbors: Spain, 1990; Korea, 1991; Brazil, 1993

	Spain		Korea		Brazil	
Predictor	b	T-value	b	T-value	b	T-value
Religiosity	.09	7.38*	.09	5.91*	.11	6.59*
Age	.06	7.01*	.04	2.11†	.05	3.78*
Education	−.12	−5.66*	−.20	−6.85*	−.16	−5.94*
Class identification	−.06	2.68*	.03	.97	.08	2.49*
Newspaper reading	.01	1.18	−.04	−.89	NA	NA
TV viewing	.01	.62	.04	2.00†	−.02	−1.20
Employed	−.02	−.55	.04	.99	−.02	−.50
Gender	.01	.20	−.01	−.16	.04	.96
Constant	2.71	32.95*	2.06	15.01*	2.57	25.75*
R²	.12		.14		.05	

NA = not available.
* Sig. < .01.
† Sig. < .10.

mode of participation in each of the three countries. Tables 6.1, 6.2, and 6.3 summarize the multivariate analyses for neighborhood ties, membership in voluntary associations, and political participation, respectively.[10]

In order to negotiate the profusion of coefficients, one should keep the central hypotheses plainly in sight. Thus, in gauging the growing impact of gender and work-force participation as we move from comparatively private to more public activities, it helps to scan across the tables, from one type of participation to another. In the case of the impact of religiosity, changes between countries (within tables) in the direction of the association are at least as important as differences between types of participation.[11]

The Main Lines of the Causal Structure

Consider first the role of gender. Women tend to be marginalized in comparison with men beyond the zone of the local. In none of the countries does gender have a significant net effect on neighborhood ties. But it exerts a powerful influence on membership in voluntary organizations and political activity. Gender differences cut more deeply as we move from the comparatively intimate relations between neighbors toward intermediate associations and political participation (Togeby 1994).

The impact of employment is similarly enhanced. Irrelevant to neighborhood ties, employment boosts the extra-parochial associational involvement of both men and women in all three countries. It does the same for political participation, except in Korea, perhaps because the employment rate is so high there to begin with.[12]

TABLE 6.2. Regression analyses: Dependent variable = membership in voluntary associations: Spain, 1990; Korea, 1991; Brazil, 1993

Predictor	Spain		Korea		Brazil	
	b	T-value	b	T-value	b	T-value
Education	.12	6.49*	.02	.49	.24	7.71*
Newspaper reading	.12	5.97*	.21	8.45*	NA	NA
Employed	.13	4.87*	.21	3.08*	.20	4.12*
Gender	.11	4.19*	.25	3.80*	.08	2.49*
Class identification	.05	2.96*	.22	4.73*	.11	2.76*
TV viewing	.01	1.64†	−.08	−2.81*	.11	5.78*
Religiosity	.00	.34	.19	8.45*	.21	11.36*
Age	.00	.25	−.04	−1.53	.01	.39
Constant	−.18	−2.57*	.62	3.04*	−.47	−4.18*
R²	.11		.23		.12	

NA = not available.
* Sig. < .01.
† Sig. < .10.

TABLE 6.3. Regression analyses: Dependent variable = political participation: Spain, 1990; Korea, 1991; Brazil, 1993

Predictor	Spain		Korea		Brazil	
	b	T-value	b	T-value	b	T-value
Newspaper reading	.18	12.92*	.13	5.80*	NA	NA
TV viewing	.11	7.81*	−.01	−.41	.15	7.85*
Education	.19	6.22*	.07	1.67*	.19	6.10*
Religiosity	−.11	−6.19*	.07	3.36*	.08	4.61*
Age	−.07	−5.40*	−.03	−1.24	−.03	−1.99†
Gender	.23	5.36†	.32	5.21*	.13	2.69*
Class identification	.13	4.42*	.10	2.21†	.12	3.27*
Employed	.18	3.91*	.05	.85	.25	5.15*
Constant	1.71	14.40*	2.34	12.23*	1.73	15.45*
R²	.23		.13		.10	

NA = not available.
* Sig. < .01.
† Sig. < .10.

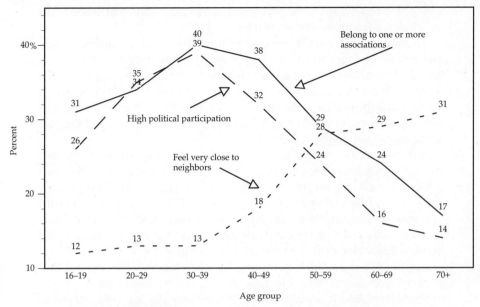

Figure 6.4 Percent of Spaniards who belong to one or more voluntary associations, who report high political participation, and who feel very close to neighbors, by age group, 1990

The impact of age varies with the type of activity. For any given mode of participation, age operates pretty consistently from country to country, but its effect changes direction as we move toward more public types of behavior. The Spanish data depicted in Figure 6.4 illustrate a pattern found, with adjustments for absolute levels of participation, in Brazil and Korea as well.[13]

So, for example, the elderly are regularly closer to their neighbors, regardless of country. This association, we surmise, is more of a historical shift than a perennial reflection of the life cycle. But for membership in voluntary associations, the connection with age is curvilinear—moderate among the young and rising toward early middle age, after which it declines.

A similar trajectory holds for political participation. Younger Spaniards, Brazilians, and Koreans show above-average political participation. The greater political activity among the young may reflect their coming of age at the right historical moment, when democratization made mass politics possible on a scale that was mostly a remote memory for older cohorts. In this view, age-specific differences in political participation, like the decline in neighborhood ties, would support a historical interpretation, even if this time the generational trend favors the young instead of the old. But it is impossible to sort out all life-cycle influences from historical readings of the evidence (compare Beckwith 1986).

To summarize: for neighborhood relations the trend is linear with age, low among younger and much higher among older cohorts. The pattern has a historical cast. Even if a few might be added on with retirement, it is improbable that local ties would grow so steeply over the life cycle, and it is likely that the decline in down-home attachments among the young mirrors a generational transformation, from the relative immobility of the past to the cosmopolitanism of today.

But membership in secondary associations, like political participation, follows an up-and-down curve with age. Social interaction of this sort peaks among thirty-to-fifty-year-olds, during the ripeness of their productive lives, and falls off as people enter retirement. Some of this decline with age may be attributable to the repression experienced by older cohorts under Franco, and some of the participatory upsurge may be indicative of good timing, coincident with the advent of democracy. It is impossible to divide the rise-and-fall trajectory in association membership and political participation exactly into life-cycle and historical-generational components. Nevertheless, it is worth noting that the curvilinear phasing of political participation corresponds to the pattern of job-market involvement over the course of the life cycle, a perennial dynamic whose form is independent of historical shifts.

The effect of religiosity varies as sharply across countries as it does among modes of sociality and participation. It has a very strong, practically uniform, and probably reciprocal connection with neighborhood ties. The more numerous such ties, the more religious the community, and vice versa. At the closely interpersonal level the parochial assumes, paradoxically, the aspect of the universal; no country-specific variations emerge. Neighborhood conviviality is thinning out, but it appears to be undergoing this change at a fairly constant rate across countries, and at a remove from larger-scale political events.[14]

As for membership in more formal associations religiosity has on the average no role in Spain but a powerfully positive effect in Brazil and Korea. In these countries, religion became a mobilizing force with democratization. The churches not only encouraged but themselves formed one of the main vehicles of collective action. The intercountry contrast is heightened in the case of political participation. In Brazil and Korea the link between religiosity and political participation is strongly positive. It is at least equally powerful, but negative, in Spain.

The spur given to antiregime mobilization by the Catholic church in Brazil has been amply documented (Bruneau 1982; Burdick 1993; Cleary 1997; Della Cava 1989). Grass-roots Christian communities developed soon after the military seized power in 1964, and by the 1970s many of them had taken on a para-political mission, allying with opposition parties and adding to the repertoire of insurgent social movements (Boschi 1987; French 1992; Ireland 1991; Keck 1992; Mainwaring 1987; Payne 1991). Increasing numbers of clerics departed from religious life and this shortfall amplified incentives for the laity to become involved in church affairs and, by extension, in politics (Adriance 1995; Hewitt 1990).[15]

Though the Korean scenario is broadly similar to the Brazilian experience, it differs in two respects. Christian denominations, though growing rapidly, have nowhere near the semimonopoly that Catholicism enjoys in Brazil and Spain; in addition, Catholics are a minority among Christians in Korea, accounting for approximately one out of four believers (WuDunn 1995). And church-sponsored mobilization got under way in the late seventies and early eighties, about a decade after such movements started in Brazil (Ham 1996; Koo 1993).[16]

Catholics made up for their comparatively small numbers by tight organization and well-orchestrated protests. Myongdong Cathedral in downtown Seoul became a rallying point for ecumenical, interclass, antigovernment demonstrations in the democratic as well as authoritarian eras. The success of the church-affiliated "people power" movement that led to the downfall of the Marcos regime in the Philippines in 1986 gave a boost to the impetus already supplied by liberation theology (Smith 1991; compare McAdam and Rucht 1993). Moreover, Catholics and some Protestant denominations formed coalitions with sectors of nationalist *minjung* ("oppressed") movements (Clark 1995; Kim 1986; Yong-Bok 1986).

Spain, by contrast, stands out among recently democratized countries for the absence of religious sentiment in the rallying of mass support. Well into the 1960s, Catholicism was linked with Francoism. The *aggiornamento* (updating) initiated by Vatican II (1962–65) about a decade before democratization encouraged the Spanish bishops to open a prudential distance between the church and the Franco regime without jeopardizing the "special position" of Catholicism (written into the democratic constitution) by calling for mass mobilization (Gunther and Blough 1981). Democratization wound up being a satisfactory outcome for the church in part because it was no longer associated with the anticlericalism of village atheists and republican enthusiasts (compare Ullman 1968). The bishops repaid this unaccustomed tolerance by preaching moderation. Although the church continued to act as an interest group, lobbying for continued public funding of its schools (with some success) and against the legalization of divorce and the sale of contraceptives (with none), the new found ethos of compromise resulted in the abandonment of political confrontation that could arouse dormant antagonisms on a large scale. The piety-and-quiescence syndrome carried over from the old days and dampened mass participation.

What happened with religion during the Spanish transition was an unprecedented separation of religion from public life at the mass level—in effect, virtual privatization (Véliz 1994: 219–20). Rather than encouraging alienation from the new order, popular Catholicism by and large stood aside. Devout Catholics were spectators, not ardent participants, or they took part in politics as mostly secular Spaniards first and as believers second (Orizo 1993; Orti 1982).

The Spanish experience represents a partial fulfillment of modernization theory: with economic development, urbanization, and allied social transformations, the public presence of religion declined (Lipset 1994). But participation did not go up as "superstition" went down. On the contrary, it has stalled, in large measure for lack of the para-political stimuli that involvement in church organizations can provide (Brady, Verba, and Schlozman 1995).

The message of this comparative exercise, articulated cogently by José Casanova (1993) and others (Keddie 1997), is that the political impact of religion is historically conditioned, varying according to legacies of church-state relations. A corollary of this message is that secularization does not constitute a uniform dynamic. Though almost everywhere the process seems to involve the differentiation of church and state together with a decline in religious faith, it does not automatically entail a privatization of religious conviction; that is, a diminution of religion-driven activism.

Privatization as an adjunct of democratization is most likely to develop in countries, such as Spain, where "politics and religion" have been associated with repressive alliances between church and state, where secularization has taken the form of a virulent anticlericalism, and where spasms of fanaticism on both sides have punctuated extended periods of apathy. But this particular history is not paradigmatic. In other countries—notably but not only those without an established church—the nature of religion-driven politics is likely to be less destructive. Thus the range of connections between religion and mass participation extends from the negative and the neutral to the possibility of a benign symbiosis between religious attachment and democratic mobilization.

Some Loose Ends

Although education and class identification do not account for absolute differences in the levels of activity between countries, they influence practically all the modes of social involvement and political participation within all three countries. Education has opposite effects on neighborhood bonds and political participation: negative on the former, positive on the latter. In boosting mobility, education undercuts local attachments. At the same time it hones political awareness and participatory skills (Verba, Schlozman, and Brady 1995).

Social class identification has no consistent impact on neighborhood ties. Lower-class Spaniards report closer relations with their neighbors but it is the middle and upper-middle sectors who do so in Brazil, and in

Korea no association shows up. When it comes to the more public types of social and political interaction, class matters in quite predictable ways. Across the countries, regardless of the mixed connection of class with neighborhood relations, positions toward the upper rungs of the class hierarchy consistently favor membership in voluntary associations and increased political participation. These public behaviors, with potential political consequences, depend to a significant degree on class in a way that the intimacies of neighborhood exchange do not (Moisés 1993, 1995).

Initially we included newspaper reading and television viewing more as baseline items than as predictors of theoretical interest. Our supposition is borne out in the case of newspaper reading. It has no effect on neighborhood ties but a great impact on association membership and political participation. Indeed, so forceful is the effect of newspaper reading that it may be considered more as a political skill itself than as a resource for participation.

Our casual treatment of television exposure may seem surprising in view of the attention this factor has received as the villain in the drama of deteriorating civic engagement elsewhere (Durant 1995; Entman 1989; Putnam 1995a, 1995b; compare Ganz 1994). And in fact its role is complex. More is known about the effect of media exposure on political opinion than on political behavior (Graber 1993; Mahan 1995). What we do know is that the relationship of television viewing and participation varies from country to country. If there is a characteristic relationship, it is curvilinear, one that entails a modified couch-potato effect. Television viewing and political participation generally go up in tandem, at least until an overdose sets in, at around median daily exposure-plus, after which participation tails off.

In summary, religiosity conditions levels of political participation among the post-authoritarian regimes. Its net impact is strongly positive in Brazil and Korea, and equally negative in Spain. The contrast fits with all that is known about the divergent functions of church-sponsored politics during the course of democratization in these countries. The effects of other predictors—notably employment status and gender—are also impressive. Economic marginalization in the sense of nonentry or unsuccessful entry into the labor market doesn't foster political participation.[17]

Our analysis began by profiling modes of participation in three countries. "Neighborliness" anchors the comparison. The level of neighborhood ties is about the same in Spain, Brazil, and Korea, and it is probably declining at similar rates among younger cohorts in all three countries. The data on membership in voluntary associations and the incidence of political participation tell a different story. On both of these dimensions Spain lags.

Having verified the disparities in civic engagement and political participation, we set about explaining them. We distinguished between causal forces that affect participation in nearly identical ways within the countries under study but whose capacity to explain intercountry differences is just about nil and those factors with explanatory potential germane to cross-national gaps. Education is a prime instance of the former type of variable, potent everywhere as a driver of political participation but irrelevant to an understanding of differences between the countries at hand. The level of education is higher in Spain than in Brazil, but civic engagement and political participation are higher in Brazil than in Spain.

As for the variables with explanatory power of comparative promise, two subtypes emerged. One set, represented by "employment status" (labor force participation and employment), works the same way within countries yet varies so greatly in absolute level across countries that it has a significant impact on gross differences in political participation. In addition, employment takes on a certain complexity because of its tie-in with gender. The interaction of these two variables highlights the participatory disadvantage of unemployed women at one extreme versus the comparative activism of working men at the other. What sets Spain apart is not the form of the relationship between gender, employment, and participation but its strength and the impact it has on the level of participation vis-à-vis other countries (Martinez Lucio and Blyton 1995; Pontusson and Smith 1995; Smith 1995).

Another factor, religiosity, furnishes explanatory leverage from a cross-national perspective, not so much on account of differences in *levels* of devotion across countries as because of the variable *form* of its relationship with participation. This systematic variation testifies to the inadequacy of universal laws linking religious sentiment and political behavior, and it belies generic structural linkages between modernization and secularization. The religious factor is more realistically construed as a highly condensed proxy for intricate histories of church-state relations at the origin of contingent, path-dependent patterns of mass participation. Our approach is indebted to formulations stressing the mutability of religion-driven politics that emphasize distinctive histories of church-state relations. This perspective alerts us to how much of what used to be taken as secularization theory was extrapolated from a limited sample of European countries—conspicuously, Spain—during a limited historical period (compare Lannon 1987 and Lawrence 1989).

The inverse association between religious practice and political activism found in Spain fits the received wisdom handsomely. But neither the Brazilian nor the Korean scenario lives up to this conflation of modernization and secularization. Indeed, the Spanish experience happens to be so uncommon among third-wave democratizers that it is tempting to speak of Iberian exceptionalism. It is difficult to think of a recently democratizing country in which the churches refrained from encouraging mass mobilization. The Spanish fluke raises a serious question. Are there any other cases of third-wave democratization in which a negative link between religiosity and participation can be detected?

Argentina may be the sole candidate. After the fashion of the Spanish bishops, though for somewhat different reasons, the ecclesiastical establishment there maintained a hands-off policy as the military regime unraveled during the 1980s in the wake of the Falklands Islands fiasco (Catterberg 1991: 47ff.; Manzetti 1993: 45 ff.). Estimates of participation put Argentina very close to Spain, at the nether end of the civic continuum (World Values Study Group 1994). The incidence of membership in voluntary associations also places Spain and Argentina side by side, far below peer democracies. In fact, Argentina is the only country aside from Spain that exhibited a recession in participation, whether conventional or in the form of protest, over the decade covered by the World Values surveys (Inglehart 1997: 308ff).

The data do not permit the exact comparisons necessary for testing the relative impact of the religious factor across a range of participatory behaviors.[18] Nevertheless, in the aggregate the Argentine outcome is consistent with the contingency model of church-driven activism. Low participation is what we would expect with a strategy of neutrality and de facto abstention on the part of organized religion, even if other possible causes cannot be held constant. Furthermore, the comparative model is upheld by evidence confirming variable rates of popular participation as a function of different church gambits in selected Central American countries (Stein 1997; compare Fleet 1985; Smith 1982). In the very few cases where, as in Spain, the church kept its distance from regime transformation, mass participation seems to have been modest. Hence, though the delinking of religion and mobilization during political transition is rare, Spain's experience is not wholly exceptional.

On most counts, then, social capital and political participation come up short in Spain. This peculiarity of the mass politics of the country, it should be remembered, cannot be attributed to some exotic constellation of causal factors. High unemployment and low female participation in the labor market, structural forces that depress political participation elsewhere, do so as well in Spain, with a vengeance traceable to the extreme levels of these parameters in Spain. Religiosity is also a common explanatory element; it is not the case that completely divergent cultural elements are at work in each of the countries we have examined. Differences in histories of church-state relations have encouraged divergent strategies of mobilization and moderation around the same religious factor.

Some puzzles remain. One concerns the flickering signs of a possible evolution of new forms of political participation. Here Spain may not be so much of a laggard as it appears when judged according to conventional standards. While evidence from the World Values Study places Spain toward the bottom on all dimensions of participation, our data suggest that protest behavior in Spain is on a par with comparable activity in Brazil and not very far below the levels elsewhere in Europe.

Perhaps the closer we get to realistic calculations of the frequency of these unconventional forms of political action, the more skittish our measures become. Almost by definition, such behavior is exceptional—that is, irregular in time and space—so that distributions of its incidence tend to be very skewed. Because it is likely to be highly concentrated, this kind of behavior may not be picked up in numbers useful for analysis except by extremely large samples, and even then timing can introduce substantial error.

Obstacles to gathering valid information about such forms of political behavior may be secondary, however, to limitations imposed by standard analytical methods. Estimation, in other words, may be less daunting than the task of explanation, once valid observations have been made. Even where political protest is found to be growing, its manifestations still tend to be discontinuous and sporadic. In such cases, reduction-in-variance techniques that draw on the stock assortment of explanatory variables (socioeconomic background, attitudinal measures of alienation, and the like) tend to max out pretty quickly, leaving upwards of two-thirds or three-quarters of the variance unaccounted for. What need to be understood, besides the role of baseline predictors, are the organizational and strategic contexts that shape surges and downturns in collective action. These are not the sort of variables that are ordinarily incorporated in survey research, though our treatment of the country-specific institutional environments behind the differential impact of the religious factor conveys an idea of how such an investigation might proceed.[19]

What is clear is that two types of civic engagement and political interaction—membership in voluntary associations and conventional political participation—are exceptionally low in Spain. So is partisan identification. At first glance, it is tempting to assign the blame for this shortfall to bad habits picked up under the demobilization of the Franco regime and to inexperience with democratic institutions. But this line of explanation falls apart as soon as Spain is compared with Brazil and Korea, two new democracies with recent authoritarian predecessors and reasonably high levels of participation. The authoritarian background is roughly constant across these countries, so the overall rate of political participation in Spain cannot be explained by reference to the authoritarian past alone.

An explanation that combines the heavily depoliticizing effects of a protracted authoritarian past with the spillover effects of a general decline in participation throughout democratic Europe may be closer to the truth. According to this scenario, after a long antidemocratic hiatus, a redemocratized Spain was born relatively free of older forms of political organization (hence the low incidence of conventional participation), and is now primed to experiment with newer modalities. The tolerance for protest activity that is a prominent feature of Spanish political culture supports this supposition. So many working hours are lost to strikes in Spain that at least one kind of protest seems to have become routinized.

Speculative as it is, this line of explanation suggests that Spain may not be so anomalous as it seems. The shortfall in conventional participation in Spain corresponds, albeit in a fashion exacerbated by unemployment, to the decline in similar modes of participation in other industrial societies. And Spain's relatively appreciable levels of protest activity resemble, though they probably don't match, the rise of such behavior in those same societies. Still, none of this makes sense of cases, such as post-authoritarian Brazil, where both conventional and unconventional political action seem to be extensive.[20]

The imperfections of cross-national point estimates can be set aside momentarily as we turn to a head-on comparison between the two countries, Spain and Brazil, for which we have fairly reliable measures of protest behavior. Table 6.4 shifts the focus from the sheer amount of this activity to its determinants.

The clearest message conveyed by these results has to do with the cross-nationally common factors that drive unorthodox participation—conspicuously, education. Age is another. By and large, younger, better-educated Brazilians and Spaniards are the ones who have the skills and the will to engage in direct political action. The employed, and those who are tuned in to the mass channels of political information, are also more likely to get

TABLE 6.4. Regression analyses: Dependent variable = protest behavior Spain, 1990; Brazil, 1993

Predictor	Spain		Brazil	
	b	T-value	b	T-value
Education	.23	10.71*	.31	14.57*
Religiosity	−.13	−10.32*	.01	.97
Newspaper reading	.06	6.47*	NA	NA
Age	−.05	−5.55*	−.10	−9.10*
Employed	.14	4.47*	.07	1.94†
TV viewing	.02	1.94†	.06	4.95*
Gender	.03	1.09	.13	4.07*
Social class identification	.01	.43	−.00	−.17
Constant	.42	5.25*	−.16	−2.13†
R^2	.25		.18	

NA = not available.
* Sig. < .01.
† Sig. < .10.

involved in this sort of behavior. These sociological underpinnings of participatory action are hardly confined to Brazil and Spain; the pattern echoes tendencies known to prevail elsewhere. If there is a sense in which these regularities are nontrivial, it is in demonstrating how stratified much political protest can be. The participatory bias favors the better-off (though it can be argued that factors beyond the socioeconomic status of the participants, such as unemployment or the threat of it, drive many instances of collective protest).

Two other features of the array transmit more intriguing information. In Spain religiosity seems to discourage direct political action even more powerfully than it does conventional behavior. The operative factor here is the conservatism built into popular religious sentiment in Spain. At the same time, in contrast to its impact on association membership and conventional participation, religious practice in Brazil tends simply to be dissociated from engagement in direct political action. The explanation is that though unconventional political behavior tends to be linked with progressive sympathies on the left-right continuum, the devout in Brazil, not to mention Spain, are not uniformly or even typically of the left. Religious mobilization in Brazil has been ideologically heterogeneous and ambiguous, at least among the rank and file.[21] Deeply religious Brazilians who favor mainstream forms of participation are a little more cautious when it comes to direct action.

Second, what this analytical approach picks up are the individual, cross-nationally generic determinants of protest behavior. Micro-level analysis tends to be less successful at pinpointing the contextual factors that shape the opportunity structures for such behavior. We have reconnoitered two questions regarding unconventional political participation: its variation in level from country to country and its cross-nationally common determinants. We have broached but not fully answered a third question—the contextual forces that condition it.

"States and organized interest groups are not the only actors that matter," Charles Maier (1997: xiv) observed, thinking mainly but not just of events leading up to the fall of the Berlin Wall. "Urban squares remain the site of decisive contests." The point, well taken as far as it goes, only hints of how much we don't know about collective action of this sort. The fugitive nature of protest behavior raises two analytical challenges: estimating its volume and diagnosing its causes—not to mention its effects. If, as we have demonstrated in our exploration of the determinants of variation in the conventional forms of civic engagement, institutional strategies play a large role in shaping older forms of political participation, there is reason to believe that such circumstantial factors should be at least as crucial in conditioning newer, sometimes anti-institutional varieties of political action.

Conclusion: The Mellowing of Mass Politics

Todo está atado y bien atado [Everything is tied down and well tied down].

—Francisco Franco

After four centuries of steadfast resistance to dangerous doctrinal innovations—bristling with pikes and swords, walled by stone and girdled with steel, armored stoutly against canonical deviations, steadfast against the progress of latitudinarian diversity, with battlements manned by sentries alert to the danger of excessive zeal and unquiet curiosity—the lofty dome of the Spanish cultural revolution has in the end proved defenseless against blue jeans, computer graphics, jogging shoes, and electric toasters. It is now crumbling, not because it has been bested by rival doctrines or pulled asunder and brought down by ideological deviations but because it has been overwhelmed by the tidal heaving and pulling of an immense multitude of inexpensive, pedestrian, readily accessible, and unpretentious products of industrial capitalism. No canonical reconsideration is required to play volleyball; nor is it necessary to abjure the faith to use a credit card, wear T-shirts, buy dishwashing machines, or enjoy heavy metal. The tail of consumption is wagging the dog of production so vigorously that the kennel is disintegrating. It was far less complicated to discourage Lutheran proclivities in the relaxed Italian city-states than to persuade the faithful of Buenos Aires, Coquimbo, or Guayaquil to abstain from watching television sitcoms; immensely easier to organize workers to march in favor of higher wages than to stop them from eating hamburgers, enjoying rock music, drinking Coca-Cola, or accepting the electronic precisions of supermarket bar code readers. It has proved virtually impossible to stop sizable numbers of consumers from responding to the entreaties of the charming, ar-

ticulate, helpful, understanding, and impeccably packaged ambas-
sadors from the world beyond the dome, a fact that has not been
overlooked by a number of Catholic writers who have tried, without much success, to alert the faithful. The ramparts, however, have
now been breached, not by outsiders fighting to get in, but by very
large numbers of insiders trekking out in the direction of supermarkets and shopping centers. It took one bite at the apple to open the
gates of Eden, but today the road that leads from the crumbling
dome is lined with hot dog stands and pizza parlors.

—Claudio Veliz, 1994

The kernel of our book is an analysis of the cooling of political passions and what it has meant for mass politics in Spain, from the
early stages of the transition to the beginning of the nineties. One way to
understand depolarization is as the gradual separation between lines of
conflict—between religious conviction versus secular militancy, for example, and right versus left positions on other issues. Cleavages that were
once conflated became compartmentalized. The upshot has been a profound transformation of Spanish political culture, or of the discourse by
which that culture was defined, from the ideological to the instrumental.
Depolarization has entailed a demystification of the grand furies that once
animated Spanish politics.

A pair of important claims can be made about this process. First, while
depolarization was encouraged by long-term societal changes, it was also
impelled by the strategic calculus of elite protagonists who were united in
their distaste for confrontation of the sort that had precipitated the Civil
War (Higley and Burton 1989). For all but a scattering of players in the
transition— those for whom the metamorphosis of a previously integrated
world view signaled fragmentation and the loss of a way of life—political
modernization meant moderation.[1]

Second, depolarization as moderation has lasted beyond the eighties.
The revitalization of the right under the guise of the Partido Popular has
not prompted a return to the days when moral-religious controversies or
regional issues were intertwined with the animosities between left and
right. On the contrary, the rise of the PP has to a large extent depended on
abandoning the culture-wars imagery of the traditional right, with its concern for symbolic-moral as well as political-economic issues. The ascent of
the neoconservatives has involved not a realignment of the political culture but instead an affirmation of a cultural transition already under way.

Depolarization in the complementary sense of the salience of interest issues over identity and ideological battles has also taken hold, albeit unevenly. Religion has declined as a source of conflict, but identity issues in

the shape of regional tensions persist in Spain. The assortment of programs promoting economic restructuring—privatization and downsizing—and compensatory benefits that brought Spain, during the golden decade of the socialists, close to Western European standards of state solvency and social protection were neither ideologically nor materially very divisive, as long as the economy boomed and European Community funds continued to underwrite infrastructural projects. But the social insurance programs and the great spurt of state expansion the socialists sponsored in the 1980s could not continue at the same clip through the 1990s without arousing the specter of zero-sum conflict. By the mid-nineties the socialists came under criticism for their economic performance not only on efficiency grounds but also for quasi-ideological reasons, for failing to remedy a chronic unemployment that was increasingly thought to be traceable to the high cost of labor. Still, there was no sign of serious nostalgia for a return to the simplified polarities of the Franco era.

Moderation, then, became a constitutive feature of democratic legitimacy in Spain. The new regime evoked little of the polarization along religious, regional, and class lines that characterized attitudes toward the Franco system. Coming as a relief after the crusading spirit and passionate intensity surrounding Francoism and anti-Francoism, a catch-all pragmatism became the dominant style of a new generation of political managers.

The snag was that ideological deflation had already been cultivated by the old regime, from the sixties onward, even if the figure of Franco himself continued to elicit very strong feelings. There was enough continuity in economic policy between democracy and its predecessor so that such terms as "moderation," "pragmatism," and "toleration" rang a bit hollow as designations of unique virtues of the new dispensation. For all the continuity between the regimes, Spaniards had no trouble telling them apart, and as the years passed, the perceived resemblance between the two faded still further. Nevertheless, depolarization alone could not do all the work of democratic legitimacy.

Two other elements, institutional trust and social fairness, entered the legitimacy equation. For many Spaniards, a modicum of confidence in democratic procedures is mediated through the figure of the king. What we have called emblematic narratives, the most dramatic of which is the story of Juan Carlos's forthright defense of democracy during the attempted coup of 1981, impart a sense of attachment to the meta-institutions, the rules, of the new regime. By the end of the twentieth century, after so much delay, democracy was welcome in Spain. But it was also derivative, less a pioneering venture than an attempt to recover what had been botched before. Gestures such as the king's helped Spaniards make democracy their own. Furthermore, the king has functioned as a bridging figure, uniting Spaniards of traditional and modern persuasions, if not their regions. Juan Carlos gave the transition an elemental coherence, adding more than just a grace note to the ground bass of depolarization. Moral drama invigorated dull calculation.

Social fairness is a more slippery phenomenon. Rejection of maximalism ushered in the reign of the pragmatic but also left room for more than a minimalist neoliberalism. Spanish political culture differs not only from that of the United States but also, though to a lesser degree, from that of most other European countries in the predominance accorded to norms of social equity and in the habit of assigning government a large responsibility for correcting social wrongs.

What Spaniards understand exactly by social fairness, however, and what it has to do with political legitimacy are not altogether clear. Three things are reasonably evident. First, the popular expectation was that democracy would not only usher in procedural fairness but also discourage a version of age-old hierarchies that impeded a more equitable distribution of material benefits. For a time, this project entailed not a leap from equality of opportunity to equality of result, or even the imposition of a ceiling above which the enterprising could not rise, but instead a raising of the floor to a level below which citizens would not be allowed to fall. Though the share of wages in the national product did not increase, social insurance programs burgeoned.

Second, just as Spaniards had no trouble distinguishing democracy from Francoism, they showed themselves quite capable of separating political from social agendas during the transition and in the years immediately following. "Social democracy" followed "liberal democracy" in rough sequence. While it would be otiose to deduce anything about definitional priorities from these phases, it is evident that an equilibrium of a kind was reached by the end of the eighties, one that would be difficult to push beyond but also extremely difficult to undo. In this respect social entitlements that are approximately on a par with those of the peer nations of Europe have become legitimizing ingredients of democracy in Spain.

Third, the strain between liberal and welfare constructions of democracy was heightened by international opinion as well as by rival domestic constituencies. Attention was directed at events in Spain not only by the likes of Alexander Haig, who held forth on the political stability of the country hours after the attempted coup in 1981, but also by the international economic community, anxious about the fate of the neoliberal project at the hands of a socialist executive that until recently had favored a nativist, populist rhetoric (compare Whitehead 1993). Democratic legitimacy in Spain grew out of a multilevel game, in which the international audience appeared at times to approach the status of actors themselves. Conceptual elegance was not its strong suit.

The evolution of partisan politics at the mass level followed a broadly similar path. On the whole, the Spanish public is supremely concerned with performance—that is, with the economic performance of the government—and with social fairness. The transition from the UCD governments to the PSOE during the early eighties corresponded to a shift in the public agenda "from politics to economics." Through the dawn of the nineties there were scarcely any signs that the days of the PSOE were numbered. It was only by the middle of the nineties, after growth had begun to level off and scandals centering on corruption and the abuse of power had gained publicity, that the trade-offs between economic expansion and social fairness took on a sharper edge.

Our analysis adds a couple of ideas to this story. Identity, ideological, and interest issues, varying in salience, cover a significant range of the concerns that shape public opinion and that influence evaluations of government. The period we have dealt with witnessed a shift from ideological to interest conflicts—in effect, toward depolarization. Identity conflicts were contained but not eliminated.[2]

Another important feature of mass politics in Spain, aside from the shift in priority of issues, is that partisan attachments have failed to expand. Just over half of the electorate probably remains without a crystallized party affiliation. Partisan undercurrents, on the other hand, are relatively strong. For example, about three-quarters of citizens place themselves on the left-right continuum, and this sort of cultural identification seems to persist without massive organizational reinforcement.

A combination of factors can be held responsible for the low to mediocre levels of partisan attachment in Spain. The long hiatus of the Franco period damaged the institutional base of autonomous political parties. In addition, for some time after democratization, association with Francoism almost certainly marginalized the right as an electoral force. More generally, by the time redemocratization got under way, much of the paraphernalia of mass politics—specifically, the spread of electronic media and the tools of survey research—had turned campaign strategists from mobilization to merchandising not only in Spain but in other industrial societies (compare Rosenstone and Hansen 1993). The debility of the parties may also have been aggravated by the neocorporatist tenor of decision making, which prizes consultation as much as competition. The result has been an extended period of stagnation in partisanship, which may have been overcome as the right became a credible element in mass politics during the mid-nineties.

The impoverished condition of partisanship in Spain is a special instance of the subdued stature of civil society during the transition and for some time after. Spain does not rank exceptionally low in electoral turnout. Nor, by cross-national standards, do Spaniards appear to be especially unneighborly—even though they are less neighborly nowadays than they used to be. People in other countries probably are, too. But Spain does come up short on at least three other dimensions of participation. In addition to partisanship, membership in voluntary associations and conventional political behavior are weak. As for participation in protest or elite-challenging activity the evidence, while mixed, is less negative. Spain is culturally indulgent with regard to direct action, and strikes, though on the decline, occur more frequently there than in the rest of Europe.

Our argument has been that a triad of structural, cultural, and organizational conditions accounts for Spain's poor showing in association membership and political behavior as conventionally understood. The lingering effects of Francoism on participation are probably small; other countries that suffered through extended bouts of authoritarianism, such as Brazil and Korea, have rates of participation appreciably higher than Spain's. What has mattered more than the toxic residues of authoritarian rule are protracted and very high unemployment, a very substantial lag in female participation in the labor force, and the exceptionally lukewarm attitude of the Catholic church toward mass mobilization. The convergence of these conditions has made for low civic engagement and political participation in Spain, even after the overall participatory slide through most of the rest of Europe is taken into account.

The least ambiguous of these trends is the decline in neighborhood linkages. Even with cross-sectional data it is pretty clear that this fall-off represents a structurally induced historical shift. The trend can scarcely be thought of as engineered from above; it does appear to be long-term and possibly irreversible. Life-cycle dynamics simply cannot account for the linear increase in neighborliness with advancing years, whereas the drop in such ties among younger cohorts does fit a generational dynamic reflecting increased social mobility.

When we come to membership in voluntary associations, however, or political participation, age-related patterns cannot be readily partitioned between generational and life-cycle interpretations. Some of the increase in participation and sociality among younger Spaniards may be attributable to the emancipatory impact of democratization. But a good deal of this bulge may also be a function of the life cycle, specifically of the timing of entry into and retirement from the job market.

In either case the prognosis for civic engagement and political participation is less inexorable than for neighborliness, and therefore possibly less grim. Because many forms of voluntary association and political activism are related to involvement in the labor market, an upturn in employment should make for improvement in civic engagement. The same goes for the repercussions of increased participation of women in the work force. The catch is that, as Spain becomes increasingly integrated in the European community, a reversal of the downward momentum of labor market conditions throughout Europe would be required for both of these indicators to pick up.[3]

The peculiarities of civic engagement in Spain raise a pair of questions that are germane to the study of participation everywhere. First, what is participation? We have touched on a gamut of behaviors, from prepolitical neighborhood bonds to unconventional protest activity. The last type is the most analytically problematic. Virtually by definition, there is less of it than of the more conventional modes of behavior, even where it is on the rise. Whether the traces we have gleaned of such activity represent a wave of the future is difficult to tell. Spaniards are among the more enthusiastic endorsers of protest. Approval is hardly the same as the act itself, but it is suggestive of a potential for new forms of political action. Such a cultural disposition fits with the persistence of relatively high levels of strike activity, to the point where it would not be unfair to speak of a low-grade ritualization of protest, so that bargaining tactics normally include disruption or the serious threat of disruption.

The challenge of assessing participation, then, is both to define it and to measure it. We have an adequate fix on neighborhood ties, membership in voluntary associations, conventional participation, and partisan identification. We have a less satisfactory purchase on unorthodox political behavior. Here the problem is in part a scarcity of data (cross-sectional only, for protest activities) and in part a discrepancy between estimates based on our own survey (medium) and those founded on the nearly simultaneous World Values survey of Spain (very low and pointing in the opposite direction from trends in most other democracies). There are grounds to be skeptical about an implacable replacement of old-line civic engagement by new types of behavior, unless we are willing to decode bits and pieces of popular culture rather indiscriminately as signs of resistance.

The second question is directed at the causal side: What factors condition differences in civic engagement? The positive conclusion is not so much that Spain is an aberration in this respect as that factors that suppress participation everywhere—for example, unemployment—have acquired greater force in Spain. The remaining problem is that we have measured some factors inadequately, especially exposure to the electronic media. We have tallied the number of days per week when Spaniards have watched television, but this is a crude proxy for the time in hours. Our suspicion is that the effect of television viewing on political participation is curvilinear, the two rising in tandem until an overdose effect sets in, and that, in addition, the impact of exposure to television is conditioned by national cultural contexts. But this, so far, is surmise (see Appendix B).

A final set of explanatory factors is composed of the shifting institutional contexts of participation. We approached this matter most systematically in our scrutiny of the religious factor—that is, the role of churches in stimulating or discouraging mobilization. We have also suggested that the neocorporatist tenor of post-authoritarian polities undermines incentives to older, election-bound forms of participation. As the channels and levels of access to decision making change with the consolidation of the European Community, so too may the forms and extent of political participation (Marks and McAdam 1996). Perhaps what until very recently was treated as "normal" participation will be squeezed at one end by the mass media and at the other by specialized agencies dealing with a range of specific policy areas.

The mathematician Henri Poincaré is reported to have observed that when social scientists are asked what they know, they tell what they know. Practitioners of the hard sciences tell what they don't know; they know enough to be clear about the limitations of their knowledge. In deference to this ideal, we can think of several areas that our research points to as fundamental to understanding the development of post-authoritarian politics and about which we have only the most tentative of answers.

We have paid a good deal of attention to religion, a traditional cultural factor, but little to a more modern force: the electronic media. Together with other countries in the third wave of democratization, Spain restarted mass politics at a time when the technology of the mass media had reached unprecedented sophistication, and few of these countries had sizable print-oriented publics in any case (Dizard 1994; Grossman 1995). There is practically universal assent that the mass media matter but *how* they affect the beliefs and behavior of ordinary citizens is less well understood. Some of this ignorance may be due to neglect of culture, norms, values, and the like by analysts of democratization, who focus on the hardware (the economics) and the software (the institutional design) of political transitions, relegating information such as attitudes to the position of so much vaporware.[4] Indifference to such information becomes less defensible to the degree that the media themselves have become a sprawl of network-like institutions rather than mere conduits for entertainment and information transmission. Though its implications are disputed, one of the few uncontested findings on the possible correlates of changes in social capital is that television and other electronic media take up an increasing amount of time that might otherwise go to doing politics the old-fashioned way (Putnam 1995b). How much imaginative energy as well as physical time these media occupy and how exactly they might stimulate or distract from political participation in any guise are questions that relate directly to the extent and the quality of citizen involvement.

A second set of questions, noted above, focuses on specifying the organizational contexts—the opportunity structures and disincentives—of different forms of participation. The apparent decay of neighborhood linkages erodes one of the traditional sources of mobilization. Other changes are implicit in the transitory, drop-in/drop-out nature of engagement in public action, with a potentially high volume of actors but fugitive commitment (Beck 1994; Davis, Diekmann and Tinsley 1994; McPherson and Rotolo 1996). Still others have to do with the shifting locus of collective action, especially but not only in Europe, toward institutional settings with a transnational reach. "The great challenge of the twenty-first century," John Markoff argues, ". . . will involve developing ways to make the transnational structures of power, from the 'emerging Europe' to the far more difficult challenge of the planetary networks of finance, responsive to those affected by their actions" (1997: 67).

Thus it is not just the repertoire of collective action that shows signs of changing but also the cultural and institutional landscape, heavily mediated and increasingly cosmopolitan, in which it takes place. And not only political parties, corporatist agencies, and otherwise solid bureaucracies are caught up in this metamorphosis of participation (Remmer 1997; compare Berman 1997c). Once thought to be contained in minor niches at the margins of public life, traditional institutions such as religious organizations and ethnic groups have undergone a revival of their mobilizing potential (Rudolph and Piscatori 1997). The diversity of participatory contexts seems as kaleidoscopic as the forms of participation itself.

Third, there are difficult questions about the links between participation or social capital in the more strictly behavioral sense (physical and usually collective activity) and its presumptive subjective coordinates, including, for example, trust (Brehm and Rahn 1997) and perhaps political legitimacy. The magnitude and variety of civic engagement are important phenomena, and it is important to estimate the causes of their variation. It is important, as well, to understand their consequences: what such activity entails not only for solidarity within groups but for the possible escalation of hostility and reciprocity among groups (Berman 1997a, 1997b).[5] The repercussions of participation are probably the weakest link in democratic theory (Parry and Moyser 1994; Pateman 1975); the effects of different styles and degrees of participation on conflict resolution, representation, and policy making are only patchily understood. A natural corollary of an assumption that runs through our analysis, that low participation harms democracy, is the idea that high participation is good for democracy. Political scientists have given this notion a cool reception. Almond and Verba (1963), echoing the earlier work of Lazarsfeld and his colleagues, applauded moderate participation and worried about excessive participation, and similar warnings have periodically been expressed about government overload. The Tocquevillian diagnosis of social capital that supposedly posits a straightforward relationship between the quantity of civic engagement and the health of democracy has come under attack.

But arguments that "political context" conditions the repercussions of social capital and participation, like the claim that "institutionalization" must outrun "mobilization" for stability to prevail (Huntington 1968), strike us as both vague and close to tautological. A promising way to understand the association between forms of participation and democratic flourishing may be to systematize the connections between both of these phenomena and variations in cleavage structures.

For starters, it is instructive to contrast two configurations, one reflecting a strong civic culture ethos, with a pervasive commitment to democratic procedures, and its polar opposite: a political culture that is actively hostile to democracy as an alien evil or spiritual pollution. If in the latter case the sequelae of social capital are likely to be lethal to democracy, in the former they can be expected to be relatively benign. Between this pair of ideal types at least two other, probably more common patterns can be envisioned: one typical of divided societies in which various cleavages run strong and in which adherence to democratic norms may be problematic, and another in which the ambience is neither of outright hostility to democracy nor full-blown commitment to it but of indifference to it or instrumental neutrality. Spain and, we suspect, a good many other democracies constitute variations on these intermediate types. The task becomes to delineate the conditions—in particular, the complex interactions between cleavage structures, or issue spaces, and political agents—under which certain types of participation may bolster or threaten the prospects for democracy.

Spain has rarely just been Spain. Three times in the twentieth century it has been caught up in larger-than-life transformations. The first was a civil war that riveted an international generation of intellectuals in the 1930s. Then, beginning in the late fifties, came a variant of authoritarianism that served as a pattern for developmental despotisms in newly industrializing countries. Finally, with the death of Franco in 1975, the country picked up the pace of redemocratization that had begun in Portugal the year before and that culminated with the collapse of the Soviet Union. Until the fall of the Berlin Wall, Spain was the case of democratization to be watched.

We have argued that democratization in Spain involved a triple transition, along cultural, economic, and political lines. For a long time the alternatives offered by Spanish history appeared to be nothing but a dispiriting cycle of anarchy and authoritarianism. The culture of great art and wretched politics held the society in thrall like a museum piece, a disfigured colossus of Gongorist beauty. The cultural dynamics of democratization in Spain have most evidently involved depolarization. To some extent, the process was straightforward, reflecting a reaction not only against obscurantism but also against the nightmare of reason that Goya depicted in the excesses of the terrible simplifiers (Pérez Sanchez and Sayre 1989).

The cultural transition has entailed other changes as well. It is not only the protagonists and their values that have changed. The landscape and technology of mass culture have been altered, too, through the electronic media and the rapid diffusion of surveys as tools of political management (Beniger 1986; Ward 1993). The transformation of the machinery of mass politics since earlier waves of democratization (Therborn 1995) makes for ambiguity and indeterminacy in Spain's politics. The processing of public opinion has become as "naturalized" as some of the new expressions of participation. We have yet to comprehend how one may affect or indeed displace the other.

It is a half-day trip from Madrid through the suburbs northwest of the city toward the Guadarrama mountains, where two monuments to Spain's past are maintained. Air-conditioned tour buses glide along the *autovía*, past sleek, well-lit factories, climatized office complexes, and residential developments, then down two-lane roads until they reach El Escorial, the monastery-palace built in the sixteenth century. The walls are of granite, the windows are slits. The interior, hung with dark portraits and heavy drapes, is as forbidding as the outside. It was in this building that Philip II, the Prudent King, a dour man who would rather have been a saint, wrote exhaustive directives in the margins of reports that arrived from the corners of his empire, from the plantations and mining ventures in the New World and from the rebellious towns and villages of the Netherlands. There is a doleful opulence to the place. Members of the royal house are entombed here in vaults and polished sepulchers.

Several kilometers farther north, up twisting roads, pine forests begin, and on top of one of the hills is a massive, Ozymandian shrine of basalt, brown stone, and veined prune-colored marble, the size of a cathedral, with a gigantic cross behind it, overlooking the vast ossuary of the *Valle de los Caídos*. Scores of combatants of the Civil War are buried in the evergreen Valley of the Fallen. Inside, under a round brass plaque, lie the remains of Francisco Franco. The domed vault of the mausoleum, built by prison labor in the years after the Civil War, is dimly lit. The stupendous design is reminiscent of the neo-Babylonian architecture that could be found on the backlots of Cinecittá when biblical epics were in favor. Sheer size makes for motionless spectacle. The enormous somber masonry is Mayan in its remoteness. Tourists are usually quiet.

In the opposite direction, far south of Madrid, in Andalucía near the Costa del Sol, a different kind of spectacle took shape in the early 1990s. In 1992 Seville hosted the World's Fair. Toward the east, in the Levant, Barcelona was the site of the summer Olympic games. Banners of primary colors flew everywhere. Loudspeakers broadcast international pop rock. Foreign visitors were plentiful. The grounds of the fair were busy with an air of ebullient impermanence. New *autovías* and high-speed rail routes shortened the geographical distance between the ponderous sites of pilgrimage in Castille and the bright and glossy theme park pavilions of Seville.

Appendix A

On Gender, Employment Status, Religion, and Civic Engagement

At the heart of our analysis of participation is a distinction among three main kinds of sociality and civic engagement: neighborhood ties, membership in voluntary associations, and conventional political participation. Here we consider a set of technical questions that bear on the substantive interpretation of our results. One concerns the historical, generational nature of changes in neighborliness. Another touches on the mixed (and with our cross-sectional data practically indeterminate) nature of changes in voluntary association membership and political participation. A third set of questions has to do with the effect of the interaction between gender and employment status on the modes of participation, as well as with the connection between gender and religiosity.

GENERATIONAL CHANGE IN NEIGHBORHOOD INTEGRATION

Neighborhood bonds in Spain, Brazil, and Korea have declined over time. Local ties have thinned out with geographic and social mobility, breaking down the insularity of the *patria chica*, the small worlds of the store on the corner and the familiar countryside (Press 1979; compare Cho and Shin 1996 and Flaquer and Iglesias de Ussel 1996). Figure A.1 shows that in all three countries, neighborhood ties are weakest among the young and grow strong with age. Most of the change we observe can be laid to historical shifts between generations. The social circles circumscribed by neighborhood, by ties of place, are on the wane. "Organic" networks located around the drugstore, parish church, primary school, barbershop, and hairdresser have shrunk and in some places are disintegrating, giving way to the anonymity encouraged by supermarkets and shopping malls. The trend affects men and women similarly, even if women may be

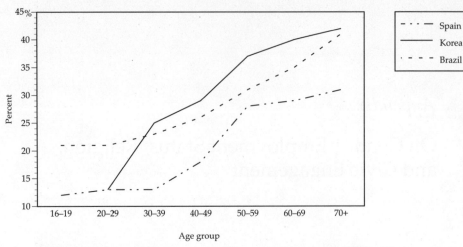

Figure A.1 Percent who feel close to neighbors by age group: Spain, 1990; Korea, 1991; Brazil, 1993

slightly more neighborhood-bound than men at any point in time; and it seems to be working its way through Spain, Brazil and Korea at a fairly constant rate, so that on this score at least something like a convergence of modernization is in sight. The historical transformations behind the erosion of neighborhood ties are more clear-cut in their operation than the mix of factors that work to alter membership in secondary associations and political activity.

MEMBERSHIP IN VOLUNTARY ASSOCIATIONS AND POLITICAL PARTICIPATION

A second trend, covering the incidence of membership in intermediate groups and the extent of political participation, probably reflects life-cycle changes at least as much as historical chances and, because men and women have different career trajectories, it affects them differently. Men enjoy an advantage in organizational affiliation and political participation because more of them are active in the work force; the proportion of women, even educated women, active in the wider world is disproportionately small.

Spain is at the bottom of the countries examined here with respect to absolute levels of employment and women's participation in the labor market (Alcobendas Tirado 1983; Bustello 1994). The size of the gender gap is likely to shrink as more women gain access to jobs outside the home, but Spain has a lot of catching up to do. Though it is possible that, with time, gender differences in rates of labor market participation will shrink between as well as within countries, and that rates of political participation

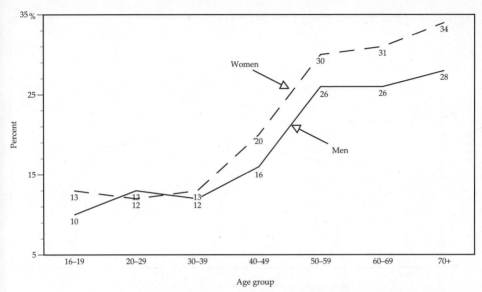

Figure A.2 Percent of men and women who feel very close to neighbors, by age group, Spain, 1990

will thereby converge, such an eventuality cannot be presumed. The variable divide between Spanish men and women in social and political activity is presented in Figure A.2, A.3, A.4. These data set the stage for consideration of the role of employment status as it affects the varieties of participation.

In the case of neighborhood relations (Figure A.2), the gender gap emerges only among the older cohorts and disappears among the younger age groups. Shawled widows in black who know all the gossip may no longer be standbys of Mediterranean life, but older women still play a larger role than men of equivalent age in knitting up the fabric of close-to-home ties.[1] It is hard to imagine how the contrast might be attributed to advancement in the life cycle and easy to see that it reflects a historical shift between generations. In the old days, women excelled in everyday intimacies because they were homebodies. This tradition is increasingly vestigial.

On the other hand, the gender gap in both association membership and political participation holds across cohorts, consistently favoring men, who are about twice as likely to take part in social groups and political activities. As the contrast with neighborhood bonds suggests, the participatory divide between the sexes increases as affiliation and interaction become more public (Verba, Burns, and Schlozman, 1997). The close association between organizational and political involvement and stages of the life cycle is the other evident regularity. For women and men alike, social engagement and civic activity rise toward the middle years, then decline.

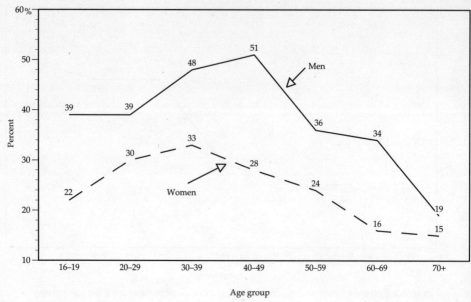

Figure A.3 Percent of men and women who belong to one or more voluntary associations, by age group, Spain, 1990

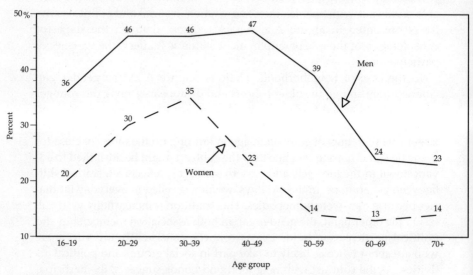

Figure A.4 Percent of men and women who report high political participation, by age group, Spain, 1990

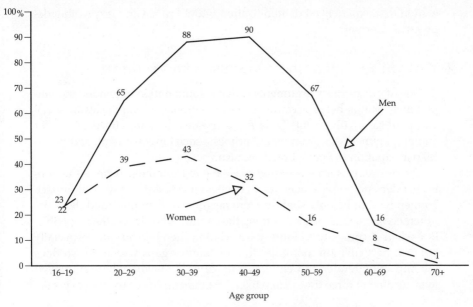

Figure A.5 Percent of men and women employed, by age group, Spain, 1990

Figure A.5 picks out a major structural factor underlying the gender gap in membership and participation over the life cycle: insertion in the labor market. Men and women begin and end at the same place, virtually outside the labor market at the extremes of the age line. The difference comes in between, with men participating in the labor market at higher and higher rates until age and retirement bring the rates together again.

The resemblance between this dual tracking in the labor market and the curves tracing association membership and political participation for men and women is not coincidental. Up to a point, the deficit among women corresponds to the life courses to which most of them are assigned, with stress on the private and the domestic over the breadwinning and the public. The shape of both curves reflects the *life-cycle* dynamics of participation in the workforce. The ballooning size of the gap between the curves can be understood as reflecting the laggard *historical* status of women. As the participation of women in the labor market increases, the distance between the male and female curves will narrow, while their bell-shaped trajectories, reflecting the life-cycle component, will stay much the same.

With cross-sectional data, however, any transfer of this reading of trends in employment status to a diagnosis of voluntary association membership and political participation can only be imperfect. It is impossible to distinguish the contribution of retirement from work to the drop-off in participation in old age from the contribution of historical effects on a generation that experienced demobilization under Franco and its possibly depressive aftermath.

GENDER, EMPLOYMENT STATUS, AND RELIGION

One of our primary arguments is that a combination of gender and employment status helps account for cross-national discrepancies in social and political involvement. Table A.1 compares the joint effects of gender and employment status on neighborliness, social involvement, and political participation in Spain, Brazil, and Korea.

The overall pattern is striking: as we move from the private to the public, gender and employment status have an increasingly powerful impact. Women tend to be only slightly more neighborly than men, and the gross differences in neighborliness among the countries border on the negligible. But when it comes to voluntary association membership and especially political participation, not only do intercountry gaps widen but so does the impact of gender and employment status. In Spain, where employed men are almost three times more likely than unemployed women to partic-

TABLE A.1. High political participation, membership in one or more associations, and close ties to neighbors, by gender and employment status: Spain, Korea, and Brazil, 1990 (percent)

| | Unemployed | | Employed | | |
	Women	Men	Women	Men	Countrywide
High political participation[a]					
Spain	16%	28%	31%	42%	27%
Korea	45	50	60	68	58
Brazil	38	48	50	56	49
Membership in one or more associations					
Spain	21	31	34	45	31
Korea	77	89	86	93	87
Brazil	59	66	69	70	49
Close ties to neighbors					
Spain	24	21	17	17	20
Korea	28	15	24	23	24
Brazil	26	26	23	24	25

[a] Includes the top quartile of respondents in Spain on a participation index of six items—that is, those who scored 10 or above on a scale from 1 to 24. The same cut points established in Spain were then applied to the Korean and Brazilian data. See note 19 in the Introduction for details.

ipate in conventional politics (42 vs. 16 percent), this interaction is most prominent. It is discernible though less pronounced in Brazil and Korea.

Another, possibly confounding interaction is that between gender and religion. The suspicion that the long-standing link between religiosity and women in Spain may render the direct link between religiosity and participation at least partially spurious is not altogether unfounded (Gallego Mendez 1994). The interaction between gender and religiosity, most marked in Spain, is less confounding than it might be, however, because it is disappearing among the young (see Table A.2).

The hold of religion remains tight among elderly women in Spain. By the same token, the youngest men and women converge toward diminished religiosity. It is a reasonable supposition, even granting some increase in religious observance over the life cycle, that this pattern reflects a generational trend toward unisex secularization. In Brazil and Korea, though the overall association is similar to that in Spain, the connection between religion and age is more tenuous to begin with, and so is the differential between men and women.

What about the impact of the gender-religion connection on participation? In all three countries, at all levels of religious observance, men tend to be more politically active than women (compare Mayer and Smith 1985). Korea furnishes the clearest instance of a simple additive distance between men and women of varying religiosity with regard to participation; there the male-female differences stay roughly parallel along the religiosity scale. In Spain and to a lesser extent Brazil, while an interaction between religion and gender emerges, a linear, additive impact of religion

TABLE A.2. Percent religious ("practicing" and "devout"), by gender and age group: Spain, Korea, and Brazil, 1990 (percent)

	Age group							
	16–19	20–29	30–39	40–49	50–59	60–69	70+	r religion/age
Spain								
Women	29%	22%	25%	43%	62%	64%	68%	.39
Men	23	12	16	25	30	36	37	.22
Korea								
Women	—	15	21	24	35	41	—	.19
Men	—	10	17	17	15	29	—	.14
Brazil								
Women	39	35	39	52	53	59	66	.19
Men	29	35	26	31	36	38	43	.10

on participation persists. Not only are women more devout than men, a tendency that is accentuated in but not unique to Spain; piety is also bound up with sexual hierarchy and privatism (Cruz Cantero and Cobo Bedia 1991; Montero, 1994). In Brazil and Korea, on the other hand, devotional practice is tied in with associational life, and church-affiliated organizations give women as well as men a chance to develop participatory skills (Ozorak 1996).[2]

Appendix B

Effects of the Media on Participation

Our indicators of media exposure are rudimentary: the number of days "during the past week" in which a newspaper was read and the number of days television was watched. What we would really like to register is how many hours people spend watching television as well as something about what they watch. Nevertheless, though it tells us nothing about content, tallying days of media exposure gives us an idea of frequency of exposure, and this is the minimum datum necessary for estimating the effects of media attention on participation.[1]

Attention to print media drives political participation more forcefully than does exposure to the electronic media. Unlike television, which places few demands on the viewer, newspaper reading is itself something of a skill, directly linked to education and political knowledge. Table 6.3 supports this idea. Newspaper reading turns out to be far and away the most powerful predictor of political participation, so much so that it might be considered an elementary form of such activity.

The origins of the difference between the print and electronic media are outlined in Figures B.1 and B.2. Formal schooling propels newspaper reading; by contrast, the effect of education on exposure to television is attenuated. In Korea, the most literate of the three societies, television viewing actually declines with years of schooling.

The effects of television viewing on participation, then, are likely to be weaker and less straightforward than those of the print media. Education is the key factor, disposing those with more of it to read. It is not difficult to account for the overall gap between the impact of print and visual media on participation. The challenge is to specify how the electronic media affect participation.

Two hypotheses can be entertained about the impact of the electronic media. On the one hand, there is the couch-potato update of the bread-and circuses hypothesis. The strong version of this argument is that it is not

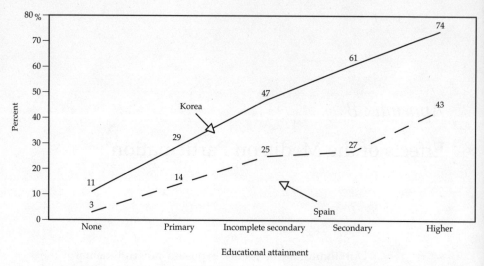

Figure B.1 Percent who read newspapers daily, by education: Spain, 1990; Korea, 1991

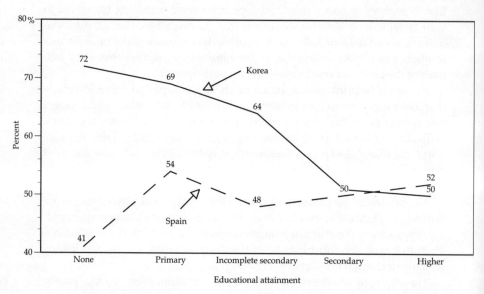

Figure B.2 Percent who watch television daily, by education: Spain, 1990; Korea, 1991

only the time spent attending to television but the content of the programs that displaces political awareness and in turn political action (Kellner 1991; Tetzlaff 1991; compare Norris 1996). Spectatorship and consumerism become surrogates for participation. Taken to the extreme, this argument posits an inverse association between exposure to television and political involvement: the more saturated the citizenry is by the former, the less there will be of the latter.

There is, on the other hand, the something-is-better-than-nothing hypothesis. With the slide in newspaper reading, television is the only mass medium capable of taking up the slack. It may increase political participation—of dubious quality perhaps, but participation nonetheless—from an otherwise abysmal low.

The complexities of television programming, together with the variable penetration of national cultures by the electronic as compared to the print media, make it unlikely that either one of these rather hyperbolic hypotheses will be universally borne out. It is nonetheless instructive to unpack the "national cultures" side of the equation along lines hinted at by the something-is-better-than-nothing hypothesis. Exposure to television is more likely to augment political participation in countries and within subcultures where the use of print media has not attained or has fallen below threshold levels; that is, where technological progress in the midst of social backwardness fortifies a popular culture with an oral-visual slant (Ong 1982).

Brazil, where literacy is less than universal and television is widely available, furnishes a prime example. In the virtual absence of stimulation from other sources, such as newspapers, television viewing generates a modicum of attention to the public sphere among sizable sectors of the population. Political participation will tend to pick up with almost any exposure to any public medium, and the most widely available medium in Brazil is television.

By the same token, in countries where functional literacy is widespread, extensive television viewing is likely to divert attention from things political. The case approaching an ideal type of this pattern seems to be Korea, with Spain somewhere behind, though certainly ahead of Brazil. To summarize: in predominantly print-oriented cultures, television tends to be something of a distraction from the business of political participation. In oral or predominantly visually oriented subcultures, on the other hand, exposure to television tends to stimulate political participation.

It would be stretching a point to contend that newspaper reading and television viewing act in divergent ways, even contingently, pulling up or pushing down levels of political participation in linear fashion depending on societal levels of effective literacy. What may in fact happen is more intriguing than this stylized conjecture. Figures B.3 and B.4 show the curve

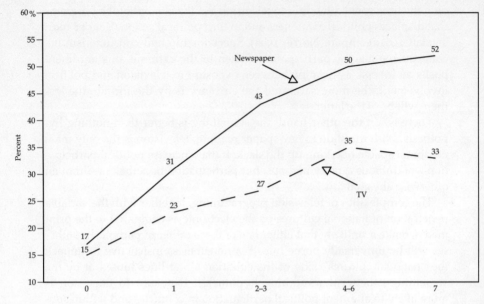

Figure B.3 Percent of Spaniards who report high political participation, by frequency of newspaper reading and television viewing, 1990

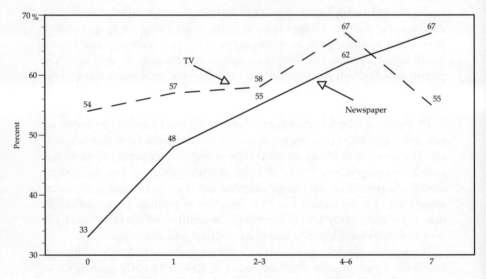

Figure B.4 Percent of Koreans who report high political participation, by frequency of newspaper reading and television viewing, 1991

of political participation as it follows newspaper reading and television viewing in Spain and Korea

The relationship between newspaper reading and participation is strongly, linearly positive not only in Spain and Korea but also in Brazil. The relation between television viewing and participation is curvilinear, however, rising with occasional and intermediate exposure only to peak, in the case of Spain, or fall off, in Korea, with greater dosages. (In Brazil from what we can tell, the link is more purely linear.) What the data pick up is a tendency, sharper in Korea than in Spain but obvious in both, for the time spent watching television to reach diminishing and ultimately counterproductive returns with regard to political participation. Heavy viewers seem to overdose and suffer a loss, slight but significant, of participatory vigor.

Even with the skimpy data at hand, more can be said about the repercussions of television viewing. Somewhat against the stereotype of youthful absorption in the electronic age, television serves in all three countries as a distraction mechanism more for the elderly than for the young. Newspaper reading and television viewing both follow life-cycle patterns but in distinctive ways. Attention to the print media peaks in the active employment years, then slopes downward. Attention to television rises pretty steadily with age. Furthermore, in Korea as compared to Spain, a clear gender difference surfaces. Korean women are less avid newspaper readers but, as typical homebodies, they are more habitual television watchers than men—a contrast that accentuates the discrepancy in participation between the sexes.

The most important configuration, however, remains the progressively curvilinear form of the relation between television viewing and political participation as we move from Brazil to Spain and on to Korea, compared to the consistently linear shape of the relation between newspaper reading and participation. Television viewing does not appear to affect the average, country-wide level of political participation. Countries with high television exposure also have high rates of political participation. Indeed, Korea comes out highest on both dimensions, and this finding confounds theories that presuppose an essentially zero-sum tradeoff between television exposure and civic engagement.

In Brazil, by and large, the more people read newspapers, the more they watch television, and the more they participate in politics. Even if the sheer amount of newspaper reading is meager and the time spent with television great, all these things go together. In Spain as well these activities tend to be mutually reinforcing but the connections are weaker (Mora 1994; Morán 1992). There the correlation between newspaper reading and television viewing (.19) is positive but mild.

The corresponding association in Korea is −.05, hardly enough to establish a massively negative link between the worlds of the print and electronic media, but suggestive of why political participation drops off at the highest levels of television viewing even as it increases regularly with newspaper reading. The environment of participation in Korea is one in which elites deal with a public—a predominantly male public—that prizes education and the written word. The seriousness accorded written communication reflects a formal style of social relations that privileges the print media. In Korea television is, if not the preserve, then the favored playground, a recreational release, for women.[2] By the Korean standard the context of participation in Brazil seems comparatively populist, allowing substantial play to television, relative to the print media, in mobilizing the public.

A final note about unconventional political behavior, or protest. There is no evidence to support the idea that new, elite-challenging forms of political action may be significantly tied to television viewing. As Figure B.5 indicates, protest activity tends to rise with newspaper reading and, in effect, with political sophistication. But aside from the difference between no and any viewing, its association with television exposure is flat.

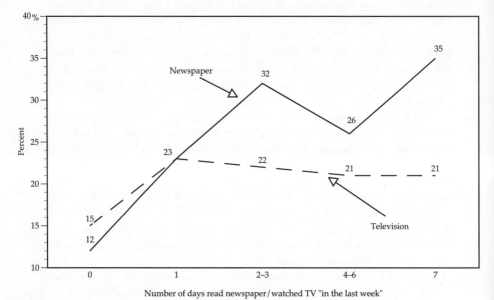

Figure B.5 Percent of Spaniards who report high political protest, by frequency of newspaper reading and television viewing, 1990

Notes

INTRODUCTION: FROM MAXIMALISM TO MODERATION

1. For example, more than a year before the death of Franco, a meeting of the "Junta Democrática" was held in Paris; this get-together was promoted by, among others, Santiago Carrillo, long-time secretary of the Communist Party of Spain, and Rafael Calvo Serer, representing the right-wing Catholic organization Opus Dei.

2. The statement, made by Manuel Fraga Iribarne, Minister of Culture during the last years of Franco and leader of the conservative Alianza Popular (later the Partido Popular) in the democratic era, has often been cited in newspaper reports. It was repeated in a personal interview with Barnes and McDonough in the early eighties.

3. Nancy Bermeo correctly makes the point that "moderation is not a prerequisite for the construction of democracy" (1997: 314). This observations holds for several cases of democratization, including that of the United States (Wood 1992). And in Spain, as we shall see, political moderation was orchestrated rather than automatic. In any case, our argument is not that moderation is a necessary, much less sufficient, condition for democratization. Instead we examine the effects of moderation—of specific tactics of conciliation—on selected aspects of the quality of democracy, e.g., participation.

4. Compare Schneider (1995: 231): "Future theory building on democracy, especially as it relates to substantive outcomes like political stability, economic reform and social justice, may be best advanced by focusing on less aggregate and sub-regime factors like intermediate organizations, state-society relations, and patterns of representation generally. Regime change has been the dominant dependent variable in the study of Latin American politics since at least the 1970s. Theorizing has been intense and stimulating but ultimately inconclusive, in part, I suspect, because the dependent variable is too aggregate."

5. The indicator of the king's popularity is drawn from a series of questions eliciting feelings about public figures. The introductory question read: "We would like to know where you stand with regard to some outstanding figures in Spain and the world today." A card was shown, with 1 signifying "Don't like" and 10 signifying "Like." The "ideology" question read: "For many people, political attitudes are of the left or the right. This is a [10-point] scale that goes from left to right. Thinking about your own political attitudes, where would you place yourself on it?" The samples are described later in this chapter.

6. The later situation corresponds approximately to the classic definition of political legitimacy, the earlier to a condition of political illegitimacy.

7. The classification of issues posits a hierarchy of volatility, not a continuum from the irrational to the rational. The tendency for identity cleavages to be less tractable than inter-

est conflicts doesn't render them—more precisely, the actors caught up in them—less rational. See Hardin 1995.

8. One issue elided here is the connection between economic modernization and political development defined as democracy, the complexities of which are examined in Feng 1997, Londregan and Poole 1996, and Przeworski and Limongi 1997.

9. Though Weingast (1997:62) doesn't consider the charisma surrounding individual elites as a way of transferring legitimacy to institutions, his comments on "veneration" come close to the understanding of political legitimacy presented here. Compare Kiser 1996.

10. The confusion about legitimacy reflects the variety of understandings of democracy found in contemporary theory, specifically with regard to substantive justice (Collier and Levitsky 1997). For a judicious coverage, see Holmes 1995. For a cogent presentation of the minimalist version, see Mueller 1992. Kekes 1997 lays out a neoconservative case for pluralistic democracy that transcends liberal proceduralism.

11. Some analyses (Foweraker 1989; Kurth and Petras 1993) suggest higher estimates of early-stage participation than we report. It should also be noted that voting turnout in Spain (about 74 percent), though below the European average (about 82 percent), is higher than in the United States (Justel 1995; Van Deth 1995: 70). Indeed, Dalton (1996: 45) equates electoral turnout in Spain with a 21-nation average, when the United States and Japan are included. However, though some of the literature on democratization in Spain stresses the "rebirth of civil society" (Carr 1993; Pérez Díaz 1993a), other analyses have revised downward early estimates or emphasized the decline or stagnation in participation (De Miguel et al. 1992; Pérez Díaz 1991b, 1993b). For a period around the death of Franco in 1975, some forms of participation—notably, strikes—surged. But by the end of 1977, well before democracy could be said to have been consolidated in Spain, such activities had trailed off (Hipsher 1996). In a recent diagnosis Pérez Díaz (1996:38) has argued that new forms of participation are emerging to make up for the shortfall in conventional participatory outlets. We discuss this possibility in the following pages.

12. The absence of comparable indicators for Portugal is especially bothersome not only because of its cultural and geographical proximity to Spain but also because of the different role that the Catholic church played in Portugal during the early years of democratization. There, a communist takeover was thought to be a serious possibility, and it wasn't until the heavily Catholic north mobilized against the communists that this threat diminished. For an overview, see Wiarda 1993. For a closer look, see Braga da Cruz 1995, 1996–1997.

13. One of the deceptively straightforward attractions of a comparison of Spain with other European democracies is that it sets up an explanation of Spain's participatory deficit as an after-effect of Francoism. Once Spain is set beside other former dictatorships with high levels of participation, such as Brazil and Korea, the spuriousness of such inferences becomes clear.

14. Tallying participation in post-authoritarian and post-communist democracies is a comparison waiting to be done. A few indicators of participation in some post-communist countries of Eastern and Central Europe can be found in Bruszt, Simon, and Wessels 1993.

15. Obligatory voting in Brazil boosts one type of participation, of course, but there is no evidence that this affects the range of behaviors we measure as political participation and voluntary association membership. See Ames 1995.

16. The negative association between religiosity and participation has often been presented as one element of a two-part package. The second part is the expected decline of religion and, with this drop, of the hold of religion as an impediment to political participation.

17. The five-point scale measuring "religiosity" derives from a pair of questions. The first elicits denominational affiliation. The second taps frequency of attendance at religious services; those without denominational attachment are at the bottom of the scale. Note 19 describes the indicators of participation.

18. The associations depicted in Figure I.3 are of the simplest, bivariate kind. Questions arise about the possible confounding effects of gender and age (among other factors),

which are known to be associated with religiosity almost everywhere. The multivariate analysis is presented in Chapter 6.

19. The participation index is adapted from Barnes, Kaase, et al. 1979. The scale was produced by summing the responses to six questions: "Some people dedicate a lot of time to politics, while others don't have time or perhaps aren't interested in taking part in political activities. I am going to read some things that people do and I would like you to tell me how often you do each one of them—frequently, sometimes, rarely, or never: (1) talk about politics with other people, (2) try to persuade someone of your political viewpoint, (3) work with people in this locality to solve local problems, (4) attend meetings or political rallies, (5) request something from a government functionary or politician, (6) work for a party or candidate." With each response scored between 1 ("never") and 4 ("frequently"), the highest possible score was 24. In Spain the lowest quartile was composed of those scoring between 4 and 6; the next quartile was made up of those scoring 7; the next-to-the-top quartile of those scoring 8 or 9; and the top quartile of those scoring 10 or above. "High political participation" describes the percentage ranking in this top quartile. The participation indices for Korea and Brazil use the cutting points set by the Spanish distribution.

20. The indicator of neighborliness comes from the question "How would you characterize your relations with your neighbors? Very close, close, off and on, or no contact?" The item is adapted from Sampson 1988. See also Litwak and Szelenyi 1969.

21. Data on membership in types of organizations are reported in Chapter 6. Ekiert 1991 draws out the distinction between "civil" and "political" society in cases of democratization. See also Linz and Stepan 1996 and Mishler and Rose 1997.

22. The correlations between associational membership and political participation are appreciable and very similar in Spain (r=.30), Brazil (.29) and Korea (.32). The correlations between neighborhood ties and associational membership and between neighborhood ties and political participation attain only borderline significance—on the order of .03. See Granovetter 1972.

23. In the 1990 Spanish survey, the following question was asked about six types of protest activity: "I would like you to tell me if you really *have* done any of these things, if you *would* do them, or if you would *not* do them under any circumstances: signing a petition; taking part in a boycott against something or somebody; participating in lawful demonstrations; participating in wildcat strikes; occupying buildings, factories, or railway stations; or filing a legal action." Responses to these indicators—that is, "yes" to whether an individual actually has taken part in such activities—are added to form a scale of "protest activity." The correlation of this scale with closeness to neighbors is −.18, with membership in voluntary associations .27, and with the conventional participation scale .45. Notice that the connection between neighborhood ties and conventional and unconventional participation is either weak (see note 22) or negative, suggesting the insulation of such bonds from "the public sphere." One case in which a forceful association between neighborhood networks and broader collective action has been documented is nineteenth-century France, e.g., during the Paris Commune (Gould 1995: 153–94).

24. The 1993 Brazilian survey asked: "We would like to know how often you participate in the following activities: sign a protest manifesto or list of demands; take part in a demonstration for or against the government or for any cause; take part in strikes." The correlation of the scale formed from these three indicators with closeness to neighbors is −.04, with voluntary association membership .29, and with conventional participation .35—quite in line with the Spanish configuration.

25. Data are composed of four national surveys of Spaniards 16 years of age and older conducted in June, 1978 (n = 3,004), in December 1979–January 1980 (3,014) in October–November 1984 (2,994), and in October-November 1990 (3000). The first two surveys were based on quota sampling at the individual level with selection by categories of age and sex. Provinces and then counties were selected by probability-proportional-to-size criteria, as were *secciones* (roughly, polling-booth areas); then quotas by age and sex were drawn. Sup-

plemental interviews, based on quota sampling, were conducted to bring the *n* to around 3,000. In 1984 and 1990, although the provinces and counties that fell in the sample differed from those in the first two surveys, the same procedure for choosing sampling points was followed. However, respondents for the third and fourth surveys were chosen by means of random selection of households and of individuals within households.

26. The Korean survey, directed by Doh C. Shin and Myung Chey, was conducted in November 1991 under the auspices of the Institute of Social Sciences at Seoul National University. A total of 1,187 personal interviews were conducted with voting-age Koreans (age 20 and older), using a probability sample to represent the adult population of South Korea resident in households. The Brazilian survey (*n* = 2,499) was directed by José Álvaro Moisés of the University of São Paulo and administered by Data Folha in March 1993. The population sampled included voting-age Brazilians (18 years and older) resident in households. The country was initially divided into four regions: South, Southeast, Northeast, and North/Center-West. Within each region, municipalities were grouped according to their socioeconomic level. Within each municipality, capitals and cities with populations larger than 500,000 were automatically included. Other localities within the municipalities were chosen according to population-size criteria. Random sampling was then used to select neighborhoods, streets, and individuals. Outside of surveys conducted by the Brazilian census bureau itself, this is probably the closest to a truly national sample of Brazilian adults.

27. De Laiglesia 1989 assembles a superb visual record of the period 1939–89, using photographic archives.

28. Senior military officers objected to taking the political opening this far. When Suárez used computer output from recent surveys to show key officers that the Communist party of Spain had the support of less than ten percent of the electorate, their opposition softened. The surveys had been conducted under the auspices of the Centro de Investigaciones Sociológicas, a research unit established during the last decade of the Franco regime, that reported directly to the head of government. Compare Brace and Hinckley 1992 and Herbst 1993.

29. The size of the electorate had doubled from Republican times: from 13.6 million to 26.8 million.

30. It took a while for the "statutes of autonomy" to be formalized. Official approval for the Basque Country accord came through in December 1979, along with that of Catalonia. The status of Madrid, the seventeenth "autonomous community," was made official in February 1983.

31. The representation of Suárez's party fell from 168 to 13 parliamentary seats.

32. In the nineties other general strikes of regional scope would be called—for example, in October 1991 in Asturias, and in Galicia in April 1992.

33. As with the use of public opinion polls to sanction the legalization of the Communist party, survey data came in handy in marketing the government's position on NATO membership. The political consultant who, after extensive polling, succeeded in framing the official question that yielded a "yes" majority was rewarded with the ambassadorship to the United States.

1. RETHINKING DEMOCRATIC LEGITIMACY

1. The percentages reporting affiliation with any religious denomination in 1978, 1980, 1984, and 1990 were, respectively, 78, 78, 83, and 83. This indicator of religion says nothing about frequency of church attendance, devotional practice, and the like. Religious affiliation in Spain over a longer period is similar to the Catholic experience in the United States: a drop in the early 1960s and early 1970s following Vatican II and then a leveling-off (Pérez Vilariño and Schoenherr, 1990; Sasaki and Suzuki, 1987). The mean positions on the left-right continuum for 1978, 1980, 1984, and 1990 were 4.4, 4.5, 4.6, and 4.4 (1 = left . . . 10 = right).

2. As noted in the Introduction, religiosity is measured along a 5-point scale running from "no religion" to "devout" (*muy practicante*). This is a powerful but unidimensional indicator. For a review of progress in measurement, confined to the American context, see Leege, Kellsted, and Wald 1990; see also Díaz Salazar and Giner 1993 and Montero 1993a.

3. The questions read: "I would like to ask you about some of the things which you might be satisfied or dissatisfied with in our country. A 1 on this scale means that you are totally dissatisfied or very unhappy, and a 10 means that you're completely satisfied or very pleased. Are you satisfied or dissatisfied with the way democracy is working nowadays in Spain? . . . Taking everything into account, are you satisfied or dissatisfied with the present government? . . . And with the governments of the last 10 years of the Franco regime?"

4. The switch from positive to negative in the correlations between left-right placement and government support, without much change in the absolute magnitude of the correlations, does not substantiate the case for overall depolarization. The reversal is readily explained as reflecting the circumstantial change from a center-right to a center-left government in 1982. It is the shrinking size of the coefficients, regardless of their sign, that indicates declining polarization.

5. Even the connection between positions on religion-related issues (e.g., abortion) and support for or opposition to the government is weak to the point of insignificance. This conclusion is documented in Chapter 4.

6. The fact that satisfaction with government and satisfaction with the way democracy has been working are partially distinct should not be taken to mean that the latter measures political legitimacy, as opposed to the "popularity" tapped by the indicator of government support. The two measures are strongly related. Nevertheless, it is worth noting that the correlations decline over the course of the 1978, 1980, 1984, and 1990 surveys. The correlations are respectively .81, .68, .57 and .59.

7. Satisfaction with "the last ten years of the Franco regime" goes up from 1978 (3.6) through 1980 (3.7) to 1984 (4.1). But this does not constitute evidence of growing nostalgia. The more recent the survey, the fewer the Spaniards who remember the Franco period; the 1984 interviews elicited many more "don't knows" than the 1978 survey. The dwindling group of those who do know are older and relatively conservative. A fuller technical discussion is given in Chapter 2, note 3.

8. As more and more regimes have democratized, survey researchers have begun to frame questions about political legitimacy in terms of comparisons with evaluations of the preceding systems (Morlino and Montero 1993). Useful as they are, these questions concentrate on whether or not people reject the old regime, while presupposing that they discern the differences between old and new. See also Montero, Gunther, and Torcal 1997.

9. The multidimensional approach to political legitimacy is "impure," that is, it mixes performance, output criteria, with presumably higher-order standards (compare Montero 1993b; Montero and Gunther 1994). But this is not the same as reducing legitimacy to effectiveness. Our point is that overall regime differences must be recognizable despite whatever functional similarities exist between them.

10. This is not to deny the possibility of estimating the (il)legitimacy of long-standing democracies. But the results so far have been inconclusive. See Weatherford 1992, Weil 1985, 1989, and the literature cited therein. Samuelson 1995 gives a nontechnical update on measures of political legitimacy for the United States.

11. A similar situation holds for emerging democracies elsewhere (Rose and Mishler 1994); see also Schuman and Scott 1989.

2. GAUGING POLITICAL LEGITIMACY

1. The items regarding trust in government, government for the few/many, and tax expenditure were translated from the standard questions originally used in the National

Election Studies conducted by the University of Michigan's Center for Political Studies (Miller, Miller, and Schneider 1980). The election question reads: "Do you believe that elections are the best system for choosing the government and the authorities of the country, or do you believe that they are not the best system?" The congress question reads: "Do you believe that we need a congress of deputies and a senate or could we get along without them?" The remaining question reads: "Do you think that Spain should be a monarchy, or that Spain should be a republic?"

2. Breakdowns of these measures by partisan identification are reported in full in McDonough, Barnes, and López Pina 1986b.

3. In 1984 the correlation between age and overall satisfaction with the Franco regime was .26; the corresponding figures for the UCD and PSOE governments were .15 and .08. Age is positively related to support for any government, although more so in the case of conservative ones. It is clear that many younger Spaniards have no opinion of Francoism. In 1984, of the cohort aged 16–19 years, one-third gave no opinion about the Franco regime. For the cohort aged 20–29 years the figure is 15%; for the cohort aged 30–39, 14%; and so on, until only 9% of 60 years of age and older expressed no opinion. Thus the steady increase in favorable ratings of Franco can be deceptive unless it is understood that they are concentrated in segments of the population that are dying off. Demographic replacement works in favor of the democratic regime.

4. We use oblique rather than orthogonal rotation. The promax algorithm is a version of oblique rotation, performed after computation of a varimax (orthogonal) rotation that gives evidence of a correlation between dimensions (Mulaik 1971: 300–304). Factor analyses of the 1978 and 1980 data, which give essentially the same configuration as that reported here, are presented in McDonough and López Pina 1984.

5. Our method can fail to pick up significant differences between political systems when functional similarities—for example, economic success or, conversely, continued economic failure—override potential contrasts in institutional form. Such cases, in which comparatively superficial differences in the type of government are blurred by underlying continuities in the performance of governments, in one or more crucial domains, are conceivable. Transitions from highly successful cases of authoritarian capitalism may be the likeliest candidate for such a nontransformation.

The Korean survey sets up a test case for just such a possibility. There, the early days of democratization were marked by perhaps even greater caution than during the onset of the Spanish transition. The economy was doing well under the old regime, and there was some reluctance to fix what did not appear to be broken. As in Spain, only more so, similarities between the economic strategies of authoritarian and democratic capitalism in Korea—not to mention continuities in the military origins of old and new political leaders—occluded the contrast between regimes (Park 1991).

As in Spain, the authoritarian system does better in the eyes of Koreans as far as law and order are concerned. What's more, the military regime outdoes its democratic successor in perceived economic performance. This invidious comparison didn't take hold in Spain (recall Table 2.2) until the early eighties, when the new democracy had been around for a while and the economy had yet to pick up. But the newborn democracy in Korea gets a slightly higher rating on social equity. And, despite the positive memories of control and prosperity under the military, Koreans give the democratic system a higher rating overall (4.4) than the authoritarian one (4.2), though the margin is not overwhelming.

Furthermore, like the Spanish, Koreans did indeed separate the regimes at the same time that they perceived a good deal of continuity between them. Two dimensions, one linked to the old and the other to the new regime, emerge. Even so, the authoritarian and democratic factors are strongly correlated. Remarkably, the correlation in Korea (.50) is almost exactly the same as in Spain (.49) for the corresponding time period—that is, for the comparison of the first democratic government with the authoritarian past reported in Figure 2.1. Since that time, especially with the prosecution of Chun Doo Whan and Roh Tae

Woo under charges of corruption and abuse of power, the popular association between the regimes has probably dropped more precipitously than it has in Spain. For a full account, see McDonough and Shin 1995.

6. Felipe González, the leader of the socialists, is seen largely as a center-left figure. The one polarizing chord struck by González occurs in 1984, in relation to the summary scores for the Franco dimension: the authoritarianism-González correlation is $-.25$. The coming to power of the PSOE aroused the potential for countermobilization on the right—a reaction encouraged by the disintegration of the center-right and substantiated by the increase in the vote for Fraga's right-wing forces in the 1982 election won by the socialists. The sign of distancing between González and the Francoists suggests a shift toward expectations of social democratic policies.

7. This progressive dissociation may seem to indicate a waning of commitment to the new regime. While the possibility cannot be ruled out, the statistical relation remains very high, and an interpretation of indifference based on this evidence would be alarmist. Furthermore, the connection between satisfaction with democracy and attachment to Franco, never very strong, became weaker, to the point that by 1984 the association turned negative, corroborating an antipathy between authoritarian and (social) democratic orientations. The 1978 correlation is .13; in 1980, .10; and in 1984, $-.17$.

8. Multiple classification analysis is used instead of ordinary least squares to unclutter presentation. For example, dealing with "region" in OLS would require a long list of dummy variables and a corresponding proliferation of coefficients. We ran estimates using standard regression analysis; the results are the same as those obtained from MCA.

9. The MCA coefficients alone are opaque regarding the direction of statistical associations. None of the coefficients has a sign, since a predictor can be a nominal attribute. Without going through a predictor-by-predictor account, one can note that the relationships work in expected ways. For example, as the beta of .30 indicates, orientations toward the Franquist system vary sharply (and linearly) with religiosity, while the link of the new regime with religiosity is irregular and washed-out (beta = .06). "Region" (of residence) is the only less-than-ordinal predictor. Basques and Catalans are the least favorable to Francoism. Although it remains important, the center-vs.-periphery conflict is considerably more attenuated in the case of the democratic factor. For an exposition of the statistical technique, see Andrews, Morgan, Sonquist, and Klem 1973.

10. The emphasis here is on trust rather than on the proliferation of voluntary associations. While the two may be related, authoritarian regimes—more precisely, authoritarian societies—can be imagined in which there are a fair number of associations, more or less autonomous, but little interpersonal trust.

11. The question reads: "To get ahead, people need to have confidence and feel that they can trust themselves and others. How much do you believe you can trust . . . ?"

12. Note that feelings toward González are correlated as strongly with the political system as with the government mechanics factor, lending González a "founding father" status and an air of indispensability that no other politician in Spain enjoyed.

3. THE TRANSFORMATION OF THE
AGENDA OF PUBLIC OPINION

1. In the 1978 survey we repeated a battery of questions concerning the responsibility of government for various issues that had been asked in eight other nations (Barnes, Kaase, et al. 1979). Spaniards assigned higher levels of responsibility to government than did citizens of the other industrial democracies. On a scale from 1 to 5, the Spanish average was 4.7 for governmental responsibility for material well-being. Britain and Italy followed at 4.4. The Spanish average for governmental responsibility for social equity was 4.0; Italy came in second at 3.1. See McDonough, Barnes and López Pina 1984.

2. The questions posed in 1980 read: "Now I'm going to ask you your impressions

about how things are going in Spain. Do you think that in some respects life in Spain has gotten worse in the past two years? (If yes, in what respects?) Do you think that in some respects life in Spain has gotten better in the past two years? (If yes, in what respects?)"

3. The 1-to-10 left-right continuum is aggregated here into a 5-point scale; 1–2 = "left", 3–4 = "left-center," etc.

4. Insofar as conservatism was bound to historical factors and not just to the life-cycle, demographic renewal also eroded the bases of political reaction.

5. The history of this shift within the Spanish parties has yet to be written. But there are all sorts of telling anecdotes, such as the refusal of the right-wing leader, Fraga Iribarne, to apply makeup before televised debates.

6. In order to avoid clutter, Figures 3.1 and 3.2 include only the three most frequent response categories. For the "How have things gotten worse?" question, "crime" (categorized separately from law and order), "everything," and "politics in general" ranked fourth, fifth and sixth, respectively. For the "How have things improved?" question, "everything" and "law and order" ranked fourth and fifth.

7. We have no direct evidence on this point. One might build a case for it using time-series data gathered by the Centro de Investigaciones Sociológicas; see, for example, *Datos de opinión* 1989.

8. As we noted in Chapter 1, the beta coefficients in multiple classification analysis carry no sign. Except for education, they can be imagined as positive. The more religious, the more supportive of the UCD government; the higher the class identification, the more supportive of the UCD government, and so on. Only in the case of education is the relationship inverse. Those with higher education tend to be less supportive of the government. In Spain as in many other countries, a penchant for political criticism goes with education. A somewhat weaker but still significant relationship between education and satisfaction/dissatisfaction with the socialist governments developed after 1982.

9. The values of the dependent variable, government support, for each category of the predictors are not shown here. The data contain no surprises.

10. The actual audience for these spectacles, however, has probably increased. Spaniards can watch bullfights on television in the comfort of their homes and bars, in living color, with instant replay.

4. THE GOLDEN DECADE OF THE SOCIALISTS

1. Interview with Julio Feo, May 7, 1988.

2. The habit of reliance on the state should not be understood as an invariant norm of Spanish political culture, though it is clearly more "traditional" than economic liberalism. As noted below, it is tied in with distributive norms—that is, with criteria of social fairness. These criteria are also very strong but they show signs of changing toward greater acceptance of inequality, as we shall see.

3. The question reads: "Do you think there should be a great deal of difference, some difference, or almost no difference in how much people in different occupations earn?"

4. When the question regarding equity of distribution was asked in a series of surveys conducted during 1990–91 in several countries of Eastern Europe, the results resembled the American pattern more closely than the Spanish—a symptom of the general though by no means uniform revulsion against the egalitarian norms of communist regimes. The surveys were directed by László Bruszt and Janos Simon. The results of applying the question in Brazil and Korea were the opposite—much closer to the Spanish configuration than to the American.

5. For an insightful discussion of the values vs. interests distinction that is pertinent to the cross-national cultural vs. economic comparison presented here, see Chong 1996.

6. The questions read as follows: "I would like to know your opinion about how Felipe González has been doing. As *president of the government* would you say that he has been

'very good' . . . 'not good at all'? How about the way he's been *handling the economy*? And how about the way he's been dealing with Spain's *relations with other countries*?"

7. The reservoir of goodwill in the foreign policy area served the socialists well in early 1986, when Spain's candidacy for membership in the European Community was accepted, and when a close referendum ratified the country's entrance into NATO.

8. The questions read as follows: "We'd like to know how people are doing economically. As for you and the members of your family who live with you, would you say that your economic situation over the past years is much better, a bit better, about the same, a bit worse, or much worse? And the economic situation of you and your family during the next year? Better, about the same, or worse? In your opinion, regarding the economic situation of you and your family, has the economic policy of the government made things much better . . . much worse? And the Spanish *economy as a whole*, over the *last twelve months*, would you say that it is much better . . . much worse? During the *next twelve months*? In your opinion, have the economic and tax policies of the government made the economy of the country much better . . . much worse?"

9. The questions (interspersed with other items not shown here) read as follows: "I'd like to ask you some questions about economic conditions. In respect to the situation of Spain during the time that the present government has been in power, since 1982, would you say that the economic situation of the country has improved, has worsened, or has stayed about the same? Regarding the future, do you expect that in the next year the economic situation of the country will improve, worsen, or stay the same? In comparison with the last ten years of the Franco government (1965–1975), could you tell me if the economic situation of the country has improved, worsened, or stayed the same? Compared with the majority of the countries of Western Europe, do you believe that economically Spain is doing better, the same, or worse? Could you tell me if, under the socialist government, corruption [*corrupción/el tráfico de influencias*] has increased, stayed the same, or decreased? Could you tell me if under the socialist government street crime [*la inseguridad ciudadana*] has increased . . . ? Regarding public morals [*la moralidad publica*], do you think that in Spain things have improved, stayed the same, or gotten worse since the last ten years of the Franco government? Do you believe that the family as an institution is stronger, the same, or weaker now than during the last ten years of the Franco government? Compared with most people around you [*que le rodea/de su ambiente*], do you think that financially you're doing better, the same, or worse? In comparison with the life your parents had at your age, do you think that financially speaking you're better off, the same, or worse off?"

10. This "surplus support" contrasts with the generally sorry state of the post-communist economies of the former Soviet-bloc countries (Bruszt and Simon 1991).

11. Of course, a negative result, in which the present government actually loses support when compared with its antecedent, is also possible, as happens in some post-communist countries (McDonough 1995).

12. Alcaide Inchausti (1989–90, 1994) gives a somewhat more cautious overview of socialist policies; see also Atkinson, Rainwater, and Smeeding 1995, Bandrés Moliné 1991, Muñoz de Bustillo Llorente 1990, and Wolf 1995.

13. The questions read: "During the time the present socialist government has been in power, would you say that the condition of the working class has improved, has gotten worse, or has stayed about the same as before? And the middle class? The upper classes? And in comparison with the situation during the last ten years of the Franco government, would you say that the working class . . . ?"

14. Not that relations between the PSOE and sectors of the working class have been smooth. The hardships associated with industrial restructuring and persistently high unemployment have led to occasional confrontations (Campos and Alvarez 1990). After 1990, economic growth slowed and unemployment, after dipping a bit, climbed again (Cohen 1992; Hooper 1993). More recent evidence indicates that the perceptions of fairness that suffuse our data have diminished; see Pradera 1992.

15. Some of the items are derived from questions developed by Feldman (1983) and used in the 1984 National Election Study in the United States. In order to streamline presentation, Table 4.6 omits the "strongly agree/strongly disagree" differentiation of response categories in the raw data.

16. Linz 1984 presents similar findings about the "contradictory" preferences of Spaniards on economic issues.

17. From the commonalities it can be seen that some of the items that remain in the analysis (for example, "fewer services" or "business taxes") do not load heavily on any of the dimensions, even though the empirical pattern is sufficiently clear to justify their retention.

18. Since the tax factor doesn't correlate with anything of relevance, it is dropped from the remainder of the presentation. Nevertheless, this set of nonfindings has some importance, since it doesn't seem to be unique to Spain. It accords with the conclusions of Hansen's study (1983) in the United States: that public opinion is irrelevant to the formation of tax policy because of, among other things, a dissociation between taxing and spending decisions. Since direct taxation and withholding are recent phenomena in Spain, it is little wonder that public opinion on such issues is unformed; compare Ladd 1985.

19. The association of the welfare-populism orientation with education and income (and class identification) is significantly negative: the better-educated and the well-to-do tend not to favor statist policies. The correlations of education and income with the free-enterprise factor are also negative, although much less strongly so. Ideological *tendance* counts for more than "objective" position in the class structure as an influence on positive commitment to the norms of laissez-faire.

20. This difference between the structural bases of the left and the cultural-ideological bases of the right should not be exaggerated. Yet it does help account for the catch-all nature of modern-day electioneering by the PSOE. A key factor reinforcing the slippage between the structural demographics of center-leftism in Spain and leftist ideology is the weakness of party organization and partisan identification (Barnes, McDonough, and López Pina 1985), a question that we explore in Chapter 5.

21. The dependent variable, government popularity, is a four-point scale formed from the responses to the following question: "We would like to know your opinion about how Felipe González is doing. As president of the government, would you say that (1) you approve of him completely, (2) approve more or less, (3) disapprove somewhat, or (4) disapprove completely?"

22. The new economic questions are: "We would like to know how people are doing economically, you and the members of your family who live with you. Would you say that over the past year your economic situation has gotten (a) much better, (b) somewhat better, (c) stayed the same ... (e) much worse?" "Now let's talk about the situation of you and your family over the next year. Do you think it will be (a) better, (b) the same, or (c) worse?" "Do you believe that the economic policy of the government has influenced how you and the members of your family are doing economically? (a) Much improved, (b) improved a bit ... (e) much worse." "And the Spanish economy as a whole, would you say that over the last twelve months it has been (a) much better ... (e) much worse?" "And for the next twelve months ... ?" "Do you believe that the economic and tax policies of the government have worked so that the economy of the country is (a) much better ... (e) much worse?" "As for the way Felipe González has been handling the economy, would you say that you (a) fully approve, (b) partly approve, (c) partly disapprove, or (d) disapprove completely." The questions are adapted from the American National Election Study.

23. A cautionary note is in order. Age is so entangled with religiosity and education that some multicollinearity is present. In the early days of democracy in Spain, when memories of Francoism were fresh, age (and religiosity) came into play as determinants of government support when the new regime was set against the old one. Younger Spaniards disproportionately favored democratic governments. It seems likely that after the socialists had

been in power for more than a decade and their distributive program had begun to take effect, the contrast with Francoism would be practically meaningless and their support among the aged would be considerable.

24. Again, the failure of the welfare populism and free-enterprise indices to correlate more strongly with left-right orientation (recall Table 4.8) is indicative of the fragility of economic substance behind popular ideology in Spain.

25. The relevant questions read: "The best thing for a woman is to keep busy with household responsibilities" (completely agree ... completely disagree), and "Abortion should be allowed for every woman on demand." "Political interest" is a 4-point scale derived from the standard query "How interested would you say you are in politics?"

26. The privatization and marketization scenarios associated with economic shock treatment in some post-communist societies are liable to be more extreme than in post-authoritarian settings (Holmes 1997).

5. IDENTITIES, IDEOLOGIES, AND INTERESTS

1. To be fair, diagnoses of Spanish political culture as less than hysterical antedate democratization, going back at least as far as Franco's later, managerial years. Some historians have pointed to evidence showing that even during the Civil War Spanish political culture was probably less radicalized than literary treatments of the period suggest (Aviv and Aviv 1981). See also Amelang 1993 and Cruz 1996.

2. Fearon and Laitin (1996) demystify the supposition of "ubiquitous violence" associated with ethnic tensions. Our point is not that all or even most such tensions erupt in violence but rather that rivalries based on identity tend to be more difficult to adjudicate than, for example, issues framed as interest conflicts.

3. The locus classicus for the analysis of the rise of nationalism over local attachments is Andersen 1991.

4. The parishes of the Catholic church have come closest to providing a built-in organizational lever for conservatives. However, although the manpower crisis is not quite so acute as in Latin America, priests have become increasingly thin on the ground, and without this clerical presence the organizational capacity of the church has weakened (Díaz Salazar 1981).

5. Geographic mobility varies greatly across regions as well as over time. Twenty-nine percent of the respondents in our 1984 survey claim to have been born outside the province in which they reside. The three regions with the highest proportions of immigrants are Catalonia (49%), Madrid (48%), and the Basque country (33%). The cosmopolitan nature of Madrid is not surprising; in Catalonia and the Basque country, the large proportions of immigrants belie the stereotypes of regionalism. It is the poorest provinces—Estremadura and Galicia—that are demographically the most nativist; few Spaniards move there from elsewhere.

6. The questions are of the form "In general, how close do you feel toward the working class? and the middle class ... ?" Close is 1, distant is 10. The Spanish questionnaire uses the official term *comunidad autónoma*—literally, "autonomous community." The *comunidad autónoma* can be either a former province or a regional agglomeration of provinces such as the Basque country.

7. Here a methodological difficulty should be recognized. Because of the large number of autonomous communities in Spain, it makes no sense to elicit respondents' feelings about each of them separately. Most Spaniards do not have *sentimientos* regarding those communities individually. Hence we use an omnibus item directed at feelings toward "people from other communities." Still, the simplification raises doubts about the comparability of the regional items with the class and religious indicators. The latter incorporate exhaustively symmetrical comparisons; the former do not. In order to mitigate this difficulty, we added two questions, one for all respondents except those resident in Catalonia

and the second for all except those resident in the Basque country. They are, respectively, "How close do you feel toward the Catalans?" and "How close do you feel toward the Basques?" The results (not shown here) indicate that the Catalans and, even more, the Basques tend to be held in lower esteem by their fellow Spaniards than the generic "people from other communities." The average closeness score for the Catalans is 4.3 and for the Basques 4.2; the corresponding score for "people from other communities," depending on whether respondents are natives or migrants, is 5.6 and 6.1. This result suggests, first, that the distance felt by Basques and Catalans toward Spain may be reciprocated by Spaniards when the objects of concern become Basques and Catalans. It also suggests that the gap between center and periphery may be wider than reliance on the tripartite Spain/own community/others approach indicates.

8. Age divisions with regard to economic issues are more prominent in post-communist societies, as opportunities open up for the energetic and the skilled and as inflation erodes fixed pensions.

9. Using a five-point agree/disagree response format, the question reads: "Lo mejor que puede hacer una mujer es ocuparse de su casa." The item was used in the 1978, 1980, 1984, and 1990 surveys.

10. This figure uses the "business factor" scores presented in Chapter 4.

11. John Paul II became pope in 1978, and his "restorationist" project did not receive the impetus in Spain that it did in Eastern Europe, notably in Poland. Beginning in the late eighties, the pope initiated a wave of beatifications—for example, of clergy martyred during the Civil War, and of the Spanish founder of Opus Dei. But the time had passed for re-founding the Spanish equivalent of a Christian Democratic party. Compare Kalyvas 1996.

12. Another difficulty with regard to "the mobilization of religion" in Spain, one that we explore in detail in Chapter 6, should be noted: the traditional link between religiosity and political nonparticipation.

13. The weakness of institutional expression and of ideological intensity in class antagonism has brought Spain close to what appears to be a Euro-American norm. See Brooks 1994, Kelley and Evans 1995, and Ringen 1998.

14. Similar correlations have been found between electoral shares of pre- and postwar parties in France and Italy (Warner 1994). See also Bennett 1995.

15. It is important to remember what lies behind the discussion of party constancy and the lack of it: the weakness of attachment to organized parties as compared to the strength of adherence to left-right *tendance*. It is equally important not to sever culture (*tendance*) from identification with party organizations as if the two inhabited "unreal" and "real" spheres of politics. The slippage between the cultural and institutional facets of partisanship is only partial. Left-right placement (along with center-periphery sentiment) acts as an aligning mechanism for the various parties, which the electorate distinguishes pretty clearly along a progressive-conservative continuum.

16. The catastrophic version of this thesis has been challenged on two grounds. First, in many countries it is the incidence of party membership, relative to the available population, that has gone down, not the absolute numbers of party members (Katz and Mair 1994). Second, patterns vary so much from country to country that it is hazardous to speak of an overall "decline" (van Deth and Janssen 1994). Nevertheless, it is clear that since their heyday in the immediate postwar period, political parties in Western Europe and the United States have lost ground as agents of mass mobilization and as objects of political identification (Lawson and Merkl 1988).

17. Nonresponse for left-right placement holds steady around 25%. This sizable minority is off the ideological spectrum, somewhat as those without partisan attachment are outside the party system.

18. To place this in context: at .53 the temporal correlation of the left-right continuum is the second highest in the 1978–80 panel. The largest is religiosity: .55.

19. There are five variations, in descending order of frequency: no partisanship at time 1

and time 2 (39%); partisanship at time 1 but not at time 2 (22%); same partisanship at time 1 and time 2 (17%); no partisanship at time 1 but partisanship at time 2 (17%); and partisanship at time 1 and different partisanship at time 2 (6%).

20. Chhibber and Torcal 1997 analyze the rise of class voting during the nineties in Spain.

6. THE PUZZLE OF PARTICIPATION

1. On the other hand, in countries such as Brazil where the churches did promote participation at the time of political transition, the effect may be fairly enduring. The mobilization of landless peasants in Brazil in the second half of the nineties draws on support from religious activists (Petras 1997).

2. Though it has nothing to do with intercountry differences, age is of some interest because it captures the interpretive ambiguity of life-cycle versus generational or historical effects in changing rates of participation. Appendix A takes up this problem.

3. In the quantitative analysis we use "employment status" to signify both labor force participation and employment. Our actual measure is of employment (working versus not working), a subcategory of labor force participation. Though the survey data do not permit precise estimates of participation in the labor market, we retain the conceptual distinction because of the evident difference between the two, especially in the experience of women.

4. The specific activities, listed in the Introduction, include (1) discussing politics, (2) trying to persuade others of one's political viewpoint, (3) working with people to solve local problems, (4) attending meetings or political rallies, (5) requesting something from a civil servant or politican, and (6) working for a party or candidate.

5. Lemann (1996) hints at such a diagnosis.

6. This is the argument espoused by Pérez Díaz 1996.

7. The comparison must be treated gingerly because the indicators of protest behavior are not exactly comparable. For Spain in 1990, the proportion who claimed to have signed a petition is 32%, participated in a lawful demonstration 26%, filed a legal action 11%, taken part in a wildcat strike 9%, taken part in a boycott 6%, and occupied a building 5%. For Brazil in 1993, 27% claimed to have signed a petition or list of demands; 24% to have taken part in a demonstration; and 19% to have taken part in a strike, authorized or wildcat. When the measures are combined in additive indices, the results are the same for Brazil and Spain: 60% without participation, 20% taking part in at least one activity, and 20% taking part in two or more.

8. One possible indication of a real consequence is that, despite the fact that strike activity has fallen off since the very early days of the transition, Spain ranks second only to Greece in the European Community in working days lost through strikes. The annual average, from 1986 through 1990 (the years that coincided with an economic boom), was 647 days per 1,000 employees. In Greece the figure was 887. Third-place Italy was far behind with 271 ("After the Fiesta" 1992: 14). The annual average from 1991 through 1995 for Spain was 342 and for Greece 623 (International Labor Office 1996: 74–84, 1061–84). See also Wozniak 1991.

9. There may be still other types of social interactions with potential political implications that we have failed to consider. There is some evidence that Spaniards spend more time than other Europeans "schmoozing"— talking with friends in tapas bars, casual (not to say anarchic) socializing, "Mediterranean lounging," and so on. (Requena and Benedicto 1988; Requena Santos 1994; "Suecos y españoles . . . " 1992). Perhaps informal socializing substitutes for membership in organized associations, not to mention political activity. The possibility is intriguing. The task would be to figure out what the linkages are between this type of behavior, for which we have no measures, and more organized interaction. See Martín Serrano 1982.

10. "Education" is a 6-point measure covering "incomplete primary or less," "complete

primary," "incomplete secondary," "complete secondary," "incomplete higher," and "complete higher." The indicator of class identification is based on the question "To which class would you say your family belongs? Upper, upper-middle, lower-middle, or working class?" The newspaper-reading and television-viewing indicators are taken from questions that measured the frequency of these behaviors as "the number of days (0–7) during the past week." There is no measure of the frequency of newspaper reading in Brazil expressed in the number of days per week. There is a question, common to the political participation battery in all countries, about "how often you follow newspaper reports about politics" (1 = never . . . 4 = often). For our purposes, the trouble with this indicator is threefold: it differs from the measure of newspaper reading in Spain and Korea; it taps political news specifically rather than newspaper reading generally; and it is embedded in the political participation scale of the questionaire. Including the Brazilian measure in the regression analysis causes the model to explode: a very high coefficient of determination is attained, and "newspaper reading" turns out to be far and away the most important predictor. For these reasons we omit it from the Brazilian analysis.

11. Since the country samples differ in design, even though the question items and response coding are identical, we follow the conventional admonition against using standardized regression coefficients (betas) to compare the impact of predictors across countries. We report unstandardized regression coefficients and their corresponding t-values. Comparisons within countries across modes of participation are of course permissible. As for cross-country comparisons: because the means and variances of the predictors are similar (though not equivalent) across countries, we can estimate the relative impact of predictors as orders of magnitude, even if the precision of the coefficients is open to debate. In addition, in the case of the religious factor, there is no reason to doubt the reversal of the direction of its impact, from negative to positive, as we move from Spain to Brazil and Korea.

12. At the time of the 1991 survey, unemployment ran at less than 5% in Korea. In Brazil in 1993, unemployment was estimated in the 5–7% range (Instituto Brasileiro de Geografia e Estatística 1993). Neither of these estimates takes account of underemployment, which has traditionally been high in Brazil. Conversely, the double-digit unemployment figures for Spain do not take account of the off-the-books job market.

13. As indicated in the description of the samples in the Introduction, the Spanish respondents are somewhat younger (minimum age of respondent = 16) than either the Brazilian (minimum age = 18) or the Korean (minimum age = 20). It might be argued that the general tendency for the very young to participate less in politics could account for some of the participatory shortfall in Spain. But this happens not to be the case, so we work with the full sets of data from the three countries rather than standardize them by age.

14. It is risky to equate neighborhood ties with conviviality because of the link between these ties and religious practice. Neighborhood ties may be divisive where multiple religious denominations flourish, insofar as they encourage religious factionalism. See Sampson 1988.

15. It is ironic that a significant number of clerical leaders in Brazil, among them several bishops, had emigrated from Spain to escape the strictures of the Franco regime. The same holds true for other parts of Latin America, e.g., El Salvador (Whitfield 1994).

16. Presbyterians form the largest Protestant denomination in Korea, with evangelicals on the increase (Kim 1994). There is also a growing pentecostal-evangelical presence in Brazil, perhaps as large as 30 percent of the population (Berryman 1995; Damazio 1994; Dixon 1995; Ireland 1995; Krischke 1991; Maríz 1993; Smith 1994). In Spain non-Catholics remain an infinitesimal fraction even though practicing Catholics are uncommon. Our analysis concentrates on religiosity rather than denominational labels as determinants of participation. However, in Brazil and Korea, where the numbers permit, we divided the samples between Catholics and Protestants (mostly evangelicals in Brazil) and found no significant difference between the two, once religiosity was taken into account.

17. The ordinary least squares models used in Tables 6.1–6.3 are simplified in some re-

spects. Since the dependent variables have limited values—i.e., a dichotomy or a small range, as happens with our ordinal measures—application of an ordered logit algorithm may be preferable to OLS. Here we stick with OLS not only because it is likely to be more familiar but also because the results are fairly robust; they do not differ substantially from those generated by ordered logit. Second, we omit indicators such as political interest for two reasons: they tend to be highly correlated with the harder, baseline measures such as media exposure, and they add little to our understanding of cross-national differences in civic engagement. Not surprisingly, the effect of political interest on neighborhood ties is vestigial. Its importance increases, sensibly enough, as the dependent variables become more explicitly political. For an analysis that employs ordered logit techniques and includes political interest, see McDonough, Shin, and Moisés forthcoming. Third, the OLS results do not specify interaction terms between gender and employment or gender and religiosity. When the models are adjusted to include interactions, the results generally do not differ from those of the additive models. For a presentation of the analysis with interaction terms and using ordered logit, see McDonough, Shin, and Moisés 1998. Wright, Baxter, and Birkelund 1995 give an interesting report of the gender-interaction factor in cross-national research.

18. While the indicators of associational membership data drawn from the World Values surveys are close to ours, the measures of political participation are spottier. Even so, the association membership data provide a useful check on our estimates. The two coincide as orders of magnitude. Thus the World Values Study estimates for the percentage of respondents belonging to one or more associations are, for Spain, 23%; for Brazil, 43%; and for South Korea, 61%. The WVS estimate for Argentina is 24%. For the record, it is 71% for the United States. It is interesting that, by Latin American standards, Argentina is "European."

19. Analysts of collective behavior typically deal with this problem by sampling events rather than individuals. See McAdam, Tarrow, and Tilly 1996 and the literature discussed therein. For an imaginative statement of the need to move beyond "the multivariate causal paradigm" toward analytical narrative approaches to social explanation, see Abbott 1997.

20. With a tradition of low levels of conventional and high levels of unconventional political behavior, France may be the European country that most resembles Spain (Dalton 1996: 73–74).

21. The way to check this contention is to correlate left–right placement with religiosity—graphically, to construct a scatter plot with religiosity as the x variable and left–right placement as the y variable. The general tendency toward a connection between religosity and conservatism, though still significant, is much weaker in Brazil than in Spain.

CONCLUSION: THE MELLOWING OF MASS POLITICS

1. For a discussion of the role of elite strategy in the timing of democratization, see Achen 1996.

2. In two respects our classification of issues differs from that formulated by Inglehart (1988). It is less teleological; interest conflicts, for example, may be easier to deal with than identity conflicts, but whether they represent a step up on the evolutionary ladder is another question. Second, our scheme has no special place for "postmaterialist" issues, although some identity conflicts may fall in that category. Our tripartite classification of issues is more capacious than the erstwhile dichotomy between "status" or "symbolic" and "interest" politics (Sears et al. 1980), and our focus on the contents of the issues represents a departure from the custom of sorting through mass publics according to levels of cognitive sophistication, regardless of the substance of issues (Converse 1964; Feld and Groffman 1988). But the taxonomy alone says nothing about the future evolution of issue types.

3. Since religious observance is already so low in Spain, significant decline in it is unlikely, and even were it to decline further, the effect on political participation is by no means certain.

4. Studies of democratization that successfully join cultural and institutional explanations are extremely rare. Garvin 1996 is one example. For a comparably imaginative and eclectic study of revolution, see Goldstone 1991.

5. We correlated the trust items analyzed toward the end of Chapter 2 with the various indicators of participation presented in Chapter 6. Construing trust as one dimension and adding responses to all fifteen items to form a single scale, we find what looks like a gullibility syndrome emerging. The correlation of trust with education, for example, is strongly negative($-.22$) and with religiosity strongly positive (.36). Correlations of trust with the public or unorthodox types of participation are increasingly negative: .26 with neighborliness, $-.02$ with voluntary association membership, $-.04$ with conventional political participation, and $-.18$ with protest behavior. But when trust is broken down into the four component dimensions of public, political, associational, and religious and then correlated with the same measures of civic engagement, a different picture emerges. Trust is specialized, so to speak. The association between trust in politicians and conventional political participation, for example, is a sizable .18, whereas the association between trust in the church and religious figures and such activity is $-.20$ ($-.29$ if the referent is protest).

APPENDIX A

1. Folkways have gone commercial. In department stores in Madrid and other large cities of Spain, professional *brujas* (witches) can be hired to tell fortunes.

2. Devout women in Spain (as in Ireland) have so internalized church teaching that they tend to be more conservative than their male counterparts in matters of sexual doctrine, such as the legalization of divorce and abortion (Inglis 1987). Korean women, though generally more conservative than men, follow their presumptive self-interest in such matters; that is, they wind up taking relatively progressive positions in this area (DeVos and Sofue 1986; Kendall and Peterson 1983; Moon 1991; Wade and Seo 1996).

APPENDIX B

1. It is important to remember that all the indicators are comparable except for the measure of newspaper reading in Brazil, where 4–5 days were coded as one category and 6–7 days as another, thus truncating the full range. We limit the statistical presentation to Spain and Korea; textual references to the Brazilian pattern are based on empirical analysis using the less-than-perfect indicator for that country.

2. Although the fact doesn't affect the present argument, a degree of gender segregation exists in television programming in Korea. Much television programming in Korea, as in the United States and Europe, is directed to the consumer market and disproportionately to housewives. But the American presence gives the Korean public access to an Armed Forces channel, which emphasizes sports programs and caters more to a male audience.

References

Abbott, Andrew. 1997. "Of Time and Space: The Contemporary Relevance of the Chicago School." *Social Forces* 75: 1149–82.

Abramson, Paul R., and Ronald Inglehart. 1995. *Value Change in Global Perspective*. Ann Arbor: University of Michigan Press.

Achen, Christopher H. 1996. "The Timing of Political Liberalization: Taiwan as the Canonical Case." Paper presented at the annual meetings of the American Political Science Association, San Francisco, August 28–September 1.

Adriance, Madelaine Cousineau. 1995. *Promised Land: Base Christian Communities and the Struggle for the Amazon*. Albany: State University of New York Press.

"After the Fiesta." 1992. *Economist*, April 25, 3–18.

Aguilar, Paloma. 1995. "Political Learning and Historical Memory in the Spanish Transition (1975–1978): The Case of the Pro-amnesty Mobilizations." Paper presented at the annual meetings of the American Political Science Association, Chicago, August 31–September 3.

Alcaide Inchausti, Julio. 1989–90. "Política de rentas" [Incomes policy]. *Información Comercial Española*, December–January, 51–97.

———. 1994. "Distribución de la renta en la década socialista" [Income distribution in the socialist decade]. *El País*, July 10.

Alcobendas Tirado, Pilar. 1983. *Datos sobre el trabajo de la mujer en España* [Data on women and work in Spain]. Madrid: Centro de Investigaciones Sociológicas.

Allman, T. D. 1992. "The King Who Saved His Country." *Vanity Fair*, August, 154–72.

Almond, Gabriel, and Sidney Verba. 1963. *The Civic Culture*. Princeton: Princeton University Press.

Altares, Pedro. 1985a. "La tecnocratización del cambio" [The technocratization of change]. *El País*, January 26.

———. 1985b. "Reforma sin cambio" [Reform without change]. *El País*, March.

Alvarez-Bolado, Alfonso. 1976. *El experimento del nacional-catolicismo, 1939–1975* [The experiment of national Catholicism]. Madrid: Cuadernos para el Diálogo.

Amelang, James. 1993. "Society and Culture in Early Modern Spain." *Journal of Modern History* 65: 357–74.

Ames, Barry. 1995. "Electoral Strategy under Open-list Proportional Representation." *American Journal of Political Science* 39: 406–33.

Andersen, Benedict R. 1991. *Imagined Communities: The Changes and Spread of Nationalism*. Rev. ed. London: Verso.

Anderson, Charles W. 1970. *The Political Economy of Modern Spain: Policy Making in an Authoritarian System*. Madison: University of Wisconsin Press.

Anderson, Kristi. 1975. "Working Women and Political Participation, 1952–1972." *American Journal of Political Science* 19: 439–54.

Anderson, Kristi, and Elizabeth A. Cook. 1985. "Women, Work, and Political Attitudes." *American Journal of Political Science* 29: 606–25.

Andrews, Frank M., James N. Morgan, John A. Sonquist, and Laura Klem. 1973. *Multiple Classification Analysis*. Ann Arbor, Mich.: Institute for Social Research.

Argandoña, Antonio, et al. 1988. *La competitividad de la economía española: Determinantes Micro- y macroeconómicas* [The competitiveness of the Spanish economy: Micro- and macroeconomic determinants]. Madrid: Círculo de Empresarios.

Arjomand, Said Amir, ed. 1993. *The Political Dimensions of Religion*. Albany: State University of New York Press.

Atkinson, Anthony B., Lee Rainwater, and Timothy M. Smeeding. 1995. *Income Distribution in OECD Countries*. Paris: Organization for Economic Cooperation and Development.

Aumente, José. 1985a. "Habría otra alternativa posible?" [Could there be another alternative?] *El País*, June 29.

———. 1985b. "Dudas y ambigüedades en nuestra situación política." [Doubts and ambiguities in our political situation]. *El País*, June 30, 20.

Aviv, Aviva, and Isaac Aviv. 1981. "The Madrid Working Class, the Spanish Socialist Party, and the Collapse of the Second Republic (1934–1936)." *Journal of Contemporary History* 16: 229–50.

Baklanoff, Eric N. 1992. "The Political Economy of Portugal's Later Estado Novo: A Critique of the Stagnation Thesis." *Luso-Brazilian Review* 24: 1–17.

Baldwin, Peter. 1992. *The Politics of Social Solidarity: Class Bases of the European Welfare State, 1875–1975*. Cambridge: Cambridge University Press.

Bandrés Moliné, Eduardo. 1991. *Los efectos de los gastos sociales sobre la distribución de la renta en España* [The effects of social expenditures on the distribution of income in Spain]. Madrid: Instituto de Estudios Fiscales.

Barnes, Samuel H., Max Kaase, et al. 1979. *Political Action*. Beverly Hills, Calif.: Sage.

Barnes, Samuel H., Peter McDonough, and Antonio López Pina. 1985. "The Development of Partisanship in New Democracies: The Case of Spain." *American Journal of Political Science* 29: 695–720.

———. 1986. "Volatile Parties and Stable Voters in Spain." *Government and Opposition* 21: 56–75.

Barnstone, Willis. 1995. *Sunday Morning in Fascist Spain: A European Memoir, 1948–1953*. Carbondale: Southern Illinois University Press.

Bayón, Miguel. 1995a. "España es un país plenamente secularizado" [Spain is a fully secularized country]. *El País*, October 24.

——. 1995b. "La primera transición fue la religiosa" [The first transition was the religious one]. *El País*, October 24.

Beck, Ulrich. 1994. "The Reinvention of Politics: Towards a Theory of Reflexive Modernization." In *Reflexive Modernization: Politics, Tradition and Aesthetics in the Modern Social Order*, ed. Ulrich Beck, Anthony Giddens, and Scott Lash. Oxford: Polity.

Beckwith, Karen. 1986. *American Women and Political Participation: The Impacts of Work, Generation, and Feminism*. New York: Greenwood.

Bedeski, Robert E. 1994. *The Transformation of South Korea*. London: Routledge.

Beetham, David. 1991. *The Legitimation of Power*. London: Macmillan.

——. 1992. "Liberal Democracy and the Limits of Democratization." *Political Studies*, special issue, 40–53.

——. 1993. "In Defense of Legitimacy." *Political Studies* 41: 488–91.

Beiner, Ronald. 1992. *What's the Matter with Liberalism?* Berkeley: University of California Press.

Bellah, Robert N., and Philip E. Hammond. 1980. *Varieties of Civil Religion*. San Francisco: Harper & Row.

Beltrán Villalba, Miguel. 1992. "Terremotos en los cimientos de la estructura social española" [Earthquakes in the firmament of the Spanish social structure]. *Sistema* 16: 31–49.

Beltrán Villalba, Miguel, et al. 1984. *Informe sociológico sobre la juventud española, 1960–1982* [Sociological report on Spanish youth]. Madrid: Santa María.

Beniger, James. 1986. *The Control Revolution: Technological and Economic Origins of the Information Society*. Cambridge: Harvard University Press.

Bennett, Anne M. 1995. "Continuity in Party Systems and Individual Parties in Redemocratizing Countries." Paper presented at the annual meetings of the American Political Science Association, Chicago, August 31–September 3.

Bennett, W. Lance. 1993. "Constructing Publics and Their Opinions." *Political Communication* 10: 101–20.

Berger, Suzanne, ed. 1981. *Organizing Interests in Western Europe: Pluralism, Corporatism, and the Transformation of Politics*. Cambridge: Cambridge University Press.

Berger, Suzanne, and Ronald Dore, eds. 1996. *National Diversity and Global Capitalism*. Ithaca: Cornell University Press.

Berman, Sheri. 1997a. "Civil Society and the Collapse of the Weimar Republic." *World Politics* 49: 401–29.

——. 1997b. "Civil Society and Political Institutionalization." *American Behavioral Scientist* 40: 562–74.

——. 1997c. "The Life of the Party." *Comparative Politics* 30: 101–22.

Bermeo, Nancy. 1994. "Sacrifice, Sequence, and Strength in Successful Dual Transitions." *Journal of Politics* 56: 601–27.

——. 1997. "Myths of Moderation: Confrontation and Conflict during Democratic Transitions." *Comparative Politics* 19: 305–22.

Berryman, Phillip. 1995. "Is Latin America Turning Pluralist? Recent Writings on Religion." *Latin American Research Review* 30: 107–22.

Blackburn, Julia. 1992. *The Emperor's Last Island: A Journey to St. Helena.* New York: Random House.

Boix, Carlos. 1995. "Building a Social Democratic Strategy in Southern Europe: Economic Policy under the González Government, 1982–93." Working paper no. 69, Centro de Estudios Avanzados en Ciencias Sociales, Instituto Juan March, Madrid.

Boschi, Renato. 1987. *A arte da associacão: política de base e democracia no Brasil* [The art of association: Grass-roots politics and democracy in Brazil]. Rio de Janeiro: Vertice.

Brace, Paul, and Barbara Hinckley. 1992. *Follow the Leader: Opinion Polls and the Modern Presidents.* New York: Basic Books.

Brading, D. A. 1991. *The First America: The Spanish Monarchy, Creole Patriots, and the Liberal State, 1492–1867.* Cambridge: Cambridge University Press.

Brady, Henry E., Sidney Verba, and Kay Lehman Schlozman. 1995. "Beyond SES: A Resource Model of Political Participation." *American Political Science Review* 89: 271–94.

Braga da Cruz, Manuel. 1994. "O presidente da república na génese e evolução do sistema de governo português" [The president of the republic in the genesis and evolution of the Portuguese system of government]. *Análise Social* 29: 237–65.

———. 1995. "A participação social e política" [Social and political participation]. In *Portugal Hoje* [Portugal Today], ed. Eduardo de Sousa Fereira and Helena Rato. Lisbon: Instituto Nacional da Administração.

———. 1996–97. "A igreja na transição democrática portuguesa" [The church in the Portuguese democratic transition]. *Lusitania Sacra* 8–9: 519–36.

Bratton, Michael, and Nicolas Van De Walle. 1994. "Neopatrimonial Regimes and Political Transitions in Africa." *World Politics* 46:453–89.

Braun, Denny. 1997. *The Rich Get Richer: The Rise of Income Inequality in the United States and the World.* 2d ed. Chicago: Nelson-Hall.

Brehm, John, and Wendy Rahn. 1997. "Individual-Level Evidence for the Causes and Consequences of Social Capital." *American Journal of Political Science* 41: 999–1023.

Bresser Pereira, Luiz Carlos, José María Maravall, and Adam Przeworski. 1993. *Economic Reforms in New Democracies: A Social-Democratic Approach.* Cambridge: Cambridge University Press.

Brooks, Clem. 1994. "Class Consciousness and Politics in Comparative Perspective." *Social Science Research* 23: 167–95.

Brownlee, Marina S., and Hans Ulrich Gumbrecht, eds. 1995. *Cultural Authority in Golden Age Spain.* Baltimore: Johns Hopkins University Press.

Bruneau, Thomas C. 1982. *The Church in Brazil: The Politics of Religion.* Austin: University of Texas Press.

Bruszt, László, and János Simon. 1991. "The Great Transformation: Opinions on Democracy and Capitalism in Hungary." Paper presented at the Georgetown University workshop on Democratization and the European Public, Washington, D.C. December 10–14.

Bruszt, László, János Simon, and Bernhard Wessels. 1993. *Codebook of the International Survey on 'Political Culture, Political and Economic Orientations in Central and Eastern Europe during Transition to Democracy, 1990–1992.'* Berlin: Wissenschaftszentrum Berlin für Sozialforschung.

Buchanan, Tom, and Martin Conway, eds. 1997. *Political Catholicism in Europe, 1918–1965.* New York: Oxford University Press.

Bull, Martin J. 1993. "The Crisis of European Socialism: Searching for a (Really) Big Idea." *West European Politics* 16 (July): 413–23.

Burdick, John. 1993. *Looking for God in Brazil: The Progressive Catholic Church in Urban Brazil's Religious Arena.* Berkeley: University of California Press.

Bustello, Carlota. 1994. "La situación de las mujeres en la Unión Europea" [The situation of women in the European Union]. *Leviatán* 56 (Summer): 61–86.

Caciagli, M. 1984. "España 1982: Las elecciones del cambio" [Spain 1982: The elections of change]. *Revista Española de Investigaciones Sociológicas* 28: 85–118.

Callahan, William J. 1992. "Church and State in Spain, 1976–1991." *Journal of Church and State* 34: 502–19.

Campos, Angel, and José Manuel Alvarez. 1990. *Ayer, hoy y mañana del 14-D* [Yesterday, today, and tomorrow from December 14]. Madrid: Asemblea.

Carr, Raymond. 1993. "How Spain Regained Civil Society." *Times Literary Supplement*, October 15, 4–5.

Casado, Demetrio, et al. 1992. *Organizaciones voluntarias en España* [Voluntary organizations in Spain]. Barcelona: Hacer.

Casanova, José. 1993. *Public Religions in the Modern World.* Chicago: University of Chicago Press.

Cassel, Carol A. 1993. "A Test of Converse's Theory of Party Support." *Journal of Politics* 55: 664–81.

Castles, Francis G. 1994. "On Religion and Public Policy: Does Catholicism Make a Difference?" *European Journal of Political Research* 22: 19–40.

———. 1995. "Welfare State Development in Southern Europe." *West European Politics* 18: 291–313.

Catterberg, Edgardo. 1991. *Argentina Confronts Politics: Political Culture and Public Opinion in the Argentine Transition to Democracy.* Boulder, Colo.: Lynne Rienner.

Cavendish, James C. 1994. "Christian Base Communities and the Building of Democracy: Brazil and Chile." *Sociology of Religion* 55: 179–95.

Cazorla Pérez, José. 1990. "La cultura política en España" [Political culture in Spain]. In *España: Sociedad y Política*, ed. Salvador Giner. Madrid: Espase-Calpe.

Cebrián, Juan L. 1984. "Entre el poder y el cambio" [Between power and change]. *El País*, December 24.

———. 1985. *Crónicas de mi país* [Chronicles of my country]. Madrid: Ediciones El País.

Cheng, Tun-jen, and Eun Mee Kim. 1994. "Making Democracy: Generalizing the South Korean Case." In *The Politics of Democratization: Generalizing East Asian Experience*, ed. Edward Friedman. Boulder, Colo.: Westview.

Chhibber, Pradeep, and Mariano Torcal. 1997. "Elite Strategy, Social Cleavages, and Party Systems in a New Democracy: Spain." *Comparative Political Studies* 30: 27–54.

Cho, Byung Eun, and Hwa-Yong Shin. 1996. "State of Family Research and Theory in Korea." In *Intercultural Variation in Family Research and Theory*, ed. Marvin B. Sussman and Roma Stoval Hanks. New York: Haworth.

Chong, Dennis. 1996. "Values versus Interests in the Explanation of Social Conflict." *University of Pennsylvania Law Review* 144: 2079–135.

Clark, Donald N. 1995. "Growth and Limitations of Minjung Christianity in South Korea." In *South Korea's Minjung Movement: The Culture and Politics of Dissidence*, ed. Kenneth M. Wells. Honolulu: University of Hawaii Press.

Cleary, Edward L. 1997. "The Brazilian Catholic Church and Church-State Relations: Nation-Building." *Journal of Church and State* 39: 253–72.

Cohen, Roger. 1992. "Spain's Progress Turns to Pain." *New York Times*, November 17.

Cohen, Youssef. 1982. "The Benevolent Leviathan: Political Consciousness among Urban Workers under State Corporatism." *American Political Science Review* 76: 46–59.

Collier, David, and Steven Levitsky. 1997. "Democracy with Adjectives: Conceptual Innovation in Comparative Research." *World Politics* 49: 430–51.

Colomer, Josep M. 1991. "Transition by Agreement: Modeling the Spanish Way." *American Political Science Review* 85: 1281–302.

———. 1995. *Game Theory and the Transition to Democracy: The Spanish Model*. Aldershok, Hants.: Edward Elgar.

Comín, Francisco. 1992. "La formación histórica del estado providencia en España" [The formation of the welfare state in Spain]. *Información Comercial Española*, December, 11–26.

Comisso, Ellen. 1991. "Property Rights, Liberalism, and the Transition from Actually Existing Socialism." *East European Politics and Societies* 5: 180–88.

Converse, Philip E. 1964. "The Nature of Belief Systems in Mass Publics." In *Ideology and Discontent*, ed. David E. Apter. New York: Free Press.

———. 1969. "Of Time and Partisan Stability." *Comparative Political Studies* 2: 139–71.

Converse, Philip E., and Roy Pierce. 1992. "Partisanship and the Party System." *Political Behavior* 14: 239–58.

Coverdale, J. F. 1984. *The Basque Phase of Spain's First Carlist War*. Princeton: Princeton University Press.

Craig, Patrica. 1994: "The PSOE: Slouching toward Hegemony, or The Party's Over." Paper presented at the annual meetings of the American Political Science Association, New York, September 1–4.

Cruz, Ann J., and Mary Elizabeth Perry, eds. 1992. *Culture and Control in Counter-Reformation Spain*. Minneapolis: University of Minnesota Press.

Cruz, Jesús. 1996. "An Ambivalent Revolution: The Public and the Private in the Construction of Liberal Spain." *Journal of Social History* 30: 5–27.

Cruz Cantero, Pepa, and Rosa Cobo Bedia. 1991. *Las mujeres españolas: Lo privado y lo público* [Spanish women: The private and the public]. Madrid: Centro de Investigaciones Sociológicas.

Curtis, James E., Edward G. Grabb, and Douglas E. Baer. 1992. "Voluntary

Association Membership in Fifteen Countries." *American Sociological Review* 57: 139–52.

Dahl, Robert A. 1971. *Polyarchy*. New Haven: Yale University Press.

——. 1985. *A Preface to Economic Democracy*. Berkeley: University of California Press.

Dalton, Russell J. 1996. *Citizen Politics: Public Opinion and Political Parties in Advanced Industrial Democracies*. 2d ed. Chatham, N.J.: Chatham House.

Dalton, Russell J., and Manfred Kuechler, eds. 1990. *Challenging the Political Order: New Social and Political Movements in Western Democracies*. Cambridge: Polity.

Damazio, Sylvia F. 1994. *Da elite ao povo: Advento e expansão do espiritismo no Rio de Janeiro* [From the elite to the people: The coming and expansion of spiritism in Rio de Janeiro]. Rio de Janeiro: Bertrand Brasil.

Datos de opinión. 1989. Reprint from *Revista Española de Investigaciones Sociológicas*, October–December.

Davis, Gerald F., Kristina A. Diekmann, and Catherine H. Tinsley. 1994. "The Decline and Fall of the Conglomerate Firm in the 1980s: The Desinstitutionalization of an Organizational Form." *American Sociological Review* 59: 547–70.

Davis, Winston. 1987. "Religion and Development: Weber and the East Asian Experience." In *Understanding Political Development*, ed. Myron Weiner and Samuel P. Huntington. Glenview, Ill.: Scott, Foresman/Little, Brown.

Dealy, Glen Caudill. 1977. *The Public Man: An Interpretation of Latin American and Other Catholic Countries*. Amherst: University of Massachusetts Press.

Dealy, Glen Caudill. 1992. *The Latin Americans: Spirit and Ethos*. Boulder, Colo.: Westview.

Dela Dehesa, Guillermo. 1991. "Pueden los servicios seguir creciendo sin una base industrial?" [Can services keep growing without an industrial base?] *El País*, March 1.

——. 1993. "Las reformas politicas y económicas en la España contemporánea" [Political and economic reforms in contemporary Spain]. *ICE* 117 (May): 155–67.

De Laiglesia, Beatriz, ed. 1989. *Efemérides, 1939–1989* [Ephemera]. Madrid: EFE.

Del Campo, Salustiano. 1994. *Tendencias sociales en España, 1960–1990* [Social tendencies in Spain]. Bilbão: Fundación BBV.

Della Cava, Ralph. 1989. "The 'People's Church,' the Vatican, and *Abertura*." In *Democratizing Brazil: Problems of Transition and Consolidation*, ed. Alfred Stepan. New York: Oxford University Press. 1993.

——. 1993. "Thinking about Current Vatican Policy in Central and East Europe and the Utility of the 'Brazilian Paradigm.'" *Journal of Latin American Studies* 25: 257–81.

De Miguel, Amando. 1975. *Sociología del franquismo* [The sociology of Francoism]. Barcelona: Euros.

De Miguel, Amando, et al. 1992. *La sociedad española, 1992–93* [Spanish society]. Madrid: Alianza.

De Vaus, David, and Ian McAllister. 1989. "The Changing Politics of Women: Gender and Political Alignment in Eleven Nations." *European Journal of Political Research* 17: 241–62.

DeVos, George A., and Takao Sofue, eds. 1986. *Religion and the Family in East Asia*. Berkeley: University of California Press.

Dews, Peter. 1995. *The Limits of Disenchantment: Essays on Contemporary European Philosophy*. London: Verso.

Diamond, Larry. 1992. "Economic Development and Democracy Reconsidered." *American Behavioral Scientist* 35: 450–99.

Díaz Salazar, Rafael. 1981. *Iglesia, dictadura y democracia: Catolicismo y sociedad en España, 1953–1979* [Church, dictatorship, and democracy: Catholicism and society in Spain]. Madrid: HOAC.

Díaz Salazar, Rafael, and Salvador Giner, eds. 1993. *Religión y sociedad en España* [Religion and society in Spain]. Madrid: Centro de Investigaciones Sociológicas.

Díez Medrano, Juan. 1994a. "The Effects of Ethnic Segregation and Ethnic Competition on Political Mobilization in the Basque Country, 1988." *American Sociological Review* 59: 873–89.

——. 1994b. "Patterns of Development and Nationalism: Basque and Catalan Nationalism before the Spanish Civil War." *Theory and Society* 23: 541–69.

Díez Medrano, Juan, Blanca García-Mon, and Juan Díez Nicolás. 1989. "El significado de ser de izquierdas en la España actual" [The meaning of leftism in Spain nowadays]. *Revista Española de Investigaciones Sociológicas* 45: 9–41.

Di Palma, Giuseppe. 1980. "Founding Coalitions in Southern Europe: Legitimacy and Hegemony." *Government and Opposition* 15: 162–89.

——. 1990. *To Craft Democracies: An Essay on Democratic Transitions*. Berkeley: University of California Press.

Dirección General de Coordinación con las Haciendas Territoriales. 1991. *La decentralización del gasto público en España, 1984–1990* [The decentralization of public expenditure in Spain]. Madrid: Ministerio de Economía y Hacienda.

Dirks, Nicholas B., Geoff Eley, and Sherry B. Ortner, eds. 1993. *Culture/Power/History*. Princeton: Princeton University Press.

Dixon, David E. 1995. "The New Protestantism in Latin America: Remembering What We Already Know, Testing What We Have Learned." *Comparative Politics* 27: 479–92.

Dizard, Wilson, Jr. 1994. *Old Media/New Media: Mass Communications in the Information Age*. New York: Longman.

Djurfeldt, Göran. 1993. "Classes as Clients of the State: Landlords and Laborers in Andalusia." *Comparative Studies in Society and History* 35: 159–82.

Dobbelaere, Karel, and Wolfgang Jagodzinski. 1995. "Religious Cognitions and Beliefs." In *The Impact of Values*, ed. Jan W. van Deth and Elinor Scarbrough. New York: Oxford University Press.

Dos Santos, Wanderley Guilherme. 1990. *Que Brasil é este? Manual de indicadores políticos e sociais* [What Brazil is this? Manual of political and social indicators]. Rio de Janeiro: Vertice.

Durant, Robert F. 1995. "The Democratic Deficit in America." *Political Science Quarterly* 110: 125–47.

Easton, David. 1975. "A Re-assessment of the Concept of Political Support." *British Journal of Political Science* 5: 435–57.

Eckstein, Harry. 1992. *Regarding Politics: Essays on Political Theory, Stability, and Change*. Berkeley: University of California Press.

Edles, Laura Desfor. 1995. "Rethinking Democratic Transition: A Culturalist Critique and the Spanish Case." *Theory and Society* 24: 355–84.

Edwards, Alister. 1994. "Democratization and Qualified Explanation." In *Democracy and Democratization*, ed. Geraint Parry and Michael Moran. London: Routledge.

Edwards, Bob, and Michael W. Foley. 1997. "Social Capital and the Political Economy of Our Discontent." *American Behavioral Scientist* 40: 669–78.

Ekiert, Gregorz. 1991. "Democratization Processes in East Central Europe: A Theoretical Reconsideration." *British Journal of Political Science* 21: 285–313.

Elorza, A. 1985. "Postsocialismo" [After socialism]. *El País*, June 13, 11–12.

Encarnación, Omar G. 1996. "The Politics of Dual Transitions." *Comparative Politics* 28: 477–92.

———. 1997. "Social Concertation in Democratic and Market Transitions: Comparative Lessons from Spain." *Comparative Political Studies* 30: 387–419.

Ensor, Paul. 1986. "Clergy to the Fore." *Far Eastern Economic Review* 131 (March 27): 47–48.

Entman, Robert M. 1989. *Democracy without Citizens: Media and the Decay of American Politics*. New York: Oxford University Press.

Esenwein, George R. 1989. *Anarchist Ideology and the Working Class Movement in Spain, 1868–1898*. Berkeley: University of California Press.

Evans, Peter William. 1995. *The Films of Luis Buñuel: Subjectivity and Desire*. Oxford: Clarendon.

Fearon, James D., and David D. Latin. 1996. "Explaining Interethnic Cooperation." *American Political Science Review* 90: 715–35.

Feld, Scott, and Bernard Groffman. 1988. "Ideological Consistency as a Collective Phenomenon." *American Political Science Review* 82: 64–75.

Feldman, Stanley. 1983. "Economic Individualism and American Public Opinion." *American Politics Quarterly* 11: 3–30.

Feldman, Stanley, and John Zaller. 1992. "The Political Culture of Ambivalence: Ideological Responses to the Welfare State." *American Journal of Political Science* 36: 268–307.

Feng, Yi. 1997. "Democracy, Political Stability and Economic Growth." *British Journal of Political Science* 27: 391–418.

Fiorina, Morris P. 1981. *Retrospective Voting in American National Elections*. New Haven: Yale University Press.

Fish, M. Steven. 1995. *Democracy from Scratch: Opposition and Regime in the New Russian Revolution*. Princeton: Princeton University Press.

Fishman, Robert M. 1990a. "Rethinking State and Regime: Southern Europe's Transition to Democracy." *World Politics* 42: 421–40.

———. 1990b. *Working-Class Organization and the Return to Democracy in Spain*. Ithaca: Cornell University Press.

Flaquer, Luis, and Julio Iglesias de Ussel. 1996. "The Sociology of the Family in Spain." In *Intercultural Variation in Family Research and Theory*, ed. Marvin B. Sussman and Roma Stovall Hanks. New York: Haworth.

Fleet, Michael. 1985. *The Rise and Fall of Chilean Christian Democracy*. Princeton: Princeton University Press.

Fliegelman, Joel. 1982. *Prodigals and Pilgrims: The American Revolution against Patriarchal Authority, 1750–1800*. Cambridge: Cambridge University Press.

Flora, Peter, and Arnold J. Heidenheimer, eds. 1981. *The Development of Welfare States in Europe and America*. New Brunswick, N.J.: Transaction Books.

Foley, Michael W., and Bob Edwards. 1996. "The Paradox of Civil Society." *Journal of Democracy* 7: 38–52.

———. 1997. "Escape from Politics? Social Theory and the Social Capital Debate." *American Behavioral Scientist* 40: 550–61.

Foweraker, Joe. 1989. *Making Democracy in Spain: Grass-Roots Struggles in the South, 1955–1975*. Cambridge: Cambridge University Press.

Foweraker, Joe, and Todd Landman. 1997. *Citizenship and Social Movements: A Comparative and Statistical Analysis*. New York: Oxford University Press.

Franklin, Mark N., et al. 1992. *Electoral Change: Responses to Evolving Social and Attitudinal Structures in Western Countries*. Cambridge: Cambridge University Press.

French, John D. 1992. *The Brazilian Workers' ABC: Class Conflict and Alliances in Modern São Paulo*. Chapel Hill: University of North Carolina Press.

Fukuyama, Francis. 1995. "The Primacy of Culture." *Journal of Democracy* 6: 7–14.

Gallego Mendez, Maria Teresa. 1994. "Women's Political Engagement in Spain." In *Women and Politics Worldwide*, ed. Barbara J. Nelson and Najma Chowdhury. New Haven: Yale University Press.

Ganz, Marshall. 1994. "Voters in the Crosshairs: How Technology and the Market Are Destroying Politics." *American Prospect* 16 (Winter): 100–109.

García Delgado, Luis, ed. 1990. *Economía española de la transición y la democracia* [The Spanish economy during the transition to democracy]. Madrid: Centro de Investigaciones Sociológicas.

García Ferrando, Manuel. 1982. *Regionalismo y autonomía en España, 1976–1979* [Regionalism and autonomy in Spain]. Madrid: Centro de Investigaciones Sociológicas.

García Santesmases, Antonio. 1993. *Repensar la izquierda: Evolución ideológica del socialismo en la España actual* [To rethink the left: Ideological evolution of socialism in contemporary Spain]. Barcelona: Anthropos.

Garrido, Luis. 1993. *Las dos biografías de la mujer en España* [The two life stories of women in Spain]. Madrid: Instituto de la Mujer, Ministerio de Asuntos Sociales.

Garton Ash, Timothy. 1995. "Catching the Wrong Bus? Europe's Future and the Great Gamble of Monetary Union." *Times Literary Supplement*, May 5, 3–4.

Garvin, Tom. 1996. *1922: The Birth of Irish Democracy*. Dublin: Gill & Macmillan.

Geddes, Barbara. 1995. "The Politics of Economic Liberalization." *Latin American Research Review* 30: 195–214.

Geer, John G. 1996. *From Tea Leaves to Opinion Polls: A Theory of Democratic Leadership*. New York: Columbia University Press.

Geyer, Robert. 1993. "Socialism and the EC after Maastricht: From Classic to New-Model European Social Democracy." In *The State of the European Community*, ed. Alan Cafruny and Glenda Rosenthal. Boulder, Colo.: Lynne Rienner.

Gibson, James L. 1989. "Understandings of Justice: Institutional Legitimacy,

Procedural Justice, and Political Tolerance." *Law and Society Review* 23: 469–96.

——. 1996. "A Mile Wide but an Inch Deep(?): The Structure of Democratic Commitments in the Former USSR." *American Journal of Political Science* 40: 396–420.

Gill, Anthony. 1998. *Rendering unto Caesar: The Catholic Church and the State in Latin America*. Chicago: University of Chicago Press.

Gillespie, Richard. 1993. "'Programa 2000': The Appearance and Reality of Socialist Renewal in Spain." *West European Politics* 16: 78–96.

Gilmore, David D. 1987. *Aggression and Community: Paradoxes of Andalusian Culture*. New Haven: Yale University Press.

Goldstone, Jack A. 1991. "Ideology, Cultural Frameworks, and the Process of Revolution." *Theory and Society* 20: 405–53.

Gomes Consorte, Josildeth, and Marcia Regina Da Costa, eds. 1988. *Religião, política, identitidade* [Religion, politics, identity]. São Paulo: PUC-SP.

Gould, Roger V. 1995. *Insurgent Identities: Class, Community, and Protest in Paris from 1848 to the Commune*. Chicago: University of Chicago Press.

Graber, Doris A. 1993. *Mass Media and American Politics*. 4th ed. Washington, D.C.: Congressional Quarterly Press.

Gracián, Baltasar. 1647/1953. *The Oracle: A Manual of the Art of Discretion*. Trans. L. B. Walton. London: J. M. Dent.

Graham, Lawrence S., and Harry M. Makler, eds. 1979. *Contemporary Portugal: The Revolution and Its Antecedents*. Austin: University of Texas Press.

Granovetter, Mark. 1972. "The Strength of Weak Ties." *American Journal of Sociology* 78: 1360–80.

Grossman, Lawrence K. 1995. *The Electronic Republic: Reshaping Democracy in the Information Age*. New York: Viking.

Guerra, Alfonso, and José Felix Tezanos, eds. 1992. *La década del cambio: Diez años de gobierno socialista, 1982–1992* [The decade of change: Ten years of socialist government]. Madrid: Sistema.

Gundelach, Peter. 1995. "Grass-Roots Activity." In *The Impact of Values*, ed. Jan W. Van Deth and Elinor Scarbrough. New York: Oxford University Press.

Gunther, Richard. 1980. *Public Policy in a No-party State: Spanish Planning and Budgeting in the Twilight of the Franquist Era*. Berkeley: University of California Press.

——. 1992. "Spain: The Very Model of the Modern Elite Settlement." In *Elites and Democratic Consolidation in Latin American and Southern Europe*, ed. John Higley and Richard Gunther. Cambridge: Cambridge University Press.

——. 1996. "Spanish Public Policy: From Dictatorship to Democracy." Working paper no. 84. Centro de Estudios Avanzados en Ciencias Sociales, Instituto Juan March, Madrid.

——. 1997. "Managing Democratic Consolidation in Spain: From Consensus to Majority in Institutions." In *Institutions and Democratic Statecraft*, ed. Metin Heper, Ali Kazancigil, and Bert A. Rockman. Boulder, Colo.: Westview.

Gunther, Richard P., and Roger A. Blough. 1981. "Religious Conflict and Consensus in Spain: A Tale of Two Constitutions." *World Affairs* 143: 366–412.

Gunther, Richard, Hans-Jürgen Puhle, and P. Nikiforos Diamandouros. 1995.

"Introduction." In *The Politics of Democratic Consolidation: Southern Europe in Comparative Perspective*, ed. Gunther, Diamandouros, and Puhle. Baltimore: Johns Hopkins University Press.

———, eds. 1995. *The Politics of Democratic Consolidation: Southern Europe in Comparative Perspective*. Baltimore: Johns Hopkins University Press.

Gunther, Richard, Giacomo Sani, and Goldie Shabad. 1985. *Spain after Franco: The Making of a Competitive Party System*. Berkeley: University of California Press.

Haggard, Stephan, and Robert R. Kaufman. 1995. *The Political Economy of Democratic Transitions*. Princeton: Princeton University Press.

Hall, Peter A. 1989. *The Political Power of Economic Ideas*. Princeton: Princeton University Press.

———. 1993. "Policy Paradigms, Social Learning, and the State: The Case of Economic Policymaking in Britain." *Comparative Politics* 25: 275–96.

———. 1997. "The Role of Interests, Institutions, and Ideas in the Comparative Political Economy of the Industrialized Nations." In *Comparative Politics: Rationality, Culture, and Structure*, ed. Mark Irving Lichbach and Alan S. Zuckerman. Cambridge: Cambridge University Press.

Ham, Se Wong. 1996. "Jungei goohyonwondong ei shidaejuk baekyong" [Background to the movement to attain social justice]. In *A Torch in Darkness*, vol. 1. Seoul: Research Institute for Joy and Hope.

Han, Sung Joo. 1990. "South Korea: Politics in Transition." In *Politics in Developing Countries*, ed. Larry Diamond, Juan Linz, and Seymour Martin Lipset. Boulder, Colo.: Lynne Rienner.

Hansen, Susan B. 1983. *The Politics of Taxation: Revenue without Representation*. New York: Praeger.

Hardin, Russell. 1995. *One for All: The Logic of Group Conflict*. Princeton: Princeton University Press.

Hart, Vivian. 1978. *Distrust and Democracy: Political Distrust in Britain and America*. Cambridge: Cambridge University Press.

Hazan, Reuven Y. 1995. "Center Parties and Systemic Polarization: An Exploration of Recent Trends in Western Europe." *Journal of Theoretical Politics* 7: 421–45.

Hehir, Bryan. 1993. "Catholicism and Democracy: Conflict, Change, and Collaboration." In *Christianity and Democracy in Global Context*, ed. John Witte, Jr. Boulder, Colo.: Westview.

Helliwell, John F. 1994. "Empirical Linkages between Democracy and Economic Growth." *British Journal of Political Science* 24: 225–48.

Herbst, Susan. 1993. *Numbered Voices: How Opinion Polling Has Shaped American Politics*. Chicago: University of Chicago Press.

Hernández, Abel. 1984. *Crónica de la cruz y de la rosa: Los socialistas y la iglesia hoy* [Chronicle of the cross and the rose: The socialists and the church today]. Barcelona: Argos Vergara.

Hewitt, W. E. 1990. "Religion and the Consolidation of Democracy in Brazil: The Role of the *Comunidades Eclesiais de Base* (CEBs)." *Sociological Analysis* 50: 139–52.

Higginbotham, Virginia. 1988. *Spanish Film under Franco*. Austin: University of Texas Press.

Higley, John, and Michael B. Burton. 1989. "The Elite Variable in Democratic Transitions and Breakdowns." *American Sociological Review* 54: 17–32.

Hipsher, Patricia L. 1996. "Democratization and the Decline of Urban Social Movements in Chile and Spain." *Comparative Politics* 28: 273–97.

Hirschman, Albert O. 1977. *The Passions and the Interests: Political Arguments for Capitalism before Its Triumph.* Princeton: Princeton University Press.

Hochschild, Jennifer. 1981. *What's Fair: American Beliefs about Distributive Justice.* Cambridge: Harvard University Press.

Hojman, David E. 1994. "The Political Economy of Recent Conversions to Market Economics in Latin America." *Journal of Latin American Studies* 26: 191–219.

Holmes, Stephen. 1993. *The Anatomy of Antiliberalism.* Cambridge: Harvard University Press.

——. 1995. *Passions and Constraint: On the Theory of Liberal Democracy.* Chicago: University of Chicago Press.

——. 1997. "What Russia Teaches Us Now: How Weak States Threaten Freedom." *American Prospect* 33 (July–August): 30–39.

Hooper, John. 1993. "Spain in Search of Itself." *Wilson Quarterly* 17 (Autumn): 8–28.

Horowitz, Irving Louis. 1972. "The Norm of Illegitimacy." In *Latin America: The Dynamics of Social Change*, ed. Stefan A. Halper and John R. Sterling. New York: St. Martin's Press.

Huber, Evelyne, Dietrich Rueschemeyer, and John D. Stephens. 1997. "The Paradoxes of Contemporary Democracy: Formal, Participatory, and Social Dimensions." *Comparative Politics* 29: 323–42.

Hunt, Lynn. 1984. *Politics, Culture, and Class in the French Revolution.* Berkeley: University of California Press.

Huntington, Samuel P. 1968. *Political Order in Changing Societies.* New Haven: Yale University Press.

——. 1991. *The Third Wave: Democratization in the Late Twentieth Century.* Tulsa: University of Oklahoma Press.

——. 1997. "After Twenty Years: The Future of the Third Wave." *Journal of Democracy* 8: 3–12.

Ignatieff, Michael. 1995. "On Civil Society: Why Eastern Europe's Revolutions Could Succeed." *Foreign Affairs* 74 (March–April): 128–36.

Inglehart, Ronald. 1988. "The Renaissance of Political Culture." *American Political Science Review* 82: 1203–30.

——. 1997. *Modernization and Postmodernization: Cultural, Economic, and Political Change in 43 Societies.* Princeton: Princeton University Press.

Inglis, Tom. 1987. *Moral Monopoly: The Catholic Church in Modern Irish Society.* Dublin: Gill & Macmillan.

Inkeles, Alex, and David H. Smith. 1974. *Becoming Modern: Individual Change in Six Developing Countries.* Cambridge: Harvard University Press.

Instituto Brasileiro de Geografia e Estatística. 1993. *Pesquisa mensal de emprego* [Monthly study of employment]. Various issues.

International Labor Office. 1996. *Yearbook of Labor Statistics.* Geneva.

Ireland, Rowan. 1991. *Kingdom Come: Religion and Politics in Brazil.* Pittsburgh: University of Pittsburgh Press.

———. 1995. "Pentecostalism, Conversions, and Politics in Brazil." *Religion* 25: 135–45.

Jackman, Mary R., and Robert W. Jackman. 1983. *Class Awareness in the United States*. Berkeley: University of California Press.

Jackman, Robert W., and Ross A. Miller. 1996. "The Poverty of Political Culture." *American Journal of Political Science* 40: 697–716.

Jagodzinski, Wolfgang, and Karel Dobbelaere. "Secularization and Church Religiosity." In *The Impact of Values*, ed. Jan W. van Deth and Elinor Scarbrough. New York: Oxford University Press.

Jalali, Rita, and Seymour Martin Lipset. 1992–93. "Racial and Ethnic Conflicts: A Global Perspective." *Political Science Quarterly* 107: 585–606.

Javier Noya, Francisco, and Antonio Vallejos. 1993. *Las actitudes ante la desigualdad en España* [Attitudes toward inequality in Spain]. Madrid: Centro de Investigaciones Sociológicas.

Jiménez, Fernando. 1994. "La batalla por la opinión pública en el escándalo político: estudio de un caso en la España contemporánea" [The battle for public opinion in political scandal: A case study of contemporary Spain]. Working paper no. 60. Centro de Estudios Avanzados en Ciencias Sociales, Instituto Juan March, Madrid.

Jiménez Fernández, Adolfo. 1993. "La seguridad social, diez años después" [Social security, ten years after]. *El País*, May 28, 56.

Johnstone, Patrick. 1993. *Operation World*. Grand Rapids, Mich.: Zondervan.

Jones, Catherine. 1990. "Hong Kong, Singapore, South Korea, and Taiwan: Oikonomic Welfare States." *Government and Opposition* 25: 446–62.

Jones, Mark P. 1996. "Assessing the Public's Understanding of Constitutional Reform: Evidence from Argentina." *Political Behavior* 18: 25–49.

Jowitt, Ken. 1992. *New World Disorder: The Leninist Extinction*. Berkeley: University of California Press.

Judt, Tony. 1998. "The Stranger." *New Republic*, Feburary 16, 25–32.

Juergensmeyer, Mark. 1995. "The New Religious State." *Comparative Politics* 27: 379–92.

Jung, Kim-Dae. 1987. *Prison Writings*. Berkeley: University of California Press.

Justel, Manuel. 1995. *La abstención electoral en España, 1977–1993* [Electoral abstention in Spain]. Madrid: Centro de Investigaciones Sociológicas.

Kalyvas, Stathis N. 1996. *The Rise of Christian Democracy in Europe*. Ithaca: Cornell University Press.

———. 1997. "Religion and Democratization: Algeria and Belgium." Working paper no. 107, Centro de Estudios Avanzados en Ciencias Sociales, Instituto Juan March, Madrid.

Kamen, Henry. 1988. "Toleration and Dissent in Sixteenth-Century Spain: The Alternative Tradition." *Sixteenth-Century Journal* 19: 3–23.

Kang, Wi Jo. 1997. *Christ and Caesar in Modern Korea: A History of Christianity and Politics*. Albany: State University of New York Press.

Kaplan, Temma. 1977. *Anarchists of Andalusia, 1868–1903*. Princeton: Princeton University Press.

Karatnycky, Adrian. 1995. "Democracies on the Rise, Democracies at Risk." *Freedom Review* 26: 5–10.

Katz, Richard S., and Peter Mair, eds. 1994. *How Parties Organize: Change and Adaptation in Party Organization in Western Democracies*. Thousand Oaks, Calif.: Sage.

Keck, Margaret. 1992. *The Worker's Party and Democratization in Brazil*. New Haven: Yale University Press.

Keddie, Nikki R. 1997. "Secularism and the State: Towards Clarity and Global Comparison." *New Left Review* 226: 21–40.

Kekes, John. 1997. *Against Liberalism*. Ithaca: Cornell University Press.

Kelley, Jonathan, and M. D. R. Evans. 1995. "Class and Class Conflict in Six Western Nations." *American Sociological Review* 60: 157–78.

Kellner, Douglas. 1991. *Television and the Crisis of Democracy*. Boulder, Colo.: Westview.

Kendall, Laurel, and Mark Peterson, eds. 1983. *Korean Women: View from the Inner Room*. New Haven, Conn.: East Rock Press.

Kiewiet, D. Roderick. 1981. "Policy-Oriented Voting in Response to Economic Issues." *American Political Science Review* 75: 448–59.

Kim, Chong Lim. 1994. "Minjuwha nen Jal Ddoeo Gago Inenga?" [Democratization: How Well Has It Progressed?] *Gaegan Sasang* 6: 211–29.

Kim, Jae-Myong. 1989. "Jungei goohyon sajaedan ei hyonsil insik" [Recognizing the realities of the Catholic priests' association for social justice]. *Monthly Joongang*, September, 356–69.

Kim, Yong-Bok. 1986. "Messianism and Minjung: Discerning Messianic Politics over against Political Messianism." In *Third World Liberation Theologies*, ed. Deanne William Ferm. Maryknoll, N.Y.: Orbis.

Kinder, Donald R., and D. Roderick Kiewiet. 1981. "Sociotropic Politics: The American Case." *British Journal of Political Science* 11: 129–61.

Kinder, Donald R., and David O. Sears. 1979. "Economic Grievances and Political Behavior." *American Journal of Political Science* 23: 495–527.

Kiser, Edgar. 1996. "The Revival of Narrative in Historical Sociology." *Politics and Society* 24: 249–71.

Kitschelt, Herbert. 1994. *The Transformation of European Social Democracy*. Cambridge: Cambridge University Press.

Knoke, David. 1990a. *Organizing for Collective Action: The Political Economies of Association*. Hawthorn, N.Y.: A. de Gruyter.

———. 1990b. *Political Networks: The Structural Perspective*. Cambridge: Cambridge University Press.

Kohli, Atul. 1993. "Democracy amid Economic Orthodoxy: Trends in Developing Countries." *Third World Quarterly* 14: 671–89.

Koo, Hagen, ed. 1993. *State and Society in Contemporary Korea*. Ithaca: Cornell University Press.

Krischke, Paulo J. 1991. "Church Base Communities and Democratic Change in Brazilian Society." *Comparative Political Studies* 24: 186–210.

Kristeller, Paul Oskar. 1990. *Renaissance Thought and the Arts: Collected Essays*. Princeton: Princeton University Press.

Kurth, James, and James Petras, with Diarmuid Maguire and Ronald Chilcote. 1993. *Mediterranan Paradoxes: The Politics and Social Structure of Southern Europe*. Providence, R.I.: Berg.

Ladd, Everett C. 1985. "Tax Attitudes." *Public Opinion* 8: 8–10.

Laitin, David D. 1986. *Hegemony and Culture: Politics and Religious Change among the Yoruba*. Chicago: University of Chicago Press.

Laitin, David D., Carlota Solé, and Stathis N. Kalyvas. 1994. "Language and the Construction of States: The Case of Catalonia in Spain." *Politics and Society* 22: 5–29.

Lancaster, Thomas D. 1979. "Toward an Assessment of the Spanish Social Security System." Paper presented at the Fourth European Studies Conference, Omaha.

———. 1984. "Economics, Democracy, and Spanish Elections." *Political Behavior* 6: 353–67.

Lannon, Frances. 1987. *Privilege, Persecution, and Prophecy: The Catholic Church in Spain, 1875–1975*. Oxford: Clarendon.

Lash, Scott, and Jonathan Friedman, eds. 1992. *Modernity and Identity*. Oxford: Blackwell.

Laufer, Romain, and Catherine Paradeise. 1990. *Marketing Democracy: Public Opinion, and Media Formation in Democratic Societies*. New Brunswick, N.J.: Transaction Books.

Lawrence, Bruce B. 1989. *Defenders of God: The Fundamentalist Revolt against the Modern Age*. San Francisco: Harper & Row.

Lawson, Kay, and Peter H. Merkl, eds. 1988. *When Parties Fail: Emerging Alternative Organizations*. Princeton: Princeton University Press.

Lee, Young-Hoon. 1992. "Katholik ei sahoejuk garechim gwa hankook ei nodongwondoing" [Catholic social teaching and labor movements in Korea]. *Reason and Religion* (Soowon Catholic University) 4: 173–208.

Leege, David, Lyman A. Kellstedt, and Kenneth D. Wald. 1990. "Religion and Politics: A Report on Measures of Religiosity in the 1989 NES Pilot Study." Unpublished paper, Center for Political Studies, University of Michigan.

Leighley, Jan E. 1996. "Group Membership and the Mobilization of Political Participation." *Journal of Politics* 58: 447–63.

Lemann, Nicholas. 1996. "Kicking in Groups." *Atlantic Monthly*, April, 22–26.

Lemke, Carl, and Gary Marks, eds. 1992. *The Crisis of Socialism in Europe*. Durham, N. C.: Duke University Press.

Lesthaeghe, Ron. 1995. "The Second Demographic Transition in Western Countries: An Interpretation." In *Gender and Family Change in Industrialized Countries*, ed. Karen Oppenheim Mason and An-Magritt Jensen. New York: Oxford University Press.

Lewis, Jane, ed. 1993. *Women and Social Policies in Europe: Work, Family and the State*. Aldershot, Hants.: Edward Elgar.

Lewis-Beck, Michael S. 1988. *Economics and Elections: The Major Western Democracies*. Ann Arbor: University of Michigan Press.

Lijphart, Arendt. 1979. "Religion vs. Linguistic vs. Class Voting: The 'Crucial Experiment' of Comparing Belgium, Canada, South Africa, and Switzerland." *American Political Science Review* 73: 442–58.

———. 1992. "The Relative Salience of the Socio-economic and Religious Issue Dimensions: Coalition Formation in Ten Western Democracies." *European Journal of Political Research* 10: 201–11.

Lilla, Mark. 1993. *G. B. Vico: The Making of an Anti-Modern*. Cambridge: Harvard University Press.

Linz, Juan J. 1964. "An Authoritarian Regime: Spain." In *Cleavages, Ideologies, and Party Systems*, ed. Erick Allardt and Ÿrjo Littunen. Helsinki: Academic Bookstore.

———. 1978. "Il sistema partitico spagnolo" [The Spanish party system]. *Rivista Italiana di Scienza Politica* 8: 363–414.

———. 1984. "La sociedad española: Presente, pasado y futuro" [Spanish society: present, past, and future]. In *España: Un presente para el futuro* [Spain: A present for the future], ed. E. García de Enterría. Madrid: Instituto de Estudios Económicos.

———. 1991. "Church and State in Spain from the Civil War to the Return of Democracy." *Daedalus* 120: 159–78.

Linz, Juan J., and Alfred Stepan. 1992. "Political Identities and Electoral Sequences: Spain, the Soviet Union, and Yugoslavia." *Daedalus* 121: 123–39.

———. 1996. *Problems of Democratic Transition and Consolidation: Southern Europe, South America, and Post-Communist Europe*. Baltimore: Johns Hopkins University Press.

Linz, Juan J., et al. 1981. *Informe sociológico sobre el cambio político en España, 1975–1981* [Sociological report on political change in Spain]. Madrid: Fundación Foessa.

Lipset, Seymour Martin. 1983. "Radicalism or Reformism: Sources of Working-Class Politics." *American Political Science Review* 77: 1–18.

———. 1994. "The Social Requisites of Democracy Revisited." *American Sociological Review* 59: 1–22.

Lipset, Seymour Martin, and Stein Rokkan. 1967. "Cleavage Structures, Party Systems, and Voter Alignments: An Introduction." In *Party Systems and Voter Alignments: Cross-National Perspectives*, ed. Lipset and Rokkan. New York: Free Press.

Litwak, Eugene, and Ivan Szelenyi. 1969. "Primary Group Structures and Their Functions: Kins, Neighbors, and Friends." *American Sociological Review* 34: 465–81.

Logan, John R., and Glenna D. Spitze. 1994. "Family Neighbors." *American Journal of Sociology* 100: 453–76.

Londregan, John B., and Keith T. Poole. 1996. "Does High Income Promote Democracy?" *World Politics* 49: 1–30.

López Pina, Antonio. 1994. "Mercado e interés público en España: A vueltas con la sociedad civil" [Market and the public interest in Spain: At odds with civil society]. Universidad Complutense de Madrid, typescript.

López Pina, Antonio, and Eduardo Aranguren. 1976. *La cultura política de la España de Franco* [The political culture of Franco's Spain]. Madrid: Taurus.

López Pintor, Rafael. 1982. *La opinión pública española: Del franquismo a la democracia* [Spanish public opinion from Francoism to democracy]. Madrid: Centro de Investigaciones Sociológicas.

Luttwak, Edward, 1995. "Turbo-Charged Capitalism and Its Consequences." *London Review of Books*, November 2, 6–7.

MacDonagh, Eileen L. 1982. "To Work or Not to Work: The Differential Impact of Achieved and Derived Status upon the Political Participation of Women, 1956–1976." *American Journal of Political Science* 26: 280–97.

MacKuen, Michael B. 1989. "Macropartisanship." *American Political Science Review* 83: 1125–42.

Maddox, Robert. 1991. *El Castillo: The Politics of Tradition in an Andalusian Town.* Urbana: Univerity of Illinois Press.

Mahan, Elizabeth. 1995. "Media, Politics, and Society in Latin America." *Latin American Research Review* 30: 128–62.

Maier, Charles S., ed. 1987. *Changing Boundaries of the Political: Essays on the Evolving Balance beween the State and Society, Public and Private in Europe.* Cambridge: Cambridge University Press.

———. 1997. *Dissolution: The Crisis of Communism and the End of East Germany.* Princeton: Princeton University Press.

Mainwaring, Scott. 1986. *The Catholic Church and Politics in Brazil, 1916–1985.* Stanford: Stanford University Press.

———. 1987. "Urban Popular Movements, Identity, and Democratization in Brazil." *Comparative Political Studies* 20: 131–59.

———. 1992–93. "Brazilian Party Development in Comparative Perspective." *Political Science Quarterly* 107: 677–707.

Mainwaring, Scott, and Timothy R. Scully, eds. 1995. *Building Democratic Institutions: Party Systems in Latin America.* Stanford: Stanford University Press.

Malefakis, Edward E. 1992. "Southern Europe in the Nineteenth and Twentieth Centuries: An Historical Overview." Working paper, Centro de Estudios Avanzados en Ciencias Sociales, Instituto Juan March, Madrid.

Mancha Navarro, Tomás. 1993. *Economía y votos en España* [Economics and votes in Spain]. Madrid: Instituto de Estudios Económicos.

Manzetti, Luigi. 1993. *Institutions, Parties, and Coalitions in Argentine Politics.* Pittsburgh: University of Pittsburgh Press.

Maravall, José Antonio. 1986. *Culture of the Baroque: Analysis of a Historical Structure.* Minneapolis: University of Minnesota Press.

Maravall, José María. 1984. *La política de la transición, 1975–1980* [The politics of the transition]. Madrid: Taurus.

———. 1993. "Politics and Policy: Economic Reforms in Southern Europe." In *Economic Reforms in New Democracies: A Social-democratic Approach*, ed. Luiz Carlos Bresser Pereira, José María Maravall, and Adam Przeworksi. Cambridge: Cambridge University Press.

———. 1997. *Regimes, Politics, and Markets: Democratization and Economic Change in Southern and Eastern Europe.* New York: Oxford University Press.

Mardones, José María. 1995. "Religión y política" [Religion and politics]. *Leviatán* 59 (Spring): 15–26.

Maríz, Cecîlia Loreto. 1993. *Coping with Poverty: Pentecostals and Christian Base Communities in Brazil.* Philadelphia: Temple University Press.

Markoff, John. 1997. "Really Existing Democracy: Learning from Latin America in the Late 1990s." *New Left Review* 223: 48–68.

Marks, Gary, and Doug McAdam. 1996. "Social Movements and the Changing Structure of Political Opportunity in the European Union." *West European Politics* 19: 249–78.

Martin, David. 1979. *A General Theory of Secularization*. New York: Harper & Row.

Martín Serrano, Manuel. 1982. *El uso de la comunicación social por los españoles* [The use of social communication by Spaniards]. Madrid: Centro de Investigaciones Sociológicas.

Martinez Lucio, Miguel, and Paul Blyton. 1995. "Constructing the Post-Fordist State? The Politics of Labor Market Flexibility in Spain." *West European Politics* 18: 340–60.

Marty, Martin E., and R. Scott Appleby, eds. 1997. *Religion, Ethnicity, and Self-Identity*. Hanover, N.H.: University Press of New England.

Marvin, Garry. 1988. *Bullfight*. Oxford: Basil Blackwell.

Maxwell, Kenneth. 1995. *The Making of Portuguese Democracy*. Cambridge: Cambridge University Press.

Maxwell, Kenneth, and Steven Spiegel. 1994. *The New Spain: From Isolation to Influence*. New York: Council on Foreign Relations Press.

Mayer, Lawrence C., and Roland E. Smith. 1985. "Feminism and Religiosity: Female Electoral Behavior in Western Europe." *West European Politics* 8: 38–49.

McAdam, Doug, John D. McCarthy, and Mayer N. Zald, eds. 1996. *Comparative Perspectives on Social Movements: Political Opportunities, Mobilizing Structures, and Cultural Framings*. Cambridge: Cambridge University Press.

McAdam, Doug, and Dieter Rucht. 1993. "The Cross-National Diffusion of Movement Ideas." *Annals of the American Academy of Political and Social Science* 528: 56–74.

McAdam, Doug, Sidney Tarrow, and Charles Tilly. 1996. "A Comparative Synthesis on Social Movements and Revolution: Toward an Integrated Perspective." Paper presented at the annual meeting of the American Political Science Association, San Francisco, August 29–September 1.

McDonough, Peter. 1995. "Identities, Ideologies, and Interests: Democratization and the Culture of Mass Politics in Spain and Eastern Europe." *Journal of Politics* 57: 649–76.

McDonough, Peter, Samuel H. Barnes, and Antonio López Pina. 1981. "The Spanish Public in Political Transition." *British Journal of Political Science* 11:49–79.

———. 1984. "Authority and Association: Spanish Democracy in Comparative Perspective." *Journal of Politics* 46:652–88.

———. 1986a. "Economic Policy and Public Opinion in Spain." *American Journal of Political Science* 30:446–79.

———. 1986b. "The Growth of Democratic Legitimacy in Spain." *American Political Science Review* 80: 735–60.

———. 1994. "The Nature of Political Support and Legitimacy in Spain." *Comparative Political Studies* 27: 349–80.

McDonough, Peter, and Antonio López Pina. 1984. "Continuity and Change in Spanish Politics." In *Electoral Change in Advanced Industrial Societies*, ed. Russell J. Dalton, Scott C. Flanagan, and Paul A. Beck. Princeton: Princeton University Press.

McDonough, Peter, and Doh C. Shin. 1995. "Conservative Democratization and the Transition to Mass Politics in Korea." In *Democracy and Communism: Theory, Reality, and the Future*, ed. Sung Chul Yang. Seoul: Korean Association of International Studies.

McDonough, Peter, Doh C. Shin, and José Álvaro Moisés. 1998. "The Churches and Political Mobilization in Brazil, Korea, and Spain." In *Comparative Political Parties and Party Elites*, ed. Birol A. Yesilada. Ann Arbor: University of Michigan Press.

———. Forthcoming. "Democratization and Participation: Comparing Spain, Brazil, and Korea." *Journal of Politics*.

McPherson, J. Miller, and Thomas Rotolo. 1996. "Testing a Dynamic Model of Social Composition: Diversity and Change in Voluntary Groups." *American Sociological Review* 61: 179–202.

Medhurst, Kenneth. 1984. "Spain's Evolutionary Pathway from Dictatorship to Democracy." *West European Politics* 7:30–49.

Méndez, Elvira. 1994. "Public Policies toward Women in Spain: An Unfinished Democratic Process." Paper presented at the Sixteenth World Congress of the International Political Science Association, Berlin, August 21–25.

Merelman, Richard A. 1992. *Partial Visions: Culture and Politics in Britain, Canada, and the United States*. Madison: University of Wisconsin Press.

Miller, Arthur M., Vicki L. Hesli, and William M. Reisinger. 1997. "Conceptions of Democracy among Mass and Elite in Post-Soviet Societies." *British Journal of Political Science* 27: 157–90.

Miller, Warren E., Arthur H. Miller, and Edward J. Schneider. 1980. *American National Election Studies Data Sourcebook, 1952–1978*. Cambridge: Harvard University Press.

Mishler, William, and Richard Rose. 1997. "Trust, Distrust, and Skepticism: Popular Evaluations of Civil and Political Institutions in Post-Communist Societies." *Journal of Politics* 59: 418–51.

Mitchell, Timothy. 1990. *Passional Culture: Emotion, Religion, and Society in Southern Spain*. Philadelphia: University of Pennsylvania Press.

Moisés, José Álvaro. 1993. "Elections, Political Parties, and Political Culture in Brazil: Changes and Continuities." *Journal of Latin American Studies* 25: 575–611.

———. 1995. *Os brasileiros e a democracia: bases sócio-políticas da legitimidade democrática* [The Brazilians and democracy: Sociopolitical bases of democratic legitimacy]. São Paulo: Ática.

Monroe, Kristin R. 1979. "Econometric Analyses of Electoral Behavior: A Critical Review." *Political Behavior* 1: 137–73.

Montero, José Ramón. 1993a. "Las dimensiones de la secularización: Religiosidad y preferencias políticas en España" [The dimensions of secularization: Religiosity and political preferences in Spain]. In *Religión y sociedad en España* [Religion and society in Spain], ed. Rafael Díaz-Salazar and Salvador Giner. Madrid: Collección Academia.

———. 1993b. "Revisiting Democratic Success: Legitimacy and the Meanings of Democracy in Spain." In *Politics, Society, and Democracy: The Case of Spain*, ed. Richard Gunther. Boulder, Colo.: Westview.

——. 1994. "Religiosidad y voto en España" [Religiosity and the vote in Spain]. *Revista de Estudios Políticos* 83: 77–111.

Montero, José Ramón, and Richard Gunther. 1994. "Democratic Legitimacy in Spain." Paper presented at the Sixteenth World Congress of the International Political Science Association, Berlin, August 21–25.

Montero, José Ramón, Richard Gunther, and Mariano Torcal. 1997. "Democracy in Spain: Legitimacy, Discontent, and Disaffection." Working paper no. 100, Centro de Estudios Avanzados en Ciencias Sociales, Instituto Juan March, Madrid.

Montero, José Ramón, and Mariano Torcal. 1990a. "La cultura política de los españoles: Pautas de continuidad y cambio" [The political culture of Spaniards: Standards of continuity and change]. *Sistema* 99: 39–74.

——. 1990b. "Voters and Citizens in a New Democracy: Some Trend Data on Political Attitudes in Spain." *International Journal of Public Opinion Research* 2: 116–40.

——. 1994. "Value Change, Generational Replacement, and Politics in Spain." Working paper no. 56, Centro de Estudios Avanzados en Ciencias Sociales, Instituto Juan March, Madrid.

Moon, Okpyo. 1991. "Korean Life Styles and the Role of Women in the 21st Century." Paper presented at the international conference on Korea and the World in the 21st Century, Seoul, October 21–23.

Moore, Barrington. 1966. *Social Origins of Dictatorship and Democracy: Lord and Peasant in the Making of Modern Society*. Boston: Beacon.

Mora, Rosa. 1994. "La mitad de los españoles no lee libros" [Fifty percent of Spaniards don't read books]. *El País*, November 10.

Morán, María Luz. 1992. "Algunas reflexiones en torno a la influencia de los medios de comunicación en la formación y características de la cultura política de los españoles" [Some reflections on the influence of the communications media on the formation and characteristics of Spanish political culture]. *Revista Española de Investigaciones Sociológicas* 57: 37–59.

——. 1996. "Renewal and Permanency of the Spanish Members of Parliament (1977–1993): Reflections on the Institutionalization of the Spanish Parliament." Working paper no. 81, Centro de Estudios Avanzados en Ciencias Sociales, Instituto Juan March, Madrid.

Moreno, Javier. 1993a. "España, a la cabeza de la OCDE en redistribución de riqueza en los ochenta" [Spain at the head of the OECD in the redistribution of wealth during the eighties]. *El País*, June 2.

——. 1993b. "Las diferencias entre los ricos y los pobres se redujeron en España en los años ochenta; las políticas neoliberales aumentaron las desigualdades en EEUU y el Reino Unido" [The differences between rich and poor shrank in Spain during the eighties; neoliberal policies increased the differences in the U.S. and the U.K.] El País, June 1.

Morgan, Edward S. 1988. *Inventing the People: The Rise of Popular Sovereignty in England and America*. New York: W. W. Norton.

Morlino, Leonardo, and José Ramón Montero. 1993. "Legitimación y democracia en el sur de Europa" [Legtimation and democracy in Southern Europe]. *Revista Española de Investigaciones Sociológicas* 64: 7–40.

Mueller, John. 1992. "Democracy and Ralph's Pretty Good Grocery: Elections, Equality, and the Minimal Human Being." *American Journal of Political Science* 36:983–1003.

Mujal-León, Eusebio. 1983. *Communism and Political Change in Spain*. Bloomington: Indiana University Press.

Mulaik, Stanley A. 1971. *The Foundations of Factor Analysis*. New York: McGraw-Hill.

Munck, Gerardo, and Carol Skalnik Leff. 1997. "Modes of Transition and Democratization: The East European and South American Cases in Comparative Perspective." *Comparative Politics* 29: 343–62.

Muñoz de Bustillo Llorente, Rafael. 1990. "Distribución de la renta" [Income distribution]. In *Relexiones sobre política económica* [Reflections on political economy], ed. Instituto Sindical de Estudios. Madrid: Editorial Popular.

Nelson, Barbara J., and Najma Chowdhury, eds. 1994. *Women and Politics Worldwide*. New Haven: Yale University Press.

Nelson, Joan. 1993. "The Politics of Economic Transformation: Is Third World Experience Relevant to Eastern Europe?" *World Politics* 45: 433–63.

Nielsen, François. 1985. "Toward a Theory of Ethnic Solidarity in Modern Societies." *American Sociological Review* 50: 133–49.

Nisbett, Richard E. 1993. "Violence and U.S. Regional Culture." *American Psychologist* 48: 441–49.

Norris, Pippa. 1996. "Does Television Erode Social Capital?" *PS: Political Science and Politics* 29: 474–80.

Noya, Francisco Javier, and Antonio Vallejos. 1995. *Las actitudes ante la desigualdad en España* [Attitudes toward inequality in Spain]. Madrid: Centro de Investigaciones Sociológicas.

Nuccio, Richard. 1979. "The Family as a Metaphor in Authoritarian-Conservative Regimes: The Case of Spain." Working paper, Latin American Studies Center, University of Massachussetts, Amherst.

Ong, Walter J. 1982. *Orality and Literacy: The Technologizing of the Word*. London: Methuen.

Orizo, Francisco Andrés. 1993. *España entre la apatía e el cambio social* [Spain between apathy and social change]. Madrid: Mapfre.

Orti, Alfonso. 1982. "El significado del desencanto: Desencanto popular y transición postfranquista" [The meaning of disenchantment: Mass disenchantment and the transition from Francoism]. *Revista Canto General* 1:21–68.

Ozorak, Elizabeth Weiss. 1996. "The Power, but Not the Glory: How Women Empower Themselves through Religion." *Journal of the Scientific Study of Religion* 36: 17–29.

Padgett, Stephen, and William Patterson. 1991. *A History of Social Democracy in Postwar Europe*. London: Longman.

Pagden, Anthony. 1995. *Lords of All the World: Ideologies of Empire in Spain, Britain, and France, 1492–1830*. New Haven: Yale University Press.

Paik, Chong Koo. 1996. "Giohoenen sunguel sunggyongjungero matjeol soo iseomnida" [Churches can conduct elections according to Bibles]. *Mokhoe wa Sinhak* 81: 34–44.

Paramio, Ludolfo. 1982. "The Crisis of a Magical Discourse: The

Disenchantment of Politics in Post-Franco Spain." Paper presented at the World Congress of the International Political Science Association, Rio de Janeiro, August.

——. 1985. "La crisis del area comunista" [Crisis among the Communists]. *El País*, January 27.

——. 1988. *Tras el diluvio: La izquierda ante el fin de siglo* [After the deluge: The left before the end of the century]. Madrid: Siglo Veintiuno.

——. 1995. "Malestar político y avance electoral de la derecha" [Political hard times and the electoral advance of the right]. *Leviatán* 60 (Summer): 13–23.

Park, Chong-Min. 1991. "Authoritarian Rule in South Korea: Political Support and Government Performance." *Asian Survey* 31:743–61.

Park, Jae-Jung. 1992. "Katholic gyohoe wa hangook jongchi" [Catholic churches and Korean politics]. Research paper no. 2, Institute of Social Sciences, Hannam University.

Parry, Garaint, and George Moyser. 1994. "More Participation, More Democracy?" In *Defining and Measuring Democracy*, ed. David Beetham. Thousand Oaks, Calif.: Sage.

Pateman, Carole. 1975. *Participation and Democratic Theory*. Cambridge: Cambridge University Press.

Payne, Leigh. 1991. "Working Class Strategies in the Transition to Democracy in Brazil." *Comparative Politics* 23: 221–38.

Payne, Stanley G. 1984. *Spanish Catholicism*. Madison: University of Wisconsin Press.

——. 1987. *The Franco Regime, 1936–75*. Madison: University of Wisconsin Press.

——. 1995. *A History of Fascism, 1914–45*. Madison: University of Wisconsin Press.

Pérez Díaz, Víctor. 1984."Políticas económicas y pautas sociales en la España de la transición: La doble cara del neocorporatismo" [Economic policies and social agendas in Spain during the transition: The two faces of neocorporatism]. In *España: Un presente para el futuro* [Spain: A present for the future], ed. E. García de Enterría. Madrid: Instituto de Estudios Económicos.

——. 1991a. "The Church and Religion in Contemporary Spain." Working paper no. 19, Centro de Estudios Avanzados en Ciencias Sociales, Instituto Juan March, Madrid.

——. 1991b. "La emergencia de la España democrática: La 'invención' de una tradición y la dudosa institucionalización de una democracia" [The emergence of democratic Spain: The "invention" of a tradition and the dubious institutionalization of a democracy]. *Claves de Razón Práctica* 1: 62–80.

——. 1992. "La precariedad de la sociedad civil" [The precariousness of civil society]. *El País*, January 11, 9.

——. 1993a. *The Return of Civil Society: The Emergence of Democratic Spain*. Cambridge: Harvard University Press.

——. 1993b. *La primacia de la sociedad civil: El proceso de formación de la España democrática* [The primacy of civil society: The formation process of democratic Spain]. Madrid: Alianza.

———. 1996. *España puesta a prueba, 1976–1996* [Spain put to the test]. Madrid: Alianza.

Pérez Sánchez, Alfonso, and Eleanor A. Sayre. 1989. *Goya and the Spirit of Enlightenment*. Boston: Bullfinch Press/Little, Brown.

Pérez Vilariño, José, and Richard Schoenherr. 1990. "La religión organizada en España" [Organized religion in Spain]. In *España, sociedad y política* [Spain, society and politics], ed. Salvador Giner, vol. 1. Madrid: Espase-Calpe.

Petras, James. 1984. "The Rise and Decline of Southern European Socialism." *New Left Review* 146: 37–52.

———. 1997. "Latin America: The Resurgence of the Left." *New Left Review* 223: 17–47.

Petro, Nicholai N. 1995. *The Rebirth of Russian Democracy: An Interpretation of Political Culture*. Cambridge: Harvard University Press.

Pierson, Chris. 1995. "Comparing Welfare States." *West European Politics* 18: 197–203.

Pierson, Paul. 1996a. "The New Politics of the Welfare State." *World Politics* 48: 143–79.

———. 1996b. "The Path to European Integration: A Historical Institutionalist Analysis." *Comparative Political Studies* 29: 123–63.

Pizzorno, Alessandro. 1981. "Interests and Parties in Pluralism." In *Organizing Interests in Western Europe*, ed. Suzanne Berger. Cambridge: Cambridge University Press.

Podolny, Joel. 1993. "The Role of Juan Carlos I in the Consolidation of the Parliamentary Monarchy." In *Politics, Society, and Democracy: The Case of Spain*, ed. Richard Gunther. Boulder, Colo.: Westview.

Pontusson, Jonas, and Suzanne M. Smith. 1995. "Gender, Employment, and Party Preference in Western Europe: A Binary Logit Analysis Using Eurobarometer Data." Paper presented at the annual meetings of the American Political Science Association, Chicago, August 31–September 3.

Pradera, Javier. 1992. "Las pasiones del poder: El PSOE tras diez años de gobierno (1982–1992)" [The passions of power: The PSOE after ten years in government]. *Claves* 5: 32–42.

Press, Irwin. 1979. *The City as Context: Urbanism and Behavioral Constraints in Seville*. Urbana: University of Illinois Press.

Pritchett, V. S. 1954. *The Spanish Temper*. New York: Knopf.

Przeworski, Adam, and Fernando Limongi. 1997. "Modernization: Theories and Facts." *World Politics* 49: 155–83.

Putnam, Robert D. 1995a. "Bowling Alone: America's Declining Social Capital." *Journal of Democracy* 6: 65–78.

———. 1995b. "Tuning In, Tuning Out: The Strange Disappearance of Social Capital in America." *PS: Political Science and Politics* 28: 664–53.

Randall, Vicki. 1982. *Women and Politics*. London: Macmillan.

Randolph, Eleanor. 1996. *Waking the Tempests: Ordinary Life in the New Russia*. New York: Simon & Schuster.

Remmer, Karen L. 1995. "New Theoretical Perspectives on Democratization." *Comparative Politics* 28: 103–22.

———. 1997. "Theoretical Decay and Theoretical Development: The Resurgence of Institutional Analysis." *World Politics* 50: 34–61.

Requena, Miguel, and Jorge Benedicto. 1988. *Relaciones interpersonales: Actitudes y valores en la España de los ochenta* [Interpersonal relations: Attitudes and values in the Spain of the eighties]. Madrid: Centro de Investigaciones Sociológicas.

Requena Santos, Félix. 1994. "Redes de amistad, felicidad y família" [Friendship networks, happiness, and family]. *Revista Española de Investigaciones Sociológicas* 66: 73–89.

Ringen, Stein. 1998. "The Great British Myth: Why the Claims of Class Inequality Fail to Take Account of Social Change." *Times Literary Supplement*, January 23, 3–4.

Rivière, Margarita. 1984. *La generación del cambio* [The generation of change]. Barcelona: Planeta.

Rogowski, Ronald. 1974. *Rational Legitimacy: A Theory of Political Support.* Princeton: Princeton University Press.

Roh, Mihye, and Yu-kyong Mun. 1994. *Statistical Yearbook on Women.* Seoul: Korean Women's Development Institute.

Roh, Mihye, Young-ok Kim, and Yu-kyong Mun. 1994. *Social Statistics and Indicators on Women.* Seoul: Korean Women's Development Institute.

Rose, Richard, and William Mishler. 1994. "Mass Reaction to Regime Change in Eastern Europe: Polarization or Leaders and Laggards?" *British Journal of Political Science* 24: 159–82.

Rosenstone, Steven J., and John Mark Hansen. 1993. *Mobilization, Participation, and Democracy in America.* New York: Macmillan.

Rudolph, Susanne Hoeber, and James Piscatori, eds. 1997. *Transnational Religion and Fading States.* Boulder, Colo.: Westview.

Rustow, Dankwart. 1970. "Transitions to Democracy: Toward a Dynamic Model." *Comparative Politics* 2: 337–63.

Sachs, Jeffrey. 1992. "Building a Market Economy in Poland." *Scientific American* 266 (March): 34–40.

———. 1993. *Poland's Jump to the Market Economy.* Cambridge: MIT Press.

Sampson, Robert J. 1988. "Local Friendship Ties and Community Attachment in Mass Society: A Multilevel Systemic Model." *American Sociological Review* 53: 766–79.

Samuelson, Robert J. 1995. *The Good Life and Its Discontents: The American Dream and the Age of Entitlement, 1945–1995.* New York: Times Books/Random House.

Sánchez, José M. 1964. *The Spanish Revolution: The Politico-Religious Background of the Spanish Civil War.* Chapel Hill: University of North Carolina Press.

Sartori, Giovanni. 1994. *Comparative Constitutional Engineering.* New York: New York University Press.

Sasaki, Masamichi, and Tatsuzo Suzuki. 1987. "Changes in Religious Commitment in the United States, Holland, and Japan." *American Journal of Sociology* 92: 1055–76.

Scalapino, Richard. 1989. *The Politics of Development: Perspectives on Twentieth-Century Asia.* Cambridge: Harvard University Press.

Schlozman, Kay Lehman, et al. 1995. "Gender and Citizen Participation: Is There a Different Voice?" *American Journal of Political Science* 39: 267–93.

Schmidt, Vivien A. 1996a. *From State to Market? The Transformation of French Business and Government*. Cambridge: Cambridge University Press.

——. 1996b. "Industrial Policies and Policies of Industry in Advanced Industrialized Nations." *Comparative Politics* 28: 225–48.

Schmitter, Philippe C., and Terry Lynn Karl. 1991. "What Democracy Is . . . and Is Not." *Journal of Democracy* 2: 75–88.

Schneider, Ben Ross. 1995. "Democratic Consolidations: Some Broad Comparisons and Sweeping Arguments." *Latin American Research Review* 30: 215–35.

Schneider, Mark A. 1993. *Culture and Enchantment*. Chicago: University of Chicago Press.

Schuessler, Alexander A. 1995. "Expressive Motivation and Mass Participation." Unpublished paper, New York University.

Schuman, Howard, and Jacqueline Scott. 1989. "Generations and Collective Memory." *American Sociological Review* 54: 359–81.

Sears, David O., et al. 1980. "Self-Interest versus Symbolic Politics in Policy Attitudes and Presidential Voting." *American Political Science Review* 74: 670–84.

Secretaría Confederal de Formación y Cultura. 1989. *De los pactos de Moncloa al AES* [From the Moncloa pacts to the business-labor accords]. Madrid: Confederación Sindical de CC.OO.

Shively, W. Phillips. 1972. "Voting Stability and the Nature of Party Attachments in the Weimar Republic." *American Political Science Review* 66: 1203–25.

Shubert, Adrian. 1990. *A Social History of Modern Spain*. London: Unwin Hyman.

Shugart, Matthew. 1989. "Patterns of Revolution." *Theory and Society* 18: 249–71.

Sikkink, Kathryn. 1991. *Ideas and Institutions: Developmentalism in Brazil and Argentina*. Ithaca: Cornell University Press.

Simons, Marlise. 1995. "Entrevista con el president del gobierno de la transición" [Interview with the president of the transition government]. *El País*, November 18, 18–19.

——. 1996. "Catalan Leader Holds Key to Madrid." *New York Times*, May 5, 8.

La Situación de la mujer en la realidad sociolaboral española [The situation of women in the Spanish social-labor context]. 1994. Madrid: Consejo Económico y Social.

Smith, Brian H. 1982. *The Church and Politics in Chile: Challenges to Modern Catholicism*. Princeton: Princeton University Press.

Smith, Christian. 1991. *The Emergence of Liberation Theology*. Chicago: University of Chicago Press.

——. 1994. "The Spirit and Democracy: Base Communities, Protestantism, and Democratization in Latin America." *Sociology of Religion* 55: 119–43.

——, ed. 1996. *Disruptive Religion: The Force of Faith in Social-Movement Activism*. New York: Routledge.

Smith, W. Rand. 1995. "Industrial Crisis and the Left: Adjustment Strategies in Socialist France and Spain." *Comparative Politics* 28: 1–24.

Sniderman, Paul M., and Richard A. Brody. 1977. "Coping: The Ethic of Self-Reliance." *American Journal of Political Science* 21: 501–21.

Sotelo, Ignacio. 1984. "El fiasco del socialismo mediterráneo" [The fiasco of Mediterranean socialism]. *El País*, December 16.

———. 1985. "La popularidad del presidente" [The popularity of the president]. *El País*, July 3.

———. 1992. "La impronta del felipismo: Diez años del gobierno socialista" [The emergence of *felipismo:* Ten years of socialist government]. *Claves* 28: 40–58.

Stein, Andrew J. 1997. "Catholic Social Activism, Religious Belief, and Protest Participation in Nicaragua, El Salvador, and Guatemala." Unpublished manuscript.

"Suecos y españoles, los que más tiempo dedican a relaciones sociales [Swedes and Spaniards are the ones who spend most time on social relations]. 1992. *El País*, November 6.

Swank, Duane. 1998. "Christian Democratic Welfare States in a Global Economy: Catholic Conservative Nations in Comparative Perspective." Paper presented at the Eleventh International Conference of Europeanists, Baltimore, February 26–28.

Taggart, Paul. 1995. "New Populist Parties in Western Europe." *West European Politics* 18: 34–51.

Tarrow, Sidney. 1994. *Power in Movement: Social Movements, Collective Action and Politics.* Cambridge: Cambridge University Press.

Tetzlaff, David. 1991. "Divide and Conquer: Popular Culture and Social Control in Late Capitalism." *Media, Culture, and Society* 13: 9–33.

Tezanos, José Felix, Ramón Cotarelo, and Andrés de Blas, eds. 1989. *La transición democrática española* [The Spanish democratic transition]. Madrid: Sistema.

Therborn, Göran. 1994. "Another Way of Taking Religion Seriously." *European Journal of Political Research* 26: 103–10.

———. 1995. *European Modernity and Beyond: A Trajectory of European Societies, 1945–2000.* Thousand Oaks, Calif.: Sage.

Togeby, Lisa. 1994. "Political Implications of Increasing Numbers of Women in the Labor Force." *Comparative Political Studies* 27: 211–40.

Toharia Cortés, José Juan. 1988. *Los españoles ante la administración de justicia* [Spaniards on the administration of justice]. Madrid: Centro de Investigaciones Sociológicas.

Topf, Richard. 1995. "Beyond Electoral Participation." In *Citizens and the State,* ed. Hans-Dieter Klingemann and Dieter Fuchs. New York: Oxford University Press.

Tusell, Javier. 1984. *Franco y los Católicos: La política interior en España entre 1945 y 1957* [Franco and the Catholics: Domestic politics in Spain between 1945 and 1957]. Madrid: Alianza.

Tusell, Javier, and Genoveva G. Queipo de Llano. 1990. *Los intelectuales y la republica* [The intellectuals and the republic]. Madrid: Nerea.

Tyler, Thomas R. 1984. "Justice in the Political Arena." In *The Sense of Injustice,* ed. Roger Folger. New York: Plenum.

Ullman, Joan Connelly. 1968. *The Tragic Week: A Study of Anticlericalism in Spain*. Cambridge: Harvard University Press.

Ullman, Pierre L. 1971. *Mariano de Larra and Spanish Political Rhetoric*. Madison: University of Wisconsin Press.

United Nations. 1995. *The World's Women, 1995: Trends and Statistics*. New York.

United Nations Development Program. 1996. *Human Development Report, 1994*. New York: Oxford University Press.

Useem, Bert, and Michael Useem. 1979. "Government Legitimacy and Political Stability." *Social Forces* 57: 840–52.

Valenzuela, Incarnación, et al. 1995. "Los jóvenes abandonan al PSOE" [Young people abandon the PSOE]. *Cambio*, June 19, 18–24.

van Deth, Jan W. 1995. "A Macro Setting for Micro Politics." In *The Impact of Values*, ed. van Deth and Elinor Scarbrough. New York: Oxford University Press.

van Deth, Jan W., and Joseph I. H. Janssen. 1994. "Party Attachments and Political Fragmentation in Europe." *European Journal of Political Research* 25: 87–109.

"Veinte años después: La transición sube al cielo" [Twenty years later: The transition goes to heaven]. 1995. *El País*, November 19.

Veliz, Claudio. 1980. *The Centralist Heritage in Latin America*. Princeton: Princeton University Press.

———. 1994. *The New World of the Gothic Fox: Culture and Economy in English and Spanish America*. Berkeley: University of California Press.

Verba, Sidney, Nancy Burns, and Kay Lehman Schlozman. 1997. "Knowing and Caring about Politics: Gender and Political Engagement." *Journal of Politics* 59: 1051–72.

Verba, Sidney, Norman H. Nie, and Jae-on Kim. 1978. *Participation and Political Equality: A Seven-Nation Comparison*. Cambridge: Cambridge University Press.

Verba, Sidney, Kay Lehman Schlozman, and Henry E. Brady. 1995. *Voice and Equality: Civic Voluntarism in America*. Cambridge: Harvard University Press.

Vidal-Beneyto, Juan. 1984. "El grado cero de lo social" [Social policy at the starting point]. *El País*, December 2.

Villaria, Manuel. 1995. "The Modernization of the Spanish Central Government." Paper presented at the annual meetings of the American Political Science Association, Chicago, August 31–September 3.

von Beyme, Klaus. 1996. "Party Leadership and Change in Party Systems: Towards a Postmodern State?" *Government and Opposition* 31: 135–59.

Wade, Larry L., and Jin Wan Seo. 1996. "Women, Education, and Political Volition in the South Korean Mass Public." *Comparative Political Studies* 29: 27–51.

Walzer, Michael. 1983. *Spheres of Justice: A Defense of Pluralism and Equality*. New York: Basic Books.

Ward, Ian. 1993. "Media Intrusion and the Changing Nature of the Established Parties in Australia and Canada." *Canadian Journal of Political Science* 26: 477–506.

Warner, Carolyn M. 1994. "Patronage, Priests, and Politicians: The Role of Institutions and Elite Strategies in the Construction of the French and Italian Christian Democratic Political Parties, 1944–1958." Ph.D. diss., Department of Government, Harvard University.

Wattenberg, Martin P. 1995. *The Decline of American Political Parties, 1952–1994.* Cambridge: Harvard University Press.

Weatherford, M. Stephen. 1983. "Economic Voting and the 'Symbolic Politics' Argument: A Reinterpretation and Synthesis." *American Political Science Review* 77: 158–74.

———. 1992. "Measuring Political Legitimacy." *American Political Science Review* 86: 149–66.

Weil, Frederick D. 1985. "A Second Chance for Liberal Democracy: Popular Support in Post-Authoritarian European Regimes with Comparisons to Long-Term European and American Liberal Democracies." Paper presented at the annual meeting of the American Political Science Association, New Orleans.

———. 1989. "The Sources and Structure of Legitimation in Western Democracies." *American Sociological Review* 54: 682–706.

Weingast, Barry R. 1997. "The Political Foundations of Democracy and the Rule of Law." *American Political Science Review* 91: 245–63.

Wells, Kenneth M., ed. 1995. *South Korea's Minjung Movement: The Culture and Politics of Dissidence.* Honolulu: University of Hawaii Press.

Whitehead, Laurence. 1993. "The Alternatives to Liberal Democracy: A Latin American Perspective." In *Prospects for Democracy*, ed. David Held. Cambridge: Polity.

Whitfield, Teresa. 1994. *Paying the Price: Ignacio Ellacuría and the Murdered Jesuits of El Salvador.* Philadelphia: Temple University Press.

Whyte, John H. 1981. *Catholics in Western Democracies.* Dublin: Gill & Macmillan.

Wiarda, Howard J. 1993. *Politics in Iberia: The Political Systems of Spain and Portugal.* New York: HarperCollins.

Wilensky, Harold L. 1981. "Leftism, Catholicism, and Democratic Corporatism: The Role of Political Parties in Recent Welfare State Development." In *The Development of Welfare States in Europe and America*, ed. Peter Flora and Arnold J. Heidenheimer. New Brunswick, N.J.: Transaction Books.

Wilson, Bryan. 1982. *Religion in Sociological Perspective.* New York: Oxford University Press.

Wilson, James Q., and Edward C. Banfield. 1964. "Public-Regardingness as a Value Premise in Voting Behavior." *American Political Science Review* 65: 876–87.

———. 1971. "Political Ethos Revisited." *American Political Science Review* 68: 1048–62.

Wilson, Richard W. 1997. "American Political Culture in Comparative Perspective." *Political Psychology* 18: 483–502.

Wolf, Edward N. 1995. *Top Heavy: A Study of Increasing Inequality of Wealth in America.* New York: Twentieth Century Fund.

Wood, Gordon S. 1992. *The Radicalism of the American Revolution.* New York: Knopf.

World Values Study Group. 1994. "World Values Survey," 1981–1984, 1990–1993 [computer file]. Ann Arbor, Mich.: ICPSR.

Wozniak, Lynne. 1991. "Industrial Modernization and Working-Class Protest in Socialist Spain." Working paper no. 165, Kellogg Institute for International Studies, University of Notre Dame.

———. 1992. "The Dissolution of Party-Union Relations in Spain." *International Journal of Political Economy* 22: 73–90.

Wright, A. 1977. *The Spanish Economy, 1959–1976*. New York: Holmes & Meier.

Wright, Eric Olin, Janeen Baxter, and Elisabeth Birkelund Gunn. 1995. "The Gender Gap in Workplace Authority: A Cross-National Study." *American Sociological Review* 60: 407–35.

WuDunn, Sheryl. 1995. "Korea's Christians: A Surging, Prayerful Force." *New York Times*, May 25.

Wuthnow, Robert. 1989. *Communities of Discourse: Ideology and Social Structure in the Reformation, the Enlightenment, and European Socialism*. Cambridge: Harvard University Press.

Youngblood, Robert L. 1991. *Marcos against the Church: Economic Development and Political Represssion in the Philippines*. Ithaca: Cornell University Press.

Zang, Baohu. 1994. "Corporatism, Totalitarianism, and Transitions to Democracy." *Comparative Political Studies* 27: 108–36.

Index

Accommodating rites, 4
Age. *See* Generational differences
Alianza Popular, 20, 43, 52, 136
Almodóvar, Pedro, 20
Anarchist movement, 17
Antiterrorist operation, 20
Argentina, 161
Attitudinal indicators, 104–7
Authoritarianism, 8, 134–35, 137, 139–40,
    162, 170; overlaps with democracy, 33–34
Autonomías, 19, 201n7
Aznar, José María, 20

Basque country, 19, 20, 53, 81, 126, 201–2n7
Brazil, 11–18; Catholic church in, 156–57;
    media and, 187–90; participation in,
    148, 149, 154; religiosity in, 12, 183–84,
    204n16
Buñuel, Luis, 19

Caetano, Marcello, 18
Carrero Blanco, Luis, 18
Carrillo, Santiago, 45, 52
Casanova, José, 158
Catalonia, 19, 53, 81, 121, 126, 201–2n7
Catholic church, 53, 121, 131, 142, 201n4; in
    Brazil, 156–57; identity and, 123–25; in
    Korea, 157; moderation and, 2, 145–46,
    157, 160–61; parochialism and, 121, 123;
    participation and, 10, 121, 123, 145–46;
    and Second Vatican Council, 28, 123, 157.
    See also Religiosity
Center-left. *See* Left; Socialists
Center-right, 61, 62, 74, 78, 84; public
    opinion and, 67–68. *See also* Right;
    Unión de Centro Democrático

Christian Democratic party, 28
Church-state relations, 2, 14, 160
Civil society, 16
Civil War, 82, 92, 101–2, 132, 166
Class: desired income differences and,
    95–96; earnings and, 75–77; economics
    and, 64, 69–71, 73–78, 99–101,
    199nn13–14; generational differences
    and, 120, 127–28; identity and, 120,
    125–26, 204n10; participation and,
    158–59; partisanship and, 131–32;
    perceptions and, 112; public opinion
    and, 68, 70–71; social fairness and,
    70–71
Cleavage structures, 6–7, 25, 53;
    democratization and, 25–26, 30, 119;
    public opinion and, 93–94, 105–6. *See
    also* Conflicts; Polarization
Communist party, 19, 20, 45, 194n28
Confianza, 37, 54
Conflicts: hierarchy of, 7; overlapping, 26,
    28–29, 33–34, 142–43; types of, 6. *See also*
    Cleavage structures
Cortes, 18, 19, 42, 66
Cross-national data, 10–15, 18, 152–53

Decentralization, 112–14, 116
Democracy: ambivalence toward, 23–25;
    imagery of, 5; overlaps with
    authoritarianism, 33–34; procedural, 9,
    65–66; satisfaction with, 26–29, 44, 51, 52,
    87–88
Democratization, 18–22; church-state
    relations and, 14; cleavage structures
    and, 25–26, 30, 119; continuity and,
    33–34, 38–39, 49–50, 80, 84;

Democratization (*cont.*)
   depolarization and, 32; partisanship and,
      134–37; as triple transition, 30, 174
Depolarization, 3, 4–8, 32, 35, 87–90;
   attitudinal indicators and, 104–7;
   democratization and, 32; evolution of,
   25–30; legitimacy and, 58–60; religiosity
   and, 16, 26, 28–29, 166–67. *See also*
   Moderation; Polarization
Desencanto, 19, 42
Dews, Peter, 39
Differentiation, 115–16
Distributive economics, 65–66, 99, 200n19;
   growth vs., 93, 112–14; public opinion
   and, 72, 75–77, 91–96, 104, 106, 200n19;
   social fairness and, 116–17. *See also*
   Economics

Economics: class and, 64, 69–71, 73–78,
   99–101, 199nn13–14; distributive, 65–66,
   72, 75–77, 91–96, 99, 112–14, 116–17,
   200n19; earnings, perception of, 75–77;
   Franco regime and, 63–64, 91–92, 98–101;
   growth vs. distribution, 93, 112–14;
   perceptions and, 75–77, 94–95, 97–98,
   101–12, 168–69, 198–99n6, 199nn8–9,
   200n22; political liberalization and,
   66–71; as predictor for support, 80–81,
   111–12, 115; preferences and, 94–95,
   101–12; private vs. public arenas, 63,
   71–79, 94; problem-solving approach
   and, 81–82, 92–93; public opinion and,
   64, 69–70; reform measures, 91–93;
   regionalism and, 93, 112–14; socialist, 61,
   63–66; voting behavior and, 90–91. *See
   also* Taxation
Education, 110, 160, 203–4n10
Egalitarianism, 9, 72, 75, 95–96. *See also*
   Social fairness
Elitism, 115–16
Employment, 1–2, 203n3; participation and,
   146, 153, 160, 163–64; strikes and, 17,
   203nn7, 8; women and, 2, 12, 13, 146,
   178–80, 182–84
España atormentada, 32, 143
Estado de las Autonomías, 81, 112, 116, 142
European Community, 19, 20, 87, 114
European Monetary System, 20

Falange, 139
Felipismo, 68
Fraga Iribarne, Manuel, 52
Franco, Francisco, 3, 102, 175

Franco regime, 3; Catholic church and, 28,
   157; economics of, 63–64, 91–92, 98–101;
   moral domain and, 98–99; nostalgia for,
   45–46, 114; partisanship and, 134;
   polarization and, 50–51, 114; public
   opinion and, 29, 87, 98; religiosity and,
   50–51; weakening of, 29–30
Franquismo, 68
Free enterprise, preference for, 104–7

Galicia, 19
Generational differences, 200–201n23; class
   and, 120, 127–28; identity and, 120,
   127–29, 131; left-right continuum and,
   87–90, 128–29; neighborliness and,
   155–56, 177–78; participation and,
   155–56; religiosity and, 127–28;
   voluntary associations and, 156
González, Felipe, 18, 20, 21, 42, 57, 68, 92,
   97, 197n6, 198–99n6. *See also* Partido
   Socialista Obrero Español
Government: decentralization of, 112–14,
   116; expectations of, 62–64, 72, 78, 91, 94;
   multiple classification analysis of
   support for, 79–82, 197n8, 198n8;
   religiosity and, 79–80; satisfaction with,
   26–29, 44, 51, 52, 87–88, 196n3; support
   for, for determinants of, 79–82, 107–12,
   197n8, 198n8; taxation and, 63–64, 116
Gramsci, Antonio, 121
Grass-roots political participation, 17–18,
   149–51, 161–64, 193n23, 203nn7–8
Gundelach, Peter, 150–51
Gunther, Richard, 24

Haig, Alexander, 168
Historical context of transition, 18–22

Identity, 6; Catholic church and, 123–25;
   class and, 120, 125–26, 204n10; contours
   of, 123–27; generational differences in,
   120, 127–29, 131; native vs. migrant, 125,
   126, 201n5; partisanship and, 130–33;
   regionalism and, 126–27, 132–33;
   religiosity and, 123–24
Identity conflicts, 6–7, 62, 118–19, 169
Ideology, 6–7; asymmetry of, 121–22;
   attitudinal indicators and, 104–7;
   economics and, 78; public opinion and,
   67–70; religiosity and, 164. *See also*
   Depolarization
Iglesias, Gerardo, 45
Inglehart, Ronald, 150

Institutions, 10, 172–74
Interest conflicts, 6–8, 65, 112
Izquierda Unida, 20

Jackman, Mary R., 95
Jackman, Robert W., 95
John Paul II, Pope, 44, 51, 57, 202n11
Juan Carlos I, King of Spain, 4–6, 18–19, 38, 51, 57–58, 167–68. *See also* Monarchy

Kim Dae Jung, 12
Kim Young Sam, 12
Korea, 11–18, 196–97n5; Catholic church in, 157; media and, 185–90; participation in, 12, 148, 150, 154; religiosity in, 12, 157, 183–84, 204n16
Kristeller, Paul, 30

Leaders: popularity of, 44, 45, 51, 57, 191n5, 192n9; responsibility and, 101. *See also individual leaders*
Left, 84–85; public opinion and, 67–69, 74, 78; regionalism and, 121. *See also* Socialists
Left-right continuum: attitudinal indicators and, 105–6; decline of divisiveness, 87–90, 121–22, 132; frequency distributions, 84, 85; generational differences and, 87–90, 128–29; monarchy and, 4–5; partisanship and, 132–33; perceptions of performance and, 66–71; as predictor of support, 79–80; public opinion and, 67–71; religiosity and, 16, 26, 28–29; satisfaction with democracy and, 29, 44, 87–88; *tendances* and, 137–42, 200n20, 202n15
Legitimacy, 3–4, 8–10, 168; alternative indicators of, 43–50; approaches to, 30–32; civil creed and, 30–31; conventional measures of, 41–43; depolarization and, 58–60; determinants of, 50–54; dimensions of, 32–35; factor analysis and, 48–49; historical context and, 35–36; holistic judgment and, 46; multiple criteria and, 32–35, 52; norms and, 30–31, 39, 59; political culture and, 31–32; public perception and, 8–9; as relational pattern, 49–50, 53; retrospective comparison and, 30–31, 35–36, 114–15; social fairness and, 96; support and, 31, 41; surplus approval and, 99; testable model of, 41; trust and, 36–38, 42, 54–60

Maastricht Treaty, 20
Maier, Charles, 164
Maravall, José María, 133
Markoff, John, 173
Maximalism, 3, 101
Media, 123, 159, 172, 204n10, 206n2; literacy and, 187–89; women and, 189–90
Military uprising of 1981, 19, 66
Moderation, 4, 10, 143, 166–67, 191n3; Catholic church and, 2, 145–46, 157, 160–61; statesmanship and, 101. *See also* Depolarization
Modernization, 5–6, 142, 158
Monarchy, 5, 37–38, 57–60, 72, 167–68. *See also* Juan Carlos I
Moncloa Pacts, 19
Moral issues, 98–99, 129, 143
Movida madrileña, 20
Mystification thesis, 91, 92

NATO (North Atlantic Treaty Organization), 20
Neighborliness, 15, 147–48, 153, 170, 193n24; generational differences and, 155–56, 177–78; women and, 178–79
Norms, 30–31, 39, 59
North Atlantic Treaty Organization (NATO), 20

Olympic Games, 21, 175

País, El (newspaper), 19
Parochialism, 121, 123
Participation, 1–2, 10–18; Catholic church and, 10, 121, 123, 145–46; class and, 158–59; comparative data on, 10–15, 18, 193n19; context of, 93–96, 172–74; education and, 160, 203–4n10; employment and, 146, 153, 160, 163–64; factors in, 153–58, 171–72; generational differences in, 155–56; modes of, 147–52; religiosity and, 12, 14, 156–58, 160–61, 192n16; women and, 146, 148–53, 179–84. *See also* Neighborliness; Political participation; Voluntary associations
Partido Communista Español (PCE), 45
Partido Popular (PP), 20, 43, 116, 121, 136, 140, 143, 166
Partido Socialista Obrero Español (PSOE), 20, 21, 43, 47–48, 77, 79, 169; economics and, 81–82, 92; organizational structure of, 87; partisanship and, 139; regionalism

Partido Socialista Obrero Español
(PSOE) (*cont.*)
and, 121. *See also* González, Felipe;
Socialists
Partisanship, 118, 122, 168–69; class and,
131–32; continuity and, 137–41; decline
of, 134–35; democratization and, 134–37;
earnings and, 75–77; identity and,
130–33; left-right continuum and, 132–33;
macropartisanship, 133–34;
nonpartisanship, 135–39; polarization
and, 142; public opinion and, 67–68;
religiosity and, 131; right and, 141, 143;
social policy and, 140; *tendances* and,
137–39
PCE (Partido Communista Español), 45
Perceptions of performance: class and, 112;
economics and, 75–77, 94–95, 97–98,
101–12, 168–69, 198–99n6, 199nn8–9,
200n22; left-right continuum and, 66–71;
legitimacy and, 8–9; preferences and,
101–12; religiosity and, 110–12; and
safety, 69, 98
Pérez Díaz, Víctor, 4
Performance. *See* Perceptions of
performance
Philip II, King of Spain, 175
Poincaré, Henri, 172
Polarization: decline of, 87–90; Franco
regime and, 50–51, 114; overlapping
conflicts and, 26, 28–29. *See also*
Depolarization; Moderation
Political behavior, 15–17, 203n9
Political culture, as dualistic, 31–32
Political orientation, 43–44
Political participation, 3, 147; grass-roots,
17–18, 149–51, 161–64, 193n23, 203nn7–8;
newer forms of, 149–51, 161–64;
religiosity and, 156–58. *See also*
Participation
Political Reform, Law of, 19
Populism, 72, 75–77, 91, 95–96, 104, 106,
200n19
Portugal, 18, 22, 23, 91, 192n12
PP (Partido Popular), 20, 43, 116, 121, 136,
140, 143, 166
Pragmatism, 9, 39, 68, 82–83, 90
Preautonomy decree, 19
Preferences: on economic policy, 94–95,
101–7; perceptions and, 101–12
Private vs. public arena, 54–57, 63, 71–79,
94
Privatization, 158

Problem-solving (pragmatic) approach,
81–82, 92–93
Protest behavior. *See* Grass-roots political
participation
PSOE. *See* Partido Socialista Obrero
Español
Public opinion: ambivalence of, 66–72, 82,
86, 91–92, 102; class and, 68, 70–71;
cleavage structures and, 93–94, 105–6;
context of, 93–96; distributive-populist
theme of, 72, 75–77, 91, 95–96, 104, 106,
200n19; economic and social preferences,
95–96, 102–4; economics and, 64, 69–70;
expectations of government, 62–64, 72,
78, 91, 94; government popularity and,
79–82; ideological orientation and, 67–70;
improvement, view of, 70–71; left-right
continuum and, 67–69, 74, 78;
partisanship and, 67–68; reformism and,
61–62; religiosity and, 67; statism and,
91, 94. *See also* Perceptions of
performance; Preferences
Public vs. private arena, 54–57, 63, 71–79,
94

Randall, Vicki, 152
Reformism, 24, 61–62, 77
Regionalism, 7, 53, 81–82, 108, 121,
201–2n7; economic growth and,
93, 112–14; identity and, 126–27,
132–33
Religiosity: depolarization and, 16, 26,
28–29, 166–67; Franco regime and, 50–51;
generational differences and, 127–28;
identity and, 123–24; ideology and, 164;
left-right continuum and, 16, 26, 28–29;
moderation and, 2, 145–46, 157, 160–61;
neighborliness and, 148; neutrality and,
145–46; parochialism, 121, 123;
participation and, 12, 14, 156–58, 160–61,
164, 192n16; partisanship and, 131–32;
perceptions and, 110–12; public opinion
and, 67; support of government and,
79–80; voluntary associations and, 148;
women and, 183–84. *See also* Catholic
church
Right: attitudinal indicators and, 105–6;
moderation and, 166; partisanship and,
141, 143; public opinion and, 67, 69, 74,
78. *See also* Center-right; Left-right
continuum
Ritos pacificadores, 4
Ruptura, 25